American Decorative
Arts and Old World
Influences

ART AND ARCHITECTURE INFORMATION GUIDE SERIES

Series Editor: Sydney Starr Keaveney, Associate Professor, Pratt Institute Library, Brooklyn

Also in this series:

AMERICAN ARCHITECTS TO THE FIRST WORLD WAR—*Edited by Lawrence Wodehouse*

AMERICAN ARCHITECTS FROM THE FIRST WORLD WAR TO THE PRESENT— *Edited by Lawrence Wodehouse*

AMERICAN DRAWING—*Edited by Lamia Doumato*

AMERICAN PAINTING—*Edited by Sydney Starr Keaveney*

AMERICAN SCULPTURE—*Edited by Janis Ekdahl*

ART EDUCATION—*Edited by Clarence Bunch*

BRITISH ARCHITECTS, 1840-1976—*Edited by Lawrence Wodehouse*

COLOR THEORY—*Edited by Mary Buckley*

HISTORIC PRESERVATION—*Edited by Arnold L. Markowitz*

INDIGENOUS ARCHITECTURE WORLDWIDE—*Edited by Lawrence Wodehouse*

POTTERY AND CERAMICS—*Edited by James E. Campbell*

STAINED GLASS—*Edited by Darlene A. Brady and William Serban**

TWENTIETH-CENTURY EUROPEAN PAINTING—*Edited by Ann-Marie Cutul*

*in preparation

The above series is part of the
GALE INFORMATION GUIDE LIBRARY

The Library consists of a number of separate series of guides covering major areas in the social sciences, humanities, and current affairs.

General Editor: Paul Wasserman, Professor and former Dean, School of Library and Information Services, University of Maryland

Managing Editor: Denise Allard Adzigian, Gale Research Company

American Decorative Arts and Old World Influences

A GUIDE TO INFORMATION SOURCES

Volume 14 of the Art and Architecture Information Guide Series

David M. Sokol

Chairperson
History of Architecture and Art Department
University of Illinois at Chicago Circle

Gale Research Company
Book Tower, Detroit, Michigan 48226

Ref
Z
5956
·A68S66

Library of Congress Cataloging in Publication Data

Sokol, David M
    American decorative arts and Old World influences.

    (Art and architecture information guide series ;
v. 14) (Gale information guide library)
    Includes indexes.
    1. Art industries and trade—United States—For-
eign influences—Bibliography. I. Title.
Z5956.A68S66 [NK805]   016.745'0973   80-18249
ISBN 0-8103-1465-7

To the Staff of the Libraries of
The Art Institute of Chicago

VITA

David M. Sokol is an associate professor and chairperson of the History of Architecture and Art Department at the University of Illinois at Chicago Circle, where he has served as president of the Chicago Circle Chapter of the American Association of University Professors. He has also served as President of the Wisconsin-Northern Illinois Chapter of the American Studies Association and sat on the national organization's Council. Other professional affiliations include the College Art Association, Midwest History Society, and the American Society for Aesthetics. He is currently treasurer of the Association of Historians of American Art. Since 1977 he has been an elected member of the Board of Trustees of the Village of Oak Park.

Sokol received his graduate training at the Institute of Fine Arts, New York University, and taught at several other institutions before coming to UICC in 1971.

He has written an exhibition catalog on the nineteenth-century American painter, John Quidor (1973), AMERICAN ARCHITECTURE AND ART: A GUIDE TO INFORMATION SOURCES (1976), and is a coauthor of the major textbook AMERICAN ART (1979). He is currently book review editor of AMERICAN ANTIQUES, and has served as coordinating bibliographer for architecture and art for AMERICAN QUARTERLY and was a member of the editorial board of AMERICAN ART REVIEW. Sokol has also written many articles and book reviews for art magazines and journals, and has lectured on American fine and decorative arts.

CONTENTS

Contents

Contents

PREFACE

The purpose of this volume is to present the reader with a guide to both basic and specialized literature in the field of American decorative arts, and to provide a guide to minimal background information on the decorative arts worldwide. The term "decorative arts" is used here to denote ceramics, furniture, glass, metals (primarily gold and silver), and textiles. Some objects of folk art, where overlapping with the basic categories listed, are also included.

There is no bibliographical volume currently covering American decorative arts in depth, the volumes listed in chapter 1 are either in-depth bibliographies covering a limited number of fields or broad in scope but not thorough in coverage. The massive work of Franklin, while having both scope and depth, lacks annotations and selectivity. AMERICAN DECORATIVE ARTS AND OLD WORLD INFLUENCES itself does not include every work on the subject. Hundreds of books and pamphlets, checklists, and price guides to a variety of decorative arts objects were omitted. Only a few examples of the many concerned with collecting carnival glass, for example were included.

In addition, as well as confining my selections to those written in English, I have also excluded most volumes written before 1940 if most of their information is to be found also in later works. When reasonable doubt exists, however, I have chosen to include the works written earlier in the century. Only material published in traditional article, book, or exhibition catalog form has been included.

Although the references contained in this volume are overwhelmingly books, there are some significant exhibition catalogs included, as exhibition catalogs, especially the substantial volumes produced by major museums, are often the most complete source of information on a subject. When an author of the catalog can be identified, even as having introduced the volume, such identification is provided. In those cases where such identification is impossible, the catalog is listed by institution.

Preface

There are also some articles included, taken from a wide variety of periodic literature. Periodicals referenced include both specialized journals, such as the noted JOURNAL OF GLASS STUDIES, and several local general history journals. Conspicuous by its absence is the magazine ANTIQUES, published and indexed since 1922. Literally hundreds of articles from its pages could have been noted, and much of the information in them would have also appeared in books by the same authors. As the magazine enjoys wide circulation and is indexed, I recommend that the reader always consult it when seeking information on the decorative arts. Similarly, the ART INDEX, which cites articles, book reviews, and major reproductions, published quarterly and in almost every important library, should be consulted for information on any and all topics in the arts.

In selecting the material for the quarter of the book that deals with general and non-American material, I have weighted selections to those that are either unusually broad or those which are of particular relevance to the student of American decorative arts. It is natural, therefore, to find many more items on British developments, and more specialized works on periods of British crafts as they affected their American counterparts.

A few good picture books have been incorporated into the listings, and are identified as such when included. If they have basic introductions, that too has been noted. For all works, the number of illustrations and the number in color have been noted, when they are numbered in the text. Similarly, the number of pages of bibliography is noted when the bibliography is paged and when it appears in one place. Pages have not been noted if there are bibliographies after each chapter or, in the case of dictionaries and encyclopedias, after each entry.

To a large extent, the amount of space devoted to each of the decorative arts is a reflection of both past and present taste. Far more people collect glass than textiles, and silver is of more value to people than copper, so the references to each reflects this. The durability factor is also important, so that it is hard to write about perishable early glass and inexpensive everyday earthenware. A balance must be struck, however, and so it is possible that extra attention has been paid to those areas where the information has been scarcest. As for the total fairness of selection, only the judgement of one individual has been involved, and I have tried to present a fair picture.

My research for this volume was primarily completed at the libraries of the Art Institute of Chicago, and I express my thanks to the staff of that institution for putting up with both me and the project for so many years. Other institutions and individuals, too numerous to mention, provided either information or leads to useful sources.

Finally, to my wife, Sandra, for her help, and to my children, Adam and Andrew, who have endured so many requests for quiet while Daddy works on his book, I extend my deepest gratitude.

Chapter 1

BIBLIOGRAPHIES

The following volumes are the basic subject bibliographies available in the English language. None are inclusive, and should be used as a point of departure in investigating any particular subject.

1 American Crafts Council. MASTER'S THESES: CRAFTS. New York: 1976. 153 p.

Each entry in the listing presents the author, date, and title of the thesis. A good guide to unpublished literature.

2 ART BIBLIOGRAPHIES: MODERN. Santa Barbara, Calif.: Clio Press, 1973-- . Semiannual.

A computerized bibliography with annotated reference to articles, books, and exhibition catalogs. Contains some references to the decorative arts.

3 Campbell, James Edward. POTTERY AND CERAMICS. Art and Architecture Information Guide Series, vol. 7. Detroit: Gale Research Co., 1978. xi, 241 p.

An annotated bibliography of world ceramics.

4 Chamberlin, Mary W. GUIDE TO ART REFERENCE BOOKS. Chicago: American Library Association, 1959. xiv, 418 p.

An old standard that includes a modest number of entries on the decorative arts.

5 Duncan, George S. BIBLIOGRAPHY OF GLASS. London: Dawson of Pallmall, 1960. 544 p.

A specialized bibliography of approximately 20,000 entries of both books and articles on glass.

6 Ehresmann, Donald L. APPLIED AND DECORATIVE ARTS: A BIBLIOGRAPHIC GUIDE. Littleton, Colo.: Libraries Unlimited, 1977. 232 p.

A specialized and detailed annotated bibliography of world-wide decorative arts, arranged by material and, within sections, by country.

7   Franklin, Linda C. ANTIQUES AND COLLECTIBLES: A BIBLIOGRAPHY OF WORKS IN ENGLISH, 16TH CENTURY TO 1976. Metuchen, N.J.: Scarecrow Press, 1978. xxiii, 1,091 p.

A massive but undifferentiated bibliography of decorative arts, home furnishings, costumes, toys, musical instruments, and other ephemera.

8   Hench, L.L., and McEldowney, B.A., eds. A BIBLIOGRAPHY OF CERAMICS AND GLASS. Columbus: American Ceramic Society, 1976. 119 p.

Both technical and historical material is referenced in this basic bibliographic tool.

9   Lackschewitz, Gertrud, comp. INTERIOR DESIGN AND DECORATION; A BIBLIOGRAPHY COMPILED FOR THE AMERICAN INSTITUTE OF INTERIOR DESIGNERS. New York: New York Public Library, 1961. 86 p.

A useful bibliographical source, primarily concerned with material oriented to practical application.

10   Lucas, E. Louise. ART BOOKS: A BASIC BIBLIOGRAPHY ON THE FINE ARTS. Greenwich, Conn.: New York Graphic Society, 1968. 245 p.

A good general bibliographic volume with some attention to the various decorative arts.

11   Solon, Louis M. CERAMIC LITERATURE. London: Griffin, 1910. 660 p.

An old but basic annotated bibliography of ceramic art. Strong on technical processes.

Chapter 2

GENERAL DICTIONARIES, ENCYCLOPEDIAS, AND

HISTORIES OF DECORATIVE ARTS

The basic handbooks, dictionaries, and encyclopedias of decorative arts in general, plus a few broad surveys are included. Some are detailed and some are essentially picture books.

12   Bernasconi, John R. THE COLLECTORS' GLOSSARY OF ANTIQUES AND FINE ARTS. 3d ed. London: Estates Gazette, 1971. 595 p. Illus.

An illustrated encyclopedia of terms, periods, and forms with attention to the decorative arts.

13   Boger, Louise A., and Boger, Batterson H. THE DICTIONARY OF ANTIQUES AND THE DECORATIVE ARTS: A BOOK OF REFERENCE FOR GLASS, FURNITURE, CERAMICS, SILVER, PERIODS, STYLES, TECHNICAL TERMS, ETC. New York: Charles Scribner's Sons, 1967. 662 p. 816 illus. Bibliog., pp. 559-66.

A well-illustrated dictionary, including both plates and line drawings. Quite comprehensive in its range and depth. Material since the first edition is included in a supplement. The well-organized bibliography is oriented toward the English language, again with a supplement of recent material.

14   Bond, Harold L. AN ENCYCLOPEDIA OF ANTIQUES. Boston: Hale, Cushman and Flint, 1937. xiii, 389 p. Illus. Bibliog., pp. 361-89.

An old standard divided into long chapters on each of the media, in encyclopedia form within categories. Line drawings supplement the plates and make terms and designs clear to the beginning viewer. Strong on names and dates.

15   Bossert, Helmuth T. PEASANT ART IN EUROPE. London: E. Benn, 1927. xii, 44 p. 2,100 illus. (some in color). Bibliog., pp. 40-43.

Over 2,000 illustrations make this one of the best picture books; examples of both decorative art objects and ornament carried through the years by European peasants.

3

Dictionaries, Encyclopedias, Histories

16 Bradford, Ernle. DICTIONARY OF ANTIQUES. London: English Universities Press, 1963. 151 p. Illus.

This compact dictionary includes information on materials, ornament and technique, with careful attention to applied arts. Major designers, craftsmen, and artists are presented in separate appendices; small, but useful.

17 Cameron, Ian, and Kingsley-Rowe, Elizabeth, eds. COLLINS ENCYCLOPEDIA OF ANTIQUES. London: Collins, 1973. 400 p. Illus. Bibliog., pp. 391-96.

This is aimed at a popular audience, with collecting as the main motif. Illustrated works are oriented toward antiques obtainable on the open market.

18 THE COMPLETE ENCYCLOPEDIA OF ANTIQUES. New York: Connoisseur, 1962. Reprint. New York: Hawthorn, 1967. 1,472 p. Illus. Bibliog., pp. 1410-22.

Aimed at the amateur scholar and serious collector. This volume, while general in its coverage, is particularly strong on British decorative arts. Arranged by media and objects. Includes essay on each area and contains a museum list organized by country.

19 Cowie, Donald P., and Henshaw, Keith. ANTIQUE COLLECTORS' DICTIONARY. London and New York: Arco, 1963. 208 p. Illus.

Contains 1,600 items in alphabetical arrangement and a checklist of marks. Particularly helpful for the collector or connoisseur who wishes to have documentation to balance out aesthetic judgements. A useful tool.

20 Coysh, Arthur W. THE ANTIQUE BUYER'S DICTIONARY OF NAMES. New York: Praeger, 1970. 278 p.

Organized by media and within categories by known craftsmen. Biographies and stylistic information in easy-to-digest form. Handy format for facts on the individual craftsmen.

21 Doane, Ethel M. ANTIQUES DICTIONARY. Brockton, Mass.: Anthoesen Press, 1949. 290 p. Bibliog., pp. 283-90.

This compilation of concise definitions was aimed at a popular market. Useful though narrow in scope, the bibliography lists key books in the English language.

22 Dreppard, Carl W. FIRST READER FOR ANTIQUE COLLECTORS. Garden City, N.Y.: Doubleday and Co., 1946. 274 p. Illus.

4

A well-written general handbook that covers the major decorative arts. Carefully illustrated with bibliographies after each chapter. A still useful older source.

23 Durdik, Jan, ed. THE PICTORIAL ENCYCLOPEDIA OF ANTIQUES. Feltham, Engl.: Hamlyn, 1970. 496 p. Illus. Bibliog.

Translation of a German manuscript, this volume covers a broad span of works, with particular attention to European objects. Bibliography in several languages.

24 Dyer, Walter A. THE LURE OF THE ANTIQUE. New York: Century Co., 1910. xii, 400 p. 159 illus.

An encyclopedia of furniture, glass, metals, and so forth, which is oriented toward questions of style, dating matter, and related scarcity. Although old, most information is still unchanged.

25 Glancross, June. THE STORY OF ANTIQUES. London: Ward Lock, 1973. 144 p. Illus.

Covers a wide range of decorative art objects up to the year 1910. Oriented to the collector.

26 Harper, George W., ed. ANTIQUE COLLECTORS GUIDE AND REFERENCE HANDBOOK. New York: Harper, 1939. 87 p. Illus.

A series of essays by Harper and others covering the whys and wherefores of antique collecting. Useful, though old, bibliographies, essay, and glossary.

27 Hayward, Helena, ed. THE CONNOISSEUR'S HANDBOOK OF ANTIQUE COLLECTING--A DICTIONARY OF FURNITURE, SILVER, CERAMICS, GLASS, FINE ART, ETC. London: Connoisseur; New York: Hawthorn, 1960. 320 p. Illus.

A brief but well-organized dictionary, aimed at the intelligent beginning collector. Broad coverage with special emphasis on British things.

28 Higgs, Percy J. THE COLLECTOR'S REFERENCE BOOK OF DATES. New York: Lent and Graff, 1927. 48 p. Illus.

An unusual reference tool, this volume emphasizes important dates from ancient times to the eighteenth century. Classification is arbitrary and subjective, but a quick way to check a date.

29 Hughes, Therle. ANTIQUES, AN ILLUSTRATED A TO Z. New York: World, 1972. 175 p. Illus.

A popular work, illustrated with line drawings. Covers media, style, and techniques.

30 McClinton, Katharine M. A HANDBOOK OF POPULAR ANTIQUES. New York: Random House, 1946. 244 p. 230 illus. Bibliog.

Although the early date causes differences in taste to be reflected, this work has a satisfactory overall coverage of basic antique collectables.

31 Macdonald-Taylor, Margaret S. A DICTIONARY OF MARKS: METALWORK, FURNITURE, CERAMICS; THE IDENTIFICATION HANDBOOK FOR ANTIQUE COLLECTORS. Rev. ed. New York: Hawthorn, 1973. 318 p. Illus. Bibliog. pp. 309-16.

A pocket handbook of the best-known marks on the three forms listed in the title, with particular concentration on American and English metal, on continental furniture, and oriental ceramics. The bibliography is restricted to the most popular volumes in English.

32 Michael, George. THE BASIC BOOK OF ANTIQUES. New York: Arco, 1975. 293 p. Illus. Bibliog.

A survey for the beginning collector with separate chapters on each of the media, from the seventeenth century to the present. Emphasis is on American with English and continental work in terms of prototypes and parallels.

33 Osborne, Harold, ed. THE OXFORD COMPANION TO THE DECORATIVE ARTS. Oxford, Engl.: Clarendon, 1975. 865 p. Illus.

Covers both decorative and applied arts, with essays on major countries, periods, and media, and short entries on the craftsmen and their materials and techniques. Bibliographical references accompanying the excellent entries. A key general work.

34 Phillips, Phoebe, ed. THE COLLECTOR'S ENCYCLOPEDIA OF ANTIQUES. New York: Crown Publishers, 1973. 704 p. 2,000 illus.

Carefully illustrated and well-rounded popular work, covering all the decorative and applied arts, including musical instruments and toys. Divided by types, with historical essays, glossary, illustrations, and bibliography.

35 Pope-Hennessy, John, ed. THE RANDOM HOUSE ENCYCLOPEDIA OF ANTIQUES. New York: Random House, 1973. 400 p. Illus. Bibliog.

A popular newer encyclopedia that obviously builds on some of the standard works in the field. Concise entries covering the entire range of decorative arts.

36 Praz, Mario. AN ILLUSTRATED HISTORY OF FURNISHING, FROM THE RENAISSANCE TO THE 20TH CENTURY. Translated from the Italian by William Weaver. New York: G. Braziller, 1964. 396 p. 400 illus. (part col.).

A translation of Praz's Italian work of 1945, this work is profusely illustrated and contains a wealth of information on the variety of forms.

37 Ramsey, Leonard Gerard Gwynne, ed. THE COMPLETE ENCYCLOPEDIA OF ANTIQUES. New York: Hawthorn, 1967. 1,472 p. 512 illus. Bibliog., pp. 1410-22.

This careful, extensive reference work includes American, English, and European works, with individual chapters, including a survey of the topic, definitions of relevant terms, and illustrations. Includes a list of important museums and a far-reaching bibliography.

38 Runes, Dagobert David, and Schrickel, Harry G. ENCYCLOPEDIA OF THE ARTS. New York: Philosophical Library, 1946. 1,064 p.

One of the few encyclopedias that cuts across both fine and decorative arts. Although dated, it contains enough useful information on all periods and styles to warrant consideration.

39 Savage, George. DICTIONARY OF ANTIQUES. New York: Praeger, 1970. 534 p. Illus. Bibliog., pp. 504-34.

One of the high-quality dictionaries to list and illustrate objects and to present well-written entries on techniques and craftsmen. A major asset is the thorough and well-organized bibliography.

Chapter 3

PERIOD STUDIES AND SURVEYS OF DECORATIVE ARTS

The following entries are broadly based studies, each covering a specific historical period.

40   Abbate, Francesco, ed. ART NOUVEAU: THE STYLE OF THE 1890'S. London: Octopus, 1972. 158 p. 92 illus. Bibliog.

Covers both the fine and applied arts throughout Europe and stresses the relationship of stylistic elements among the various forms.

41   Addison, Julia D. ARTS AND CRAFTS IN THE MIDDLE AGES. Boston: L.C. Page, 1933. 378 p. Illus. (some in color). Bibliog.

Discusses both the style and the craftsmen of both the Middle Ages and the Renaissance. Covers both the traditional decorative arts and ephemera.

42   Aslin, Elizabeth. THE AESTHETIC MOVEMENT: PRELUDE TO ART NOUVEAU. New York: Frederick A. Praeger, 1969. 183 p. 121 illus. Bibliog.

A broad survey of the arts and crafts movement in both fine and applied arts. Explores its origins and its spread throughout the West. Stresses aesthetics and the philosophical frame of reference.

43   Battersby, Martin. ART NOUVEAU. Feltham, Engl.: Hamlyn, 1969. 40 p. 48 plates.

A general introduction and survey of the Art Nouveau period from 1889 to 1903. Primarily a picture book, with some text.

44   _____ . THE DECORATIVE THIRTIES. New York: Walker, 1971. 208 p. Illus. Bibliog., pp. 204-5.

A popular survey of the Art Deco style in a wide variety of individual and architecturally related forms.

9

45   Bridgeman, Harriet, and Drury, Elizabeth, eds. ENCYCLOPEDIA OF
      VICTORIANA. New York: Macmillan, 1975. 368 p. Illus. (some
      in color). Bibliog.

      Covers both British and American objects.

46   Drexler, Arthur, ed. THE DESIGN COLLECTION: SELECTED OB-
      JECTS. New York: Museum of Modern Art, 1970. Unpaged. Illus.
      (some in color).

      Good to excellent illustrations of some of the excellently de-
      signed objects from the fine collection at MOMA. We could
      wish for a text.

47   Field, June. COLLECTING GEORGIAN AND VICTORIAN CRAFTS.
      New York: Charles Scribner's Sons, 1973. 162 p. 238 illus.
      Bibliog., pp. 154–57.

      Concerned more with ephemera than the traditional crafts,
      this chatty and nonscholarly book does have the advantage of
      reproducing many types of objects of Britain, Europe, and
      America. General information on how things were made is
      useful.

48   Haslam, Malcolm. MARKS AND MONOGRAMS OF THE MODERN
      MOVEMENT, 1875-1930. New York: Charles Scribner's Sons, 1977.
      192 p. Illus.

      A rather detailed biographical dictionary of artists, craftsmen,
      distributors, and manufacturers during the years encompassed
      by the title. Marks, stamps, and descriptions of their use are
      all carefully explained and illustrated.

49   Hillier, Bevis. ART DECO OF THE 20'S AND 30'S. London: Studio
      Vista, 1968. 168 p. Illus. (some in color).

      Covers both European and American Art Deco, with emphasis
      on popular and way-out examples. Written in a breezy style
      that belies the careful study behind the writing.

50   _____ . THE DECORATIVE ARTS OF THE FORTIES AND FIFTIES
      AUSTERITY BINGE. New York: C.N. Potter, 1975. 200 p. Illus.
      Bibliog. ref.

      A chatty, often tongue-in-cheek look at the two decades,
      with the illustrations emphasizing only the most way-out cul-
      tural artifacts. Concerned more with design concepts rather
      than the traditional decorative arts, but some craft items are
      included.

51   Katzenberg, Dena S. BLUE TRADITIONS: INDIGO DYED TEXTILES
     AND RELATED COBALT GLAZED CERAMICS FROM THE 17TH
     THROUGH THE 19TH CENTURY. Baltimore: Baltimore Museum of
     Art, 1973. 214 p. 2,000 illus. Bibliog.

     The catalog of an exhibition which included 119 textiles and
     over sixty ceramic pieces from throughout the world, presents
     the scope and depth of interest in this "blue period." His-
     tory of the trade in ceramic and textile goods and technical
     information on the methods of dyeing and glazing.

52   Lichten, Frances. DECORATIVE ART OF VICTORIA'S ERA. New
     York: Charles Scribner's Sons, 1950. 274 p. Illus. Bibliog., pp.
     265-70.

     Arranged in large groupings, both British and American decora-
     tive arts of this period are covered. The illustrations are
     taken from Victorian written sources. Useful for the begin-
     ning collector.

53   McClinton, Katharine M. ART DECO: A GUIDE FOR COLLECTORS.
     New York: C.N. Potter, 1972. 288 p. Illus.

     A general popular guide to a wide range of Art Deco objects:
     ceramics, furniture, glass, metals, textiles, and graphics.
     Oriented toward the would-be collector.

54   MacKay, James A. TURN-OF-THE-CENTURY ANTIQUES: AN EN-
     CYCLOPEDIA. New York: E.P. Dutton and Co., 1975. 320 p.
     Illus. (some in color).

     Contains 350 entries covering the years from 1890 to 1910 in
     a wide range of collectible forms. Includes late Victoriana
     and various arts and crafts objects.

55   Madsen, Stephen T. ART NOUVEAU. New York: McGraw-Hill,
     1967. 256 p. Illus. Bibliog.

     A broad and scholarly study of the era, the ideas and philos-
     ophy behind the style, and the units of form in both fine and
     decorative arts.

56   Mebane, John. THE COMPLETE BOOK OF COLLECTING ART NOU-
     VEAU. New York: Coward-McCann, 1970. 256 p. Illus.

     A collector's guide that covers furniture, glass, and so on.
     Particular attention to objects made by Guimard, Lalique, and
     Tiffany.

57   Paz, Octavio. IN PRAISE OF HANDS: CONTEMPORARY CRAFTS
     OF THE WORLD. Greenwich, Conn.: New York Graphic Society,

1974. 223 p. 243 illus. Bibliog., pp. 212-18.

A broad survey of current crafts and craftsmen in a wide range of media. The only major study of this nature with good illustrations and an across-the-board bibliography.

58   Pignati, Terisio. THE AGE OF ROCOCO. New York: Hamlyn, 1969. 157 p. 69 color illus.

A study of the first half of the eighteenth century in Europe with attention to a sampling of decorative art objects.

59   THE RANDOM HOUSE COLLECTOR'S ENCYCLOPEDIA: VICTORIANA TO ART DECO. New York: Random House, 1974. 302 p. Illus. Bibliog., pp. 297-302.

A basic encyclopedia of the era. Includes craftsmen, materials, periods, techniques, and a wide variety of objects. Substantial information on major subperiods and styles.

60   Scarisbrick, Diana. BAROQUE: THE AGE OF EXUBERANCE. London: Orbis, 1973. 64 p. Illus. Bibliog.

A picture book of baroque decorative objects and ornament.

61   Schmutzler, Robert. ART NOUVEAU. New York: Abrams, 1962. 322 p. 439 illus. (12 in color). Bibliog.

A very thorough and scholarly treatment of the Art Nouveau manifestations in several countries. Ties the work together and relates the decorative arts forms to the style as a whole. Excellent bibliography.

62   Veronesi, Giulia. STYLE AND DESIGN, 1909-1929. New York: Braziller, 1968. 372 p. 256 illus. (10 in color).

A well-illustrated broad survey of the era, with much attention to various decorative art objects. The rise of a modernist Art Deco aesthetic.

63   Woodhouse, Charles P. THE VICTORIANA COLLECTOR'S HANDBOOK. New York: St. Martin's, 1970. 237 p. Illus.

A popular introduction to the ceramics, furniture, glass, and metalwork of the period. Individual chapters on particular craftsmen. Tips on collecting and a guide to marks.

Chapter 4

GENERAL AND PERIOD SURVEYS OF THE DECORATIVE ARTS OF INDIVIDUAL COUNTRIES AND REGIONS

Chapter 4 includes a selection of books in English on the docorative arts in various countries and several period studies of some important background material in the countries most relevant to the study of American decorative arts. Unfortunately, there are no suitable works in English on many of the countries or on important periods within those countries.

AFRICA

64   Trowell, Kathleen M. AFRICAN DESIGN. New York: Frederick A. Praeger, 1960. 78 p. Illus. Bibliog.

A collector's handbook of both the traditional decorative art forms and the specialized work in wood, ivory, and other materials common throughout most of the continent.

CANADA

65   Lessard, Michel. COMPLETE GUIDE TO FRENCH-CANADIAN AN-TIQUES. New York: Hart Publishing Co., 1974. 255 p. Illus. Bibliog., pp. 248-51.

The furniture and furnishings of the French Canadians. Explores sources of style and continuation of traditional forms.

66   Smith, Jean, and Smith, Elizabeth. COLLECTING CANADA'S PAST. Scarborough, Ont.: Prentice-Hall, 1974. 220 p. Illus.

A broad survey of the authors' collection of Canadian decorative arts. Mentions periods and styles and provides pointers on connoisseurship for the collector.

67   Stevens, Gerald F. THE CANADIAN COLLECTOR. Rexdale, Ont.: Coles, 1974. 100 p. Illus. Bibliog.

Covers the basic decorative art objects and some specialized objects such as firearms. Many illustrations in a collector's guide.

68   Webster, Donald B., ed. THE BOOK OF CANADIAN ANTIQUES. New York: McGraw-Hill, 1974. 352 p. 400 illus. (some in color). Bibliog.

A major illustrated survey of Canadian objects, both furniture and furnishings. Covers periods and stylistic changes.

CHINA

69   Crossman, Carl L. THE CHINA TRADE: EXPORT PAINTINGS, FURNITURE, SILVER AND OTHER OBJECTS. Princeton, N.J.: Pyne Press, 1972. 288 p. 290 illus. (40 in color). Bibliog.

A major illustrated study of the Chinese work sent out to both European and American ports from the 1780s through the 1850s.

70   Feddersen, Martin. CHINESE DECORATIVE ARTS; A HANDBOOK FOR COLLECTORS AND CONNOISSEURS. New York: T. Yoseloff, 1961. 286 p. Illus. Bibliog.

A solid history of Chinese decorative arts: ceramics, furniture, metalwork, and textiles through the nineteenth century. Includes the popular ivory and lacquer work so eagerly sought by both European and American collectors.

71   Foreign Languages Press. CHINESE ARTS AND CRAFTS. Peking: Light Industry Publishing House, 1973. Unpaged. 222 color illus.

A beautifully illustrated picture book which covers the entire range of Chinese decorative arts, with particular emphasis on high-quality pieces.

72   Forman, Werner. A BOOK OF CHINESE ART. London: Spring, 1966. 74 p. 212 plates. Bibliog.

A picture survey of the entire history of Chinese fine and decorative arts. Fine examples of porcelain, jade, and lacquer work.

73   Hobson, Robert L., comp. CHINESE ART. Rev. ed. London: Spring, 1964. 21 p. 100 color plates. Bibliog.

A picture book of Chinese porcelain, jades, lacquer work, furniture, and so forth, with a brief survey of Chinese art.

74 Jenyns, R. Soame, and Watson, William. CHINESE ART: THE MINOR
    ARTS. 2 vols. New York: Universe, 1963–64. Vol. 1: 462 p.
    143 illus. Vol. 2: unpaged. Illus. Bibliog.

    Large plates with descriptions and captions. Volume 1 covers
    metals, cloisonne, lacquer work, and furniture. Volume 2 is
    devoted to glass, ivory, work in semiprecious stones, and tex-
    tiles.

FRANCE

75 Ericksen, Svend. EARLY NEO-CLASSICISM IN FRANCE: THE CREA-
    TION OF THE LOUIS XVI STYLE IN ARCHITECTURE, DECORATION,
    FURNITURE, ORMOLU, GOLD AND SILVER, AND SEVRES PORCELAIN
    IN THE MID-18TH CENTURY. London: Faber, 1973. 432 p. Illus.
    Bibliog.

    A valuable recent survey of this much-admired French era.
    Includes both practical arts and ornament, and illustrations
    include both rooms and objects. Important background read-
    ing.

76 Gonzalez-Palacios, Alvar. THE FRENCH EMPIRE STYLE. Feltham,
    Engl.: Hamlyn, 1970. 157 p. Illus. (some in color).

    A general history that includes both the fine and decorative
    arts during the period. The quality of the color plates is
    good and the material, while not presented in a scholarly
    way, can be relied upon.

77 Oglesby, Catherine. FRENCH PROVINCIAL DECORATIVE ART. New
    York: Charles Scribner's Sons, 1951. 214 p. Illus. Bibliog., pp.
    212-14.

    Less important to the history of American decorative arts than
    court styles, provincial work as described in this handbook is
    still important background. Ceramics, furniture, metals, and
    textiles are included, with concentration on useful household
    objects.

78 McClinton, Katharine M. MODERN FRENCH DECORATION. New
    York: Putnam's, 1930. 219 p. 27 illus.

    Discusses the evolution of French decorative arts and places
    them within a broader decorative context.

79 Savage, George. FRENCH DECORATIVE ART, 1638-1793. New York:
    Frederick A. Praeger, 1969. 189 p. Illus. Bibliog., pp. 179-80.

    A compact but scholarly history conveying all the important

decorative arts. Inventories and lists supplement material on style, objects, and decoration.

80 Strange, Thomas A. AN HISTORICAL GUIDE TO FRENCH INTERIORS. London: Methuen, 1950. 370 p. Illus.

A survey of French interiors from the neoclassical through the romantic eras.

81 Verlet, Pierre. THE 18TH CENTURY IN FRANCE: SOCIETY, DECORATION, FURNITURE. Rutland, Vt.: Charles E. Tuttle Co., 1967. 291 p. Illus. (24 in color).

Although this work is primarily concerned with furniture, it also discusses French furnishings and decorative design of the eighteenth century. Well illustrated.

GERMANY

82 Hirschfield-Mack, Ludwig. THE BAUHAUS: AN INTRODUCTORY SURVEY. London: Longmans, 1963. 54 p. Illus. Bibliog.

An introduction to the art and decorative arts of the Bauhaus, including an explanation of the role of the workshop in the course of instruction.

83 Naylor, Gillian. THE BAUHAUS. London: Studio Vista, 1968. 159 p. Illus.

A picture book of the early years of the Bauhaus, from 1919 to 1928, with some introductory text.

84 Scheidig, Walther. CRAFTS OF THE WEIMER BAUHAUS, 1919-1924: AN EARLY EXPERIMENT IN INDUSTRIAL DESIGN. London: Studio Vista, 1967. 150 p. 81 illus. Bibliog.

A well-illustrated popular study of the work of the crafts shops at the Bauhaus and their impact on modern technology and design.

GREAT BRITAIN

85 Beard, Geoffrey W. GEORGIAN CRAFTSMEN AND THEIR WORK. S. Brunswick, N.J.: A.S. Barnes, 1967. 207 p. 124 illus. Bibliog., pp. 190-98.

A solid, well-researched history, covering technical and stylistic material. Includes an appendix of important craftsmen.

Valuable bibliography includes primary sources. A scholarly study of interior design in England during the eighteenth century.

86 Finlay, Ian. SCOTTISH CRAFTS. London: Harrap, 1948. 728 p. Illus.

An older but still unsurpassed general survey of both the fine and decorative arts in Scotland from the Middle Ages to the middle of the twentieth century.

87 Gloag, John [E.]. VICTORIAN COMFORT: A SOCIAL HISTORY OF DESIGN FROM 1830-1900. London: Newton, Abbott, David and Charles, 1973. 252 p. Illus.

A general social survey of the decorative arts in Britain during the Victorian era. Includes information on applied work and ornamentation.

88 Harding, Arthur. COLLECTING ENGLISH ANTIQUES. London: W. and G. Foyle, 1963. 92 p. Illus.

An introduction to the various English decorative art forms from the late Middle Ages through the middle of the nineteenth century. Illustrations of a variety of forms.

89 Hayward, Charles H. ENGLISH ROOMS AND THEIR DECORATION AT A GLANCE. London: Architectural Press, 1925. 289 p. Illus.

A picture book of English interiors that covers the period from 1066 to 1800.

90 Howarth, Thomas. CHARLES RENNIE MACKINTOSH AND THE MODERN MOVEMENT. London: Routledge and K. Paul, 1952. 329 p. 96 illus.

A study of Mackintosh, his work, and his place within the British arts and crafts movement. Illustrations of Mackintosh interiors.

91 Hughes, George B. COLLECTING ANTIQUES. New York: Macmillan, 1961. 391 p. Illus. Bibliog.

A guide to collecting various popular British objects: Battersea enamels, pewter, Sheffield plates, samplers, Tunbridge wares, and so on.

92 Lavine, Sigmund. HANDMADE IN ENGLAND: THE TRADITION OF BRITISH CRAFTSMEN. New York: Dodd, Mead, 1968. 148 p. Illus. Bibliog., pp. 135-37.

A survey of English decorative art from the Middle Ages to the end of the rococo era. Covers all major forms except textiles.

93   Reade, Brian. REGENCY ANTIQUES. London: Batsford, 1953. 270 p. Illus. Bibliog.

Decorative arts in Britain in the first third of the nineteenth century.

94   Stacpoole, George, ed. A GUIDE TO IRISH ANTIQUES AND AN-TIQUE DEALERS. Cork, Ire.: Mercier, 1967. 104 p.

One of the few volumes to discuss traditional Irish decorative arts and to point out their distinctive qualities.

95   Wintersgill, Donald. ENGLISH ANTIQUES, 1700-1830. New York: Morrow, 1975. 256 p. Illus. (some in color). Bibliog.

A study of Georgian decorative arts. Covers the changes in style and provides hints for the collector.

INDIA

96   Coomaraswamy, Ananda K. THE ARTS AND CRAFTS OF INDIA AND CEYLON. London: T.N. Foulis, 1913. 255 p. 225 illus. (some in color). Bibliog.

An old but standard survey of the fine and decorative arts of the old Indian area.

ISLAMIC

97   Kuhnel, Ernst. THE MINOR ARTS OF ISLAM. Ithaca, N.Y.: Cornell University Press, 1971. 255 p. Illus. Bibliog., pp. 247-50.

A scholarly survey of a wide range of decorative and ornamental arts of the Islamic empire. Fine illustrations and a strong bibliography on a seldom-documented field.

ITALY

98   Detroit Institute of Arts. DECORATIVE ARTS OF THE ITALIAN RE-NAISSANCE, 1400-1600. Detroit: 1958. 179 p. Illus.

The catalog of a major exhibition of Italian Renaissance metalwork, ceramics, and glass. Descriptive entries on catalog items.

99   Hunter, George L. ITALIAN FURNITURE AND INTERIORS. 2d ed.
      New York: Architectural Book Publishing Co., 1920. Unpaged.
      200 plates.

      Folio illustrations of Italian rooms from the time of the Re-
      naissance.

JAPAN

100   Lee, Sherman E. JAPANESE DECORATIVE STYLE. New York: Harry
      N. Abrams, 1961. 161 p. Illus. Bibliog., pp. 155-58.

      A well-documented, scholarly history arranged by chronologi-
      cal periods. The bibliography depends on both Oriental and
      Western languages, and the illustrations are enriched with de-
      scriptive commentary.

101   Munsterberg, Hugo. THE FOLK ARTS OF JAPAN. Rutland, Vt.:
      Charles E. Tuttle Co., 1958. 168 p. 110 illus. (some in color).

      An informative but simply written discussion of the various
      craft forms in traditional Japan, with a chapter on the con-
      temporary scene. Very little in the way of chronology and no
      documentation. Concerned with folk traditions.

102   Turk, Frank A. JAPANESE OBJETS D'ART. New York: Sterling,
      1963. 156 p. Illus. Bibliog.

      A survey of Japanese decorative arts with attention to individ-
      ual periods and styles. Oriented to the beginning collector.

103   Yamada, Chisaburoh F., ed. DECORATIVE ARTS OF JAPAN. Tokyo:
      Kodansha International, 1964. 262 p. 110 illus. (some in color).

      A scholarly study and survey of Japanese decorative arts, with
      individual chapters on the different media by known authori-
      ties. Fine color plates accompanied by detailed descriptive
      material.

MEXICO

104   Shipway, Verna C. DECORATIVE DESIGN IN MEXICAN HOMES.
      New York: Architectural Book Co., 1966. 249 p. Illus.

      A broad survey of Mexican arts and crafts with particular at-
      tention to folk and country pieces.

NETHERLANDS

105   Bromberg, Paul. DECORATIVE ARTS IN THE NETHERLANDS. New York: Netherland Information Bureau, 1944. 62 p. Illus. Bibliog.

> A brief, illustrated guide to Dutch decorative arts for the casual viewer and potential tourist.

NEW ZEALAND

106   Daalder, Truus. HUNTING ANTIQUES IN NEW ZEALAND. Dunedin, N.Z.: J. McIndoe, 1969. 187 p. Illus.

> An informal survey of New Zealand decorative arts for the beginning collector. Points out major period styles.

NORWAY

107   Hopstock, Carsten. NORWEGIAN DESIGN FROM VIKING AGE TO INDUSTRIAL REVOLUTION. Oslo: Dreyer, n.d. 212 p. Illus.

> A general survey of the range of Norwegian decorative arts, including ornament. A wide variety of illustrations makes for painless perusal.

POLAND

108   Bochnak, Adam. DECORATIVE ARTS IN POLAND. Warsaw: Arkady, 1972. 331 p. Illus. (some in color). Bibliog.

> A general survey of both decorative and folk arts, with good illustrations.

RUSSIA

109   Rybakov, Boris A. RUSSIAN APPLIED ART OF THE 10TH TO 13TH CENTURIES. Leningrad, 1971. 125 p. 161 illus.

> A pictorial survey of Russian late medieval work.

110   Verdier, Philippe. RUSSIAN ART: ICONS AND DECORATIVE ARTS FROM THE ORIGIN TO THE 20TH CENTURY. Baltimore: Walters Art Gallery, 1959. 86 p. Illus.

> The catalog of an exhibition of Russian decorative arts. Catalog objects are described and discussed, and many are illustrated.

SWEDEN

111   Nylén, Anna-Maja. SWEDISH HANDCRAFT. New York: Van Nostrand Reinhold, 1977. 428 p. Illus. Bibliog., pp. 416–20.

A solid study of the decorative arts traditions in Sweden. Includes illustrations of objects usually not seen in the United States and a basic bibliography on a variety of Swedish forms.

112   Plath, Iona. THE DECORATIVE ARTS OF SWEDEN. New York: Dover, 1966. 218 p. Illus.

Covers the era from the Middle Ages to modern times. Includes the basic folk and decorative arts as well as some fine arts. The only source for basic material in English.

Chapter 5

SUBJECT SURVEYS OF DECORATIVE ARTS

The following entries are divided by specific form--ceramics, furniture, glass, metals, and textiles. In each section, general works are followed by entries on specific periods and countries. General works include bibliographies, dictionaries, encyclopedias, and historical surveys. All of these works present useful background for the understanding of developments in American decorative arts.

CERAMICS: GENERAL WORKS

113 Barber, Edwin A. THE CERAMIC COLLECTOR'S GLOSSARY. New York: Walpole Society, 1914. Reprint. New York: Da Capo, 1967. 119 p. Illus.

An old but valuable dictionary of ceramic art. Definitions cover material, style, and technique. Illustrations are of line drawings.

114 Boger, Louise A. THE DICTIONARY OF WORLD POTTERY AND POR- CELAIN. New York: Charles Scribner's Sons, 1971. 533 p. 210 illus. (60 in color). Bibliog., pp. 525-33.

A well-written and carefully illustrated dictionary of ceramics, covering all aspects of ceramic activity.

115 Brooklyn Institute of Arts and Sciences. The Brooklyn Museum. THE ART & TECHNIQUE OF CERAMICS: AN EXHIBITION PRESENTED BY THE ROCKEFELLER FOUNDATION INTERNES OF THE BROOKLYN MUSEUM. Brooklyn, N.Y.: 1937. 112 p. Illus. Bibliog., pp. 109-10.

Brief essay on the three main developments of ceramic ware: porous pottery, glazed pottery, and vitreous ware. Organization is geographical.

116 Burton, William. A GENERAL HISTORY OF PORCELAIN. 2 vols.
New York: Funk and Wagnalls, 1921. 112 illus. (32 in color).
Bibliog., pp. 207-8.

An old but scholarly and comprehensive history of porcelain,
covering both its manufacture and its decoration. Provides
the basis for much later bibliographical work in the field.

117 Chaffers, William. THE KERAMIC GALLERY. 2d ed. Revised and
edited by H.M. Cundall. 2 vols. London: Reeves S. Turner, 1926. Vol.1:
468 p. 227 illus. (5 in color); Vol. 2: 694 p. 700 illus. (8 in color).

A companion volume to his MARKS & MONOGRAMS ON
POTTERY AND PORCELAIN (1863). An old but still useful
pictorial survey of worldwide ceramic work. Descriptions of
the illustrated examples.

118 _____. MARKS AND MONOGRAMS ON EUROPEAN AND ORIEN-
TAL POTTERY AND PORCELAIN. 2 vols. 15th rev. ed. New York:
Dover, 1965. Vol. 1: vii, 636 p. 56 illus.; Vol. 2: vii, 443 p.
12 illus.

A substantial and comprehensive dictionary. Organized by
country and includes brief histories. Facsimiles of marks are
accompanied by descriptions.

119 Charleston, Robert J., ed. WORLD CERAMICS. New York: Mc-
Graw-Hill Book Co., 1968. 352 p. Illus. (64 in color).

A profusely illustrated popular survey of ceramics to the present. Covers African, British, continental, Oceanic, Oriental,
and pre-Columbian work.

120 Cooper, Emmanuel. A HISTORY OF POTTERY. New York: St.
Martin's Press, 1972. 276 p. Illus. (8 in color). Bibliog., pp.
265-70.

A popular historical survey, with particular attention to British
and American work. Useful maps and chronology with a glossary of relevant terms.

121 Cox, Warren E. THE BOOK OF POTTERY AND PORCELAIN. 2 vols.
Rev. ed. New York: Crown Publishers, 1970. 1,158 p. 3,000
illus. (8 in color).

A collector's guidebook to identification of various ceramic
pieces. Includes a large number of illustrations and an extensive survey of ceramic marks.

122 Cushion, John P., and Honey, William B. HANDBOOK OF POTTERY
AND PORCELAIN MARKS. Rev. ed. London: Faber and Faber,
1965. 477 p. Illus.

Begins with a chapter on the historical use of pottery marks.
The body of the volume is a country-by-country alphabetical
listing of ceramic makers and line drawings of their marks.
Includes a brief historical narrative before each country's listings.

123 Dillon, Edward. PORCELAIN. Connoisseur's Library. New York:
G.P. Putnam's Sons; London: Methuen and Co., 1904. xxxv, 420 p.
49 illus. Bibliog., pp. xxvi-xxxii.

An old but still useful study that emphasizes decorated pieces.

124 Dodd, Arthur E. DICTIONARY OF CERAMICS. New York: Philosophical Library, 1964. 327 p.

Emphasis on the technical vocabulary of industrial ceramics,
trade names, and specialized terminology.

125 Eberlein, Harold D., and Ramsdell, Roger W. THE PRACTICAL BOOK
OF CHINAWARE. Rev. ed. Philadelphia: J.B. Lippincott Co.,
1948. 440 p. 189 illus. (13 in color). Bibliog., pp. 307-10.

An introductory survey for the beginning collector. Covers
both American and European wares and includes a good variety of illustrations of typical pieces.

126 Haggar, Reginald. CONCISE ENCYCLOPEDIA OF CONTINENTAL
POTTERY AND PORCELAIN. New York: Frederick A. Praeger, 1968.
533 p. Illus. Bibliog., pp. 523-33.

An illustrated dictionary that covers countries, decoration,
individuals, material, and techniques. Facsimiles of marks.
One of the best general reference tools.

127 Hannover, Emil. POTTERY AND PORCELAIN. New York: Charles
Scribner's Sons, 1925. 3 vols. Vol. 1: 589 p. 684 illus. Bibliog.,
pp. 564-73. Vol. 2: 287 p. 402 illus. Bibliog., pp. 269-72.
Vol. 3: 571 p. 858 illus. Bibliog., pp. 546-54.

This very old trilogy remains one of the most solidly researched
and presented works in the field of ceramics. Volume 1 covers earthenware and stoneware of Europe and the Near East;
volume 2, the Far East; and volume 3, European porcelain.

128 Kovel, Ralph M., and Kovel, Terry H. DICTIONARY OF MARKS:
POTTERY AND PORCELAIN. New York: Crown Publishers, 1953.
278 p. Bibliog.

An alphabetical listing of about 5,000 pottery marks, with attention to both the shapes and symbols of the marks.

129 LeFevre, Leon. ARCHITECTURAL POTTERY. Translated by K.H. Bird
and W. Moore Binns. London: Scott, Greewood and Co., 1900. xv,
496 p. 5 plates. 950 figs. Tables. Bibliog., pp. 485-86. Index,
pp. 492-96.

A technical study of pottery with attention to the qualities of
clays, the preparation of it in working form, and the various
industrial uses to which it is put. Mention of bricks, architectural pottery, tiles, and pipes.

130 Rosenthal, Ernest. POTTERY & CERAMICS: FROM COMMON BRICK
TO FINE CHINA. Hammondsworth, Middlesex, Engl.: Penguin Books,
1949. 304 p. 31 illus.

A materials and technological study of ceramic art. Traces
the developments from prehistoric times to the current innovations of contemporary industry. Some examination of the qualities and properties of various clays.

131 Savage, George. CERAMICS FOR THE COLLECTOR: AN INTRODUC-
TION TO POTTERY & PORCELAIN. New York: Macmillan Publishing
Co., 1949. 224 p. 114 illus. Bibliog.

An introduction to ceramics for the would-be collector. Illustrations of typical pieces available and a glossary of basic
terms.

132 _____. PORCELAIN THROUGH THE AGES. Baltimore: Penguin
Books, 1963. 352 p. Illus. Bibliog.

A general study of the subject, useful as background for understanding American porcelain, with particular attention paid to
technical matters such as ceramic bodies, glazes, and so on.
Includes a glossary of terms, a table of marks, and a selected
general bibliography.

133 Savage, George, and Newman, Harold. AN ILLUSTRATED DICTIO-
NARY OF CERAMICS. New York: Van Nostrand Reinhold Co., 1974.
320 p. 626 illus. (24 in color).

A detailed comprehensive reference work, including all types
of entries: location, techniques, periods, and styles.

134 Thorn, C. Jordan. HANDBOOK OF OLD POTTERY AND PORCELAIN
MARKS. New York: Tudor Publishing Co., 1947. xiii, 176 p. 44
illus.

Approximately 4,000 marks are arranged by countries, with
about 1,000 in the American section. Includes many marks
not found in earlier collections, plus some assigned on a spec-
ulation basis. Worthwhile research tool.

135 Weiss, Gustav. THE BOOK OF PORCELAIN. New York: Frederick
A. Praeger, 1971. 335 p. Illus. (some in color). Bibliog.,
pp. 318-20.

The history of porcelain in a cultural setting, from ancient
China on. Surveys major porcelain-producing centers and includes a survey of ceramic marks and information on technical
matters.

136 Wykes-Joyce, Max. 7,000 YEARS OF POTTERY AND PORCELAIN.
New York: Philosophical Library, 1958. 276 p. 85 illus. Bibliog.,
pp. 262-67.

A popular and easy-to-read overall survey of ceramics from
earliest times to the current era. Concentrates on European
developments and is so weighted in the illustrations.

CERAMICS: COUNTRIES AND PERIODS

137 Barrett, Franklin A. WORCESTER PORCELAIN. London: Faber &
Faber, 1953. xiv, 53 p. 100 plates (4 in color). Bibliog., p. 49.

A short text, followed by large clear illustrations with descriptive notes, covers the output of this popular nineteenth-
century factory. The breadth of work of the factory is stressed.

138 Barrett, Franklin A., and Thorpe, Arthur L. DERBY PORCELAIN 1750-
1848. London: Faber & Faber, 1971. xv, 206 p. 185 illus. (8 in
color). Bibliog., pp. 199-200.

The individual craftsmen and firms in the Derby porcelain
field, with particular emphasis on the Chelsea-Derby period
(1770-1784). Useful appendices include biographies, marks,
pattern books, references to technical material, and sale catalogs.

139 Buerdeley, Michel, and Buerdeley, Cecile. A CONNOISSEUR'S
GUIDE TO CHINESE CERAMICS. New York: Harper & Row, 1974.
318 p. Illus.

A general history and survey of the range and variety of Chinese ceramics from the earliest times through the late nineteenth century. Oriented to the collector and would-be connoisseur.

140 Bushnell, George H., and Digby, Adrian. ANCIENT AMERICAN
POTTERY. London: Faber & Faber, 1955. 51 p. 84 plates (4 in
color). Bibliog., pp. 47-48.

A concise history of pottery in Central America, South America,

and Southwest United States to the time of the conquest
(1550 A.D.).

141   Charles, Rollo. CONTINENTAL PORCELAIN OF THE EIGHTEENTH
CENTURY. London: Benn, 1964. 198 p. Illus.

A popular handbook of the styles of porcelain during the era,
with a survey of the major centers of production and a catalog of their marks.

142   Charleston, Robert J. ROMAN POTTERY. London: Faber & Faber,
1955. 48 p. Illus. Bibliog., pp. 41-44.

A brief but carefully done introduction to Roman pottery and
its place in world ceramic developments.

143   Ducret, Siegfried. GERMAN PORCELAIN AND FAIENCE. New York:
Universe, 1962. 466 p. Illus. Bibliog., pp. 452-56.

A solid handbook of specific pieces with extended descriptive
material on each illustration and organized in terms of location and individual factories. Includes a selection of ceramic
marks.

144   Fisher, Stanley W. ENGLISH BLUE AND WHITE PORCELAIN OF THE
EIGHTEENTH CENTURY. London: B.J. Batsford, 1948. xv, 190 p.
45 illus.

Important survey of the major patterns which were so much
appreciated in eighteenth-century America. Contains separate
chapters on marks, materials, and so on, and a valuable chronology.

145   Folsom, Robert S. HANDBOOK OF GREEK POTTERY; A GUIDE FOR
AMATEURS. Greenwich, Conn.: New York Graphic Society, 1967.
213 p. Illus.

A general popular survey of Greek work from approximately
1000 to 145 B.C. Oriented to the beginning collector, it
includes a classification of major shapes and provides basic
terminology.

146   Giacommoti, Jeane. FRENCH FAIENCE. New York: Universe, 1963.
266 p. Illus. Bibliog., p. 258.

A solid survey of French faience up to the end of the nineteenth century. Organized by geographical areas, with an
introduction to each region being supported by descriptive
plates and marks.

147   Godden, Geoffrey A. BRITISH POTTERY AND PORCELAIN, 1780–
1850. New York: A.S. Barnes, 1963. 144 p. Illus. Bibliog.,
pp. 138–40.

A good general survey of the types of work which flooded the
American market after the Revolution. One of a series of
the author's writings about British ceramic wares.

148   _____. AN ILLUSTRATED ENCYCLOPEDIA OF BRITISH POTTERY
AND PORCELAIN. New York: Crown Publishers, 1966. xxvi,
390 p. 679 illus. (16 in color).

A companion volume to Godden's ENCYCLOPEDIA OF BRIT-
ISH POTTERY AND PORCELAIN MARKS (1964). A brief history of British ceramic activity is followed by illustrations of
the work itself. Organized by artist and location. Includes
a useful glossary of terms.

149   _____. MASON'S PATENT IRONSTONE CHINA. New York: Frederick A. Praeger, 1977. xiv, 175 p. 149 illus. (8 in color).
Bibliog. note.

Discusses Mason ironstone in great detail and includes reference to similar wares of other manufacturers. The Mason family was one of the most influential potting families in England.

150   Gorham, Hazel N. JAPANESE AND ORIENTAL CERAMICS. Rutland,
Vt.: Charles E. Tuttle Co., 1970. 256 p. Illus. Bibliog., pp.
237–41.

A popular survey of both Japanese and Korean ceramics with
background information on Oriental ceramics in general. Oriented to the beginning collector, it includes information on
aesthetic and decorative material.

151   Hillier, Bevis. POTTERY AND PORCELAIN 1700–1914: ENGLAND,
EUROPE AND NORTH AMERICA. New York: Meredith Press, 1968.
386 p. 217 illus. Bibliog., pp. 361–68.

Chapters on the social status of the potter, on collectors, and
on other material clearly establish this work as one in a series
of social histories. However, the chapters on the various periods and revivals are well written and carefully documented.
Illustrations are more interesting than useful.

152   Honey, William B. THE CERAMIC ART OF CHINA AND OTHER
COUNTRIES OF THE FAR EAST. London: Faber & Faber, 1945. vii,
238 p. 192 illus. (3 in color). Bibliog., pp. 218–26.

Heavily weighted toward the ceramic ware of China, with
brief sections on Korea, Siam, and Japan. Organized by

major dynastic periods and covers the entire variety of stonewares and porcelains. An old but excellent survey. Includes
appendixes on marks; a glossary of Chinese names for shapes,
colors, and so on; one on patterns and subjects used in decoration; and one on forgeries.

153 _____. DRESDEN CHINA: AN INTRODUCTION TO THE STUDY OF
MEISSEN PORCELAIN. London: Faber & Faber, 1954. 233 p. 175
illus. Bibliog., pp. 174-76.

A comprehensive study of the eighteenth-century Meissen porcelain of Saxony. Traces the general development of the ware
and provides basic information about technical developments.
Illustrations of specifically documented pieces. Mentions some
major "made to order" sets. Includes a brief chapter on
marks.

154 _____. ENGLISH POTTERY AND PORCELAIN. 6th ed. London:
A. & C. Black, 1969. xvi, 284 p. Illus. Bibliog., pp. 269-75.

A concise history of English ceramic art in three sections:
earthenware and stoneware to the end of the eighteenth century; English porcelain of the eighteenth century (over one-
third of the book); and nineteenth-century pottery and porcelain. Discusses questions of taste and technological innovations.

155 _____. EUROPEAN CERAMIC ART: FROM THE END OF THE MID-
DLE AGES TO ABOUT 1815. Vol. 1: ILLUSTRATED HISTORICAL SUR-
VEY; Vol. 2: A DICTIONARY OF FACTORIES, ARTISTS, TECHNICAL
TERMS, AND GENERAL INFORMATION. London: Faber & Faber,
1952. 788 p. Illus. Bibliog., pp. 17-27.

A combination dictionary-encyclopedia, covering all terms,
periods, styles, ceramic companies, and so on, in the period
covered. Line drawings of marks and forms. A very useful
tool for basic research.

156 _____. FRENCH PORCELAIN OF THE 18TH CENTURY. London:
Faber & Faber, 1950. xv, 78 p. 100 illus. (some in color).
Bibliog., pp. 70-71.

A solid historical treatment of French porcelain of the eighteenth century. Organized by centers of manufacture and presents the major factories and their marks. Places the porcelain
work within a broader context of French decorative arts of the
century.

157 Hyde, John A. ORIENTAL LOWESTOFT, CHINESE EXPORT PORCE-
LAIN, PORCELAINE DE LA CIE DES INDES. 3d ed., rev. Newport,

Engl.: Ceramic Book Co., 1964. viii, 168 p. 35 illus.

Discusses and illustrates the variety of porcelains made for foreign markets and ordered from Canton. Concentrates on the wares destined for the American market, particularly those objects decorated with American subjects. Scholarly and comprehensive.

158   Jenyns, [R.] Soame. JAPANESE PORCELAIN. London: Faber & Faber, 1973. 252 p. Illus. Bibliog., pp. 321-23.

The major general but carefully presented survey of Japanese porcelain since the seventeenth century. Organized in terms of types with particular attention to the work that was heavily exported to Europe, Britain, and the United States.

159   _____. MING POTTERY AND PORCELAIN. London: Faber & Faber, 1953. xi, 160 p. 124 illus. (some in color). Bibliog., pp. 156-57.

A scholarly monograph worth reading by the student of ceramics. Provides a basis for understanding the later European, English, and American attempts to produce fine wares. Beautifully illustrated.

160   Koyamu, Fujio. THE HERITAGE OF JAPANESE CERAMICS. New York: Weatherhill, 1973. 256 p. Illus. Bibliog.

A general survey of the history of Japanese ceramic ware from the beginning to the end of the nineteenth century.

161   Laidacker, Sam. ANGLO-AMERICAN CHINA: PART II. Bristol, Pa.: Privately printed, 1956. xiii, 144 p. Illus.

Records non-American scenes in transfer-printed English pottery, 1815-1860. Illustrations of identifying borders. Lists the views pictured and discusses various connoisseurship problems. Companion volume to his standard catalog.

162   Lane, Arthur. ITALIAN PORCELAIN. London: Faber & Faber, 1954. 79 p. Illus. Bibliog., pp. 74-75.

A careful though brief survey of Italian porcelain up to 1820. Discusses the major centers of ceramic manufacture and lists their marks.

163   Lehmann, Henri. PRE-COLUMBIAN CERAMICS. New York: Viking Press, 1962. 127 p. Illus. Bibliog., pp. 122-25.

A popular history of the pre-Columbian ceramic societies and a careful study of both their aesthetics and their technology.

164 Liverani, Giovanni. FIVE CENTURIES OF ITALIAN MAJOLICA. New York: McGraw-Hill, 1960. 258 p. Illus. Bibliog.

A general survey of the Italian work that has proved to be so enduringly popular.

165 McCauley, Robert H. LIVERPOOL TRANSFER DESIGNS ON ANGLO-AMERICAN POTTERY. Portland, Maine: Southworth-Anthoesen, 1942. xxi, 150 p. 32 illus. Bibliog., p. 141.

A comprehensive study of this popular ware, including a detailed check list of subjects concerned with the American trade.

166 Mackenna, Francis S. CHELSEA PORCELAIN: THE GOLD ANCHOR WARES. Leigh-On-Sea, Engl.: F. Lewis, 1952. xviii, 122 p. 64 illus.

Discusses the final phase of the creation of this ware, including the final years of the Chelsea works (1770-84) under William Duesbury. Biographical checklist of artists and craftsmen, marks, and description notes on the plates all serve to make this the standard work on the subject.

167 Mankowitz, Wolf, and Haggar, Reginald. CONCISE ENCYCLOPAEDIA OF ENGLISH POTTERY AND PORCELAIN. 2d ed. New York: Frederick A. Praeger, 1968. 312 p. Illus. Bibliog., pp. 300-311.

A substantial encyclopedia of individual artists, materials, techniques, and so on. Oriented to the collector and includes illustrations of typical quality pieces. Facsimiles of marks and signatures.

168 New Haven Colony Historical Society. AN EXHIBITION OF CHINA TRADE PORCELAIN. New Haven, Conn.: 1968. 99 p. Illus. Bibliog.

The catalog of an exhibition of the various porcelain ware imported from China through the port of New Haven.

169 Penkala, Maria. FAR EASTERN CERAMICS: MARKS AND DECORATION. The Hague: Mouton, 1963. 263 p. Illus. Bibliog., pp. 235-41.

A scholarly history of Far Eastern work, organized by country and including a checklist of marks after each brief survey. Valuable glossaries cover a variety of Oriental terms.

170 Savage, George. EIGHTEENTH-CENTURY ENGLISH PORCELAIN. New York: Macmillan, 1952. xx, 435 p. 112 plates.

A carefully written guide to an important century in English ceramics. A survey of the major English factories and American production with a section of biographies on important figures, both craftsmen and manufacturers. Includes an index of marks and analysis of the illustrations.

171 _____. ENGLISH POTTERY AND PORCELAIN. New York: Universe, 1961. 431 p. Illus. Bibliog., p. 428.

A popular survey and history of English ceramics. Organized in terms of major pottery centers and includes a list of important pottery marks.

172 Theil, Albert W.R. CHINESE POTTERY AND STONEWARE. Los Angeles: Bordon, 1953. xiv, 204 p. Illus.

A carefully illustrated history of this popular ware, so often imitated and collected by Americans. Good background for understanding of later Western developments.

173 Ware, George W. GERMAN AND AUSTRIAN PORCELAIN. New York: G.E. From, 1952. 244 p. Illus. (some in color). Bibliog., pp. 227-28.

Aimed at the beginning collector, chapters cover technique and decorating, as well as the major period styles. Also valuable connoisseurship hints and, for all readers, histories of the major factories to the present. Includes list of marks, maps, and charts.

FURNITURE: GENERAL WORKS

174 Aronson, Joseph. THE NEW ENCYCLOPEDIA OF FURNITURE. Rev. ed. New York: Crown Publishers, 1967. 484 p. Illus. Bibliog., pp. 476-79.

An encyclopedia of definitions and material on styles, technique, and craftsmen. Includes some information about designers in a glossary and contains many good illustrations.

175 Boger, Louise A. THE COMPLETE GUIDE TO FURNITURE STYLES. New York: Charles Scribner's Sons, 1969. 520 p. 524 illus. Bibliog., pp. 506-8.

Each chapter, from the ancient world through the modern era, begins with a general discussion of the period and its style, and is followed by brief treatments of individual pieces. Contains over 500 photographs of individual objects and a good general text.

176 Bradford, Ernle D. ANTIQUE FURNITURE. London: English Universities Press, 1970. 248 p. Illus.

   A survey of furniture that ends with the turn of the century.
   Good for comparison of styles from country to country.

177 Davis, Frank A. PICTURE HISTORY OF FURNITURE. New York:
Macmillan Publishing Co., 1959. 160 p. Illus.

   A general picture book that covers furniture from earliest civilization to the middle of the twentieth century.

178 Gloag, John E. A SHORT DICTIONARY OF FURNITURE. Rev. ed.
London: Allen and Unwin, 1969. 813 p. 630 illus. Bibliog.,
pp. 779-84.

   This valuable reference tool defines 1,754 terms used in England and America. Provides historical background and useful
   information on furniture styles.

179 _____. A SOCIAL HISTORY OF FURNITURE DESIGN, FROM B.C.
1300 TO A.D. 1960. New York: Crown Publishers, 1966. 202 p.
340 illus. (4 in color). Bibliog., p. 192.

   A survey of Western furniture up to the twentieth century.
   The author places his discussion of furniture in a historic context of the societies and their institutions.

180 GREAT STYLES OF FURNITURE. New York: Viking Press, 1963.
308 p. 800 illus.

   A picture book which covers the period from the beginning of
   the Renaissance through the nineteenth century. Concentrates
   on English, French, Dutch, Italian, and Spanish work.

181 Hayward, Helena, ed. WORLD FURNITURE: AN ILLUSTRATED HIS-
TORY. New York: McGraw-Hill, 1965. 320 p. Illus. Bibliog.,
p. 312.

   A series of essays by authorities written for a general audience. Covers the furniture of the world, from early civilization through the middle of the twentieth century. Illustrations
   include views and interiors as well as specific objects.

182 Hunter, George L. DECORATIVE FURNITURE. Philadelphia: J.B.
Lippincott, 1923. 480 p. 900 illus. (23 in color).

   A large picture book covering both the Orient and the Western world, from ancient Egypt through American mission furniture.

183 Kimerly, William L. HOW TO KNOW PERIOD STYLES IN FURNI-
TURE. 3d ed. Grand Rapids, Mich.: Grand Rapids Furniture Record,
1931. 147 p. Illus.

A history of furniture from the earliest Egyptian forms through
the beginning of the twentieth century. Illustrations of selected popular forms.

184 McClinton, Katharine M. AN OUTLINE OF PERIOD FURNITURE.
New York: Putnam, 1929. Reissue. New York: Putnam, 1972.
259 p. 195 illus. Bibliog.

A richly illustrated survey of furniture, emphasizing changes
in style of several basic forms.

185 Molesworth, Hender D., and Kenworthy-Browne, John. THREE CEN-
TURIES OF FURNITURE IN COLOR. New York: Viking Press, 1972.
328 p. 544 color plates.

A major picture book with hundreds of color plates of furniture
from the seventeenth century to the end of the nineteenth.

186 Philip, Peter. FURNITURE OF THE WORLD. New York: Galahad,
1974. 128 p. Illus.

A general popular survey for the collector. Background information on technical matters, the evolution of the use of materials, and the development of styles. The second part of
the volume is a series of chapters on individual furniture forms
in both the Occident and the Orient.

187 Pinto, Edward H. TREEN OR SMALL WOODWORK THROUGHOUT THE
AGES. London: B.T. Batsford, 1949. viii, 120 p. 137 illus.

Divided into chapters on various types of wooden objects, with
fascinating historical background material. Written by an in-
tensely interested collector, this must still stand as one of the
few major sources of knowledge in the field. Carefully selected illustrations of good quality.

188 Ramsey, L.G., and Comstock, Helen, eds. ANTIQUE FURNITURE:
A GUIDE FOR COLLECTORS, INVESTORS, AND DEALERS. New
York: Hawthorn, 1969. 362 p. 144 illus. (9 in color). Bibliog.

A well-illustrated view of furniture viewed from the collector's
vantage point. How to recognize period styles and geographical differences within a historical period. A good general introduction for any nonspecialist.

189 Schmitz, Hermann, comp. THE ENCYCLOPEDIA OF FURNITURE.

Rev. ed. New York: Frederick A. Praeger, 1957. 63 p. 659 illus.

A brief text with 320 plates of European, Middle Eastern, and Oriental furniture, from the ancient world to the middle of the nineteenth century.

190 Wanscher, Ole. THE ART OF FURNITURE: 5000 YEARS OF FURNITURE AND INTERIORS. New York: Reinhold, 1967. 419 p. Illus. Bibliog. pp. 411-14.

A thorough, popular history of both furniture and furnishings from Egyptian civilization to current developments. Includes views of interiors and covers both the Orient and Western Europe.

FURNITURE: COUNTRIES AND PERIODS

191 Baker, Hollis S. FURNITURE IN THE ANCIENT WORLD: ORIGINS AND EVOLUTIONS, 3100-475 B.C. New York: Macmillan Publishing Co., 1966. 351 p. Illus.

A thorough survey of ancient furniture: Egyptian, Near Eastern, and Early Greek. Each chapter includes a chronology and bibliographic references in its notes. Includes information on technical questions in an appendix.

192 Barany-Oberschall, Magda. HUNGARIAN FURNITURE. Budapest: Officina Press, 1939. 28 p. 32 plates.

A brief introduction to Hungarian furniture as an official presentation of the government. Illustrates local variations of basic furniture forms.

193 Brackett, Oliver. ENGLISH FURNITURE ILLUSTRATED. London: Spring, 1958. 403 p. Illus.

Primarily a history based on well-documented plates and a brief text. Covers English furniture from the Middle Ages through the nineteenth century, introducing new forms as well as new styles.

194 Byne, Arthur, and Byne, Mildred. SPANISH INTERIORS AND FURNITURE. New York: Helburn, 1922. Reprint. New York: Dover, 1969. 330 p. Plates.

A pictorial survey of both Spanish furniture and interiors.

195 Cescinsky, Herbert. ENGLISH FURNITURE FROM GOTHIC TO SHERATON. New York: Crown Publishers, 1958. Reprint. New York: Dover, 1968. 406 p. Illus.

A thorough survey of English furniture from the Gothic era to the end of the eighteenth century. Various popular aspects of the later years are included, such as lacquer ware and coverings of needlepoint. Traces styles and the introduction of new forms.

196   Dobson, Henry, and Dobson, Barbara. THE EARLY FURNITURE OF ONTARIO AND THE ATLANTIC PROVINCES. Toronto: M.F. Feheley, 1975. 188 p. 209 illus.

A well-illustrated survey of the various furniture forms and their local variations. Illustrated with a variety of basic types; interesting for a comparison with American examples.

197   Eberlein, Harold D., and Ramsdell, Roger W. THE PRACTICAL BOOK OF ITALIAN, SPANISH, AND PORTUGUESE FURNITURE. Philadelphia: J.B. Lippincott, 1927. 354 p. Illus.

A general history and survey of furniture in the three countries from the beginning of the Renaissance through the end of the seventeenth century. Concentrates on various forms, their development, and varying decoration.

198   Ecke, Gustave. CHINESE DOMESTIC FURNITURE. Rutland, Vt.: Charles E. Tuttle Co., 1962. 49 p. 161 plates.

A brief text on Chinese furniture forms is devoted to an analysis of materials and technique rather than style. The rest is a picture book surveying the various forms.

199   Edwards, Ralph. THE SHORTER DICTIONARY OF ENGLISH FURNITURE; FROM THE MIDDLE AGES TO THE LATE GEORGIAN PERIOD. London: Country Life, 1964. 684 p. Illus.

A very valuable condensation of the author's THE DICTIONARY OF ENGLISH FURNITURE. Covers accessories, materials, styles, and techniques. Also examines decoration during the years covered by the author. Information on both designers and furniture makers.

200   Edwards, Ralph, and Jourdain, Margaret. GEORGIAN CABINET-MAKERS. 3d ed. London: Country Life, 1955. 247 p. Illus. Bibliog.

A well-written valuable biographical dictionary of English cabinetmakers of the eighteenth century. Organized chronologically by individual. Presents all available references to records as well as the usual biographical material. A separate section covers the lesser-known carvers and cabinetmakers.

201   Gloag, John [E.]. THE ENGLISHMAN'S CHAIR: ORIGINS, DESIGN, AND SOCIAL HISTORY OF SEAT FURNITURE IN ENGLAND. London: Allen and Unwin, 1964. xviii, 307 p. 64 illus. Bibliog., pp. 265–77.

      Puts the chair in England in a social and historical context. Follows changes in style and form.

202   Grandjean, Serge. EMPIRE FURNITURE, 1800–1825. New York: Taplinger, 1966. 120 p. Illus. Bibliog., pp. 112–14.

      A survey of Empire furniture, emphasizing French contributions during the first quarter of the nineteenth century. The most frequently found forms of the era are both illustrated and discussed.

203   Hayward, Charles H. ENGLISH PERIOD FURNITURE. Rev. ed. New York: Charles Scribner's Sons, 1971. 270 p. Illus.

      A carefully done general survey of English furniture from the Tudor era through the Empire period. Oriented toward tracing methods of construction rather than style. Presents useful hints for the connoisseur who follows the evolution of decoration.

204   Himmelheber, Georg. BIEDERMEIER FURNITURE. London: Faber & Faber, 1973. 115 p. Illus. Bibliog., pp. 104–5.

      A carefully organized history of Biedermeier furniture in the German-speaking countries. Covers both styles and basic forms, and includes information on upholstery and technical matters.

205   Hinckley, F. Lewis. A DIRECTORY OF ANTIQUE FRENCH FURNITURE, 1735–1800. New York: Crown Publishers, 1967. 220 p. Illus. Bibliog., pp. 213–14.

      A picture history of French furniture, organized by geographical area, follows an introductory essay. Includes a list of the major known French furniture makers and provides a glossary of terms.

206   Jervis, Simon. VICTORIAN FURNITURE. London: Ward Lock, 1968. 96 p. Illus.

      A brief popular survey of English furniture from 1850 to 1900. Emphasizes Victorian exuberance and flourishes as part of design.

207   Jourdain, Margaret. ENGLISH INTERIOR DECORATION, 1500 TO 1830: A STUDY IN THE DEVELOPMENT OF DESIGN. London: Batsford, 1950. xii, 84 p. Illus.

A useful pioneering study of early English furniture with basic material on woods and technical developments in interior design.

208 Jourdain, Margaret, and Rose, Fred. ENGLISH FURNITURE: THE GEORGIAN PERIOD (1750-1830). London: Batsford, 1953. 210 p. 172 illus.

Valuable material on woods and technical processes supplement this well-written text on eighteenth-and early nineteenth-century British furniture. Names of cabinetmakers as well as fashion setters such as Robert Adam.

209 Kates, George N. CHINESE HOUSEHOLD FURNITURE. New York: Harper, 1948. Reprint. New York: Dover, 1962. 125 p. Illus. Bibliog., p. 125.

Starts with a study of both Oriental and Western attitudes toward Chinese furniture. Discusses the inherent problems in classifying and dating furniture from China and presents a general survey of the field. Individual chapters on major furniture forms.

210 Macdonald-Taylor, Margaret S. ENGLISH FURNITURE FROM THE MIDDLE AGES TO MODERN TIMES. New York: G.P. Putnam's Sons, 1966. 299 p. Illus. Bibliog.

A dictionary-handbook of furniture styles and types in this era of English history. Includes a chronology and information for the collector. A glossary is devoted to furniture terms.

211 Northcote-Bade, Stanley. COLONIAL FURNITURE IN NEW ZEALAND. Wellington, N.Z.: Read, 1971. 164 p. Illus. Bibliog.

An interesting study of colonial developments in an English colony. Shows how basic English furniture forms evolved in an isolated environment.

212 Richter, Gisela M. THE FURNITURE OF THE GREEKS, ETRUSCANS AND ROMANS. London: Phaidon, 1966. 369 p. Illus. Bibliog., pp. 341-43.

A substantial and scholarly treatment of the furniture of classical antiquity, covering the full range of Greek and Roman civilization. High-quality illustrations develop the evolution of various furniture forms while an important section discusses technical issues.

213 Ritz, Gislind M. THE ART OF PAINTED FURNITURE. New York: Van Nostrand Reinhold, 1971. 175 p. Illus. Bibliog., pp. 169-73.

A concise and careful study of European and Pennsylvania-German painted furniture with particular emphasis on Scandinavian production. An examination of various approaches to furniture painting, amply illustrated.

214 Souchal, Genevieve. FRENCH EIGHTEENTH CENTURY FURNITURE. New York: G.P. Putnam's Sons, 1961. 128 p. Illus.

A popular history of an important era that greatly influenced American styles. Discusses various furniture forms and the variations on each type.

215 Symonds, Robert W., and Ormsbee, Thomas H. ANTIQUE FURNITURE OF THE WALNUT PERIOD. New York: Robert M. McBride, 1947. 143 p. 72 illus.

This is a reissue of the standard work on English furniture from 1660 to 1745, to which several chapters on the related American work have been added. Obvious emphasis on New England.

216 Symonds, Robert W., and Whineray, B.B. VICTORIAN FURNITURE. London: Country Life, 1962. 232 p. Illus.

A history and survey of Victorian furniture, with emphasis on both styles and technical material.

217 Verlet, Pierre. FRENCH ROYAL FURNITURE. New York: C.N. Potter, 1963. 200 p. Illus.

A carefully organized and scholarly study of eighteenth-century Royal furniture. Useful in tracing the influences down to a broader audience. Discusses the major designers and furniture makers. Illustrations include excellent captions.

218 Viaux, Jacqueline. FRENCH FURNITURE. New York: G.P. Putnam's Sons, 1964. 200 p. Illus.

A careful survey of French furniture from the Middle Ages to the mid-twentieth century. Presents a history of succeeding styles and includes a study of materials and technique. The glossary of relevant furniture terms is valuable.

219 Wolsey, Samuel W., and Luff, R.W.P. FURNITURE IN ENGLAND: THE AGE OF THE JOINER. New York: Frederick A. Praeger, 1969. 104 p. Illus.

An introduction to early English furniture of the mid-sixteenth century to the middle of the seventeenth. Emphasizes joining techniques and presents material of use to the collector and connoisseur.

GLASS: GENERAL WORKS

220   Belknap, Eugene M. MILK GLASS. New York: Crown Publishers, 1959. 327 p. 450 illus. Bibliog.

Still a useful guide to all opaque glass. Illustrations are arranged by categories--plates, bowls, and so on--with valuable captions. Brief text for each chapter and an important chapter on reproductions.

221   Bergstrom, Evangeline H. OLD GLASS PAPERWEIGHTS. Chicago: Lakeside Press, 1940. xi, 120 p. 20 color illus. Bibliog., p. 120.

A thorough treatment of both European and glass paperweights. Provides us with a history of both their creation and their use, and stylistic distinctions between various periods. The basic reference tool in the area of glass paperweights of interest to the collector.

222   Davis, Derek C. GLASS FOR COLLECTORS. Feltham, Engl.: Hamlyn, 1971. 159 p. Illus. Bibliog.

A basic general survey for the novice. Illustrates the major period styles and common types of glass objects.

223   Elville, E.M. A COLLECTOR'S DICTIONARY OF GLASS. New York: Taplinger, 1961. 194 p. 275 illus. Bibliog., pp. 193-94.

An English authority on glass provides a carefully detailed presentation on British, continental, and American glass. Both familiar and exotic terms are defined and discussed in this valuable reference work.

224   Gros-Galliner, Gabriella. GLASS: A GUIDE FOR COLLECTORS. New York: Stein and Day, 1970. 175 p. Illus. Bibliog., pp. 163-66.

A popular survey of glass covering some 4,000 years. Concerned with the materials and techniques of glassmaking, and how processes have changed through the years. Provides a glossary of glass-related terms.

225   Harden, Donald B., comp. MASTERPIECES OF GLASS: A SELECTION. London: British Museum, 1968. 199 p. 300 illus. Bibliog.

The catalog of a massive exhibition of historical glass with 300 individual pieces illustrated. Covers from early times through 1862.

226   Honey, William B. GLASS. London: Ministry of Education, 1946.

169 p. 72 illus. Bibliog.

A handbook-survey of Eastern and Western glass, from antiquity to the present. Based on the important glass collection in the Victoria and Albert Museum.

227 Kampfer, Fritz, and Beyer, Klaus G. GLASS: A WORLD HISTORY; THE STORY OF 4000 YEARS OF FINE GLASSMAKING. Greenwich, Conn.: New York Graphic Society, 1967. 314 p. 243 illus. Bibliog., pp. 295-315.

A wide-ranging survey of glassmaking. Emphasizes the introduction and reintroduction of techniques and forms throughout history. Points out the evolution of basic functional forms into aesthetic ones. Includes a very useful glossary.

228 Middlemas, Robert K. ANTIQUE GLASS IN COLOR. Garden City, N.Y.: Doubleday and Co., 1971. 120 p. Illus. (many in color).

A picture-book survey of various types of glass throughout the world.

229 Moore, Hannah H. OLD GLASS, EUROPEAN AND AMERICAN. New York: Tudor Publishing Co., 1944. xvi, 394 p. 165 illus.

A history of both glass styles and its manufacture by major and minor firms. Good quality illustrations of fine pieces present a cross sample of types and decoration.

230 Newman, Harold. AN ILLUSTRATED DICTIONARY OF GLASS. London: Thames and Hudson, 1977. Unpaged. 600 illus. (17 in color).

Approximately 2,500 terms in this dictionary, which covers all periods and all geographic areas. Carefully cross-indexed; with bibliographic references and excellent illustrations. Includes an essay on the history of glassmaking by Richard Charleston and a preface by Newman.

231 Robertson, Richard A. CHATS ON OLD GLASS. New York: A-A Wyn, 1954. 179 p. 46 illus. Bibliog.

A compact popular history of glassmaking and styles from Egyptian to the present, including American production. An appendix lists the major public collections.

232 Savage, George. GLASS. New York: G.P. Putnam's Sons, 1965. 128 p. Illus.

A generously illustrated survey of glassmaking from the time of the Egyptians to the revivals of the mid-nineteenth century.

233 Vose, Ruth H. GLASS. New York: Hearst, 1976. 222 p. 350 illus. (32 in color).

A good general survey, oriented toward the collector. Illustrates the changing styles and the introduction of new glass forms.

234 Weiss, Gustav. THE BOOK OF GLASS. New York: Frederick A. Praeger, 1971. 353 p. Illus. Bibliog., pp. 346-49.

A scholarly survey of glass from prehistoric times to the current age. Provides a valuable chronology and information about technological developments in glassmaking, and traces the introduction of various important types of glass.

235 Wilkinson, Oliver N. OLD GLASS: MANUFACTURE, STYLES, USES. New York: Philosophical Society, 1968. 200 p. Illus. Bibliog., pp. 187-89.

A popular survey of Western glass throughout the centuries. Particular attention to the changes of technical production as well as the evolution of style.

GLASS: COUNTRIES AND PERIODS

236 Blair, Dorothy. A HISTORY OF GLASS IN JAPAN. New York: Corning Museum of Art, 1973. 479 p. Illus. Bibliog., pp. 461-69.

A scholarly study of glass in Japan up to the early twentieth century. Chronological material establishes the Japanese periods. Notes accompanying the illustrations supplement the text.

237 Butterworth, Lionel M. BRITISH TABLE AND ORNAMENTAL GLASS. London: L. Hill, 1956. 123 p. Illus.

Covers the major firms and types of English table glass with some attention to ornamental wares. Major producers under discussion include Bristol, Narlsea, Stourbridge, and Waterford.

238 Crompton, Sidney, ed. ENGLISH GLASS. New York: Hawthorn Books, 1968. 255 p. 206 illus. Bibliog., pp. 86-87.

A series of essays by noted authorities on English glass. Covers the period from the Middle Ages through the nineteenth century and traces changes in style and form.

239 Davis, Derek C. ENGLISH AND IRISH ANTIQUE GLASS. New York: Frederick A. Praeger, 1965. 151 p. 40 illus. Bibliog., pp. 145-46.

Covers both English and Irish glass from 1700 to about 1850, tracing the changes in style and the introduction of new types of forms. Includes a glossary of terms, and information on dating and the major active glass companies.

240 Elville, E.M. ENGLISH TABLE GLASS. New York: Charles Scribner's Sons, 1952. Rev. ed. London: Country Life, 1960. 274 p. 136 illus.

One of the better works about English glass. Good introductory chapters on physical properties, methods of manufacture, decoration, and stylistic developments. Names and dates are presented clearly, and careful perusal provides a good background for the understanding of American glass.

241 Frothingham, Alice W. SPANISH GLASS. London: Faber and Faber, 1963. 96 p. 96 illus. (4 in color). Bibliog.

A well-illustrated survey of Spanish and Portuguese glass from the medieval era to the beginning of the nineteenth century.

242 Grover, Ray, and Grover, Lee. ART GLASS NOUVEAU. Rutland, Vt.: Charles E. Tuttle Co., 1967. 231 p. 423 color illus. Bibliog.

A profusely illustrated survey of Art Nouveau glass. Includes a checklist of marks and an ownership list covering the years 1870-1918. A must for the collector.

243 _____. CONTEMPORARY ART GLASS. New York: Crown Publishers, 1977. 208 p. 435 illus. (135 in color).

A broad survey of the major creative glass craftsmen of the last score of years. Includes the work of ninety-eight artists and emphasizes the influence of Littleton and Labino as founders of the U.S. studio movement. Worldwide coverage.

244 Hettes, Karel. GLASS IN CZECHOSLOVAKIA. Prague: SNTL, 1958. 64 p. Illus.

A general survey of Czechoslovakian glass from the Renaissance to the twentieth century. Concerned with styles and the evolution of basic forms.

245 _____. OLD VENETIAN GLASS. London: Spring Books, 1960. 46 p. 72 plates. Bibliog.

An examination of the popular Venetian glass, so much sought by collectors. Discusses and illustrates the various forms and color processes used in its creation.

246 Hughes, George B. ENGLISH GLASS FOR THE COLLECTOR, 1660-

1860. New York: Frederick A. Praeger, 1968. 251 p. 103 illus. Bibliog., p. 251.

A popular history and handbook for the general reader and collector. Arrangement is by glass type.

247 _____. ENGLISH, SCOTTISH AND IRISH TABLE GLASS: FROM THE SIXTEENTH CENTURY TO 1820. London: B.T. Batsford, 1956. 410 p. 310 illus. Bibliog., p. 393.

Primarily devoted to English glass, with brief chapters on Irish and Scottish wares. Chapters on the early history of English glassmaking are followed by specific studies of both types and forms of decoration, engraving, cutting, enamelling, and gilding. Clear illustrations and descriptive entries.

248 Mariacher, Giovanni. ITALIAN BLOWN GLASS FROM ANCIENT ROME TO VENICE. New York: McGraw-Hill, 1961. 248 p. 84 illus. Bibliog., pp. 61-62.

A survey of Italian blown glass from the ancient Roman world to the great colored glass of Venice. Detailed captions to the illustrations supplement the brief text.

249 Neuburg, Frederic. ANCIENT GLASS. Toronto: University of Toronto Press, 1962. 110 p. Illus. Bibliog., pp. 106-7.

A scholarly history of glass from ancient Egyptian civilization to the end of the fourth century A.D. A chronology and carefully described illustrations make this a useful book for both the casual student and the collector.

250 Pesatova, Zuzana. BOHEMIAN ENGRAVED GLASS. Feltham, Engl.: Hamlyn, 1968. 63 p. 110 plates. Bibliog.

A survey of the engraved glass of Czechoslovakia that so influenced the engraved glass of Western Europe and the United States. Many excellent illustrations and information about engraving technique.

251 Polak, Ada. MODERN GLASS. London: Faber & Faber, 1962. 94 p. 96 illus. (some in color). Bibliog., pp. 89-90.

A good detailed survey of twentieth century glass, divided into chapters on fin de siècle, functionalism, and neofunctionalism through 1960. Both scholarly and easy reading; much useful biographical material included.

252 Revi, Albert C[hristian]. NINETEENTH CENTURY GLASS: ITS GENESIS AND DEVELOPMENT. Rev. ed. London and New York: Thomas Nelson and Co., 1967. 301 p. Illus. Glossary.

A thorough yet general history which documents influences
and explains the spread of styles. Hundreds of illustrations
supplement the easy-to-read text. Includes some material on
technical innovations.

253 Steenberg, Elisa. SWEDISH GLASS. New York: Barrows, 1950.
     168 p. Illus.

     A general history of Swedish glass covering the time since
     the Gothic era. Illustrates changes in style and decoration.

254 Thorpe, William A. ENGLISH GLASS. 3d ed. New York: Macmil-
     lan Publishing Co., 1961. 302 p. 30 illus. Bibliog.

     Traces the history of English glass to the present time. A
     general history that introduces new forms and technology with-
     in the broader range of society's artifacts.

255 Turnbull, George, and Herron, Anthony. THE PRICE GUIDE TO
     ENGLISH 18TH CENTURY DRINKING GLASSES. Suffolk, Engl.:
     Baron, 1970. 359 p. Illus. Bibliog.

     A priced collection of illustrations of the glasses of eighteenth-
     century England.

256 Wilkinson, Reginald. THE HALLMARKS OF ANTIQUE GLASS. Lon-
     don: R. Madley, 1968. 220 p. Illus.

     The glass made by a variety of English firms throughout the
     years. An introduction to identification for the collector.

METALS: GENERAL WORKS

257 Blakemore, Kenneth. THE BOOK OF GOLD. New York: Stein and
     Day, 1971. 224 p. Illus. Bibliog.

     A general history of objects made of gold from the ancient
     world to 1970. Both aesthetic and technical questions are
     discussed.

258 Burgess, Frederick W. CHATS ON OLD COPPER AND BRASS. Lon-
     don: Benn, 1954. Reprint. Wakefield, Engl.: E.P. Pubing, 1973.
     400 p.

     A popular history with worldwide treatment of brass, copper,
     and bronze. Oriented toward the collector, the illustrations
     serve to respond to questions of connoisseurship.

259 Culme, John, and Strang, John G. ANTIQUE SILVER AND SILVER

COLLECTING. Feltham, Engl.: Hamlyn, 1973. 96 p. Illus.
Bibliog.

An introduction to the various styles and periods in silver from
the baroque era to the present. Aimed at the collector.

260 Fletcher, Lucinda. SILVER. London: Orbis, 1973. 64 p. Illus.
Bibliog.

A picture book of silver from the beginning of the fifteenth
century to the present.

261 Haedeke, Hanns-Ulrich. METALWORK. New York: Universe, 1970.
227 p. Illus. Bibliog., pp. 213-18.

A scholarly study of brass, bronze, copper, iron, and pewter
in the Western world. Covers the period from the Romanesque
era to the end of the nineteenth century. Studies the various
forms for which metals were used, and the changes in style
through the years.

262 Henderson, James. SILVER COLLECTING FOR AMATEURS. London:
F. Muller, 1968. 144 p. Illus.

A beginning collector's introduction to the styles and basic
forms of silver.

263 Honour, Hugh. GOLDSMITHS AND SILVERSMITHS. New York:
G.P. Putnam's Sons, 1971. 320 p. Illus. (some in color). Bibliog.,
pp. 313-16.

A study of both goldsmiths and silversmiths in a chronological
treatment. Covers the ninth to the middle of the twentieth
century.

264 Jones, Edward A. OLD SILVER OF EUROPE AND AMERICA. Philadelphia: J.B. Lippincott, 1928. xii, 376 p. 96 plates.

Covers both European and American work, with concentration
on important presentation pieces and sets. High-quality plates
with descriptions and measurements.

265 Link, Eva M. THE BOOK OF SILVER. New York: Frederick A.
Praeger, 1973. 301 p. Illus. Bibliog., pp. 291-96.

Covers the Western civilization from classical antiquity to the
middle of the twentieth century. Presents valuable information
on marks, guild history, and a glossary of important terms.
Treats both handmade and manufactured objects.

266   Luddington, John. ANTIQUE SILVER: A GUIDE FOR WOULD-BE CONNOISSEURS. London: Pelham, 1971. 126 p. Illus.

        Individual objects through the various stylistic periods. Introduces new objects as reflections of the taste of an era.

267   Sutherland, Carol H. GOLD: ITS BEAUTY, POWER AND ALLURE. Rev. ed. New York: McGraw-Hill, 1959. 196 p. 47 plates. Bibliog., pp. 187-91.

        A popular history of gold, from discussion of its mining and technical handling to its utilization in jewelry and vessels and for coinage.

268   Wyler, Seymour B. THE BOOK OF OLD SILVER, ENGLISH, AMERICAN, FOREIGN. New York: Crown Publishers, 1937. x, 447 p. Illus.

        Essentially a guide to British, European and American hallmarks, including those on Sheffield plates.

METALS: COUNTRIES AND PERIODS

269   Anderson, Lawrence. THE ART OF THE SILVERSMITH IN MEXICO 1519-1936. Vols. 1 and 2. New York: Oxford University Press, 1941. Vol. 1: 460 p. Illus. Bibliog., pp. 435-51. Vol. 2: 183 illus.

        A massive study of the art, including detailed history of forms and their cultural background, a chapter on marks, and large clear plates. Appendixes give the text ordinances relating to the control of the craft and list of smiths, their dates and biographical material.

270   Belli-Barsali, Isa. MEDIEVAL GOLDSMITHS' WORK. London: Hamlyn, 1969. 157 p. Illus.

        A popular survey of goldsmithing from the fourth century to the end of the fifteenth. A brief text and informative captions to the illustrations. Discussion of changes in forms.

271   Berry-Hill, Henry, and Berry-Hill, Sidney. ANTIQUE GOLD BOXES. New York: Abelard Press, 1953. xiii, 223 p. Illus. Bibliog., pp. 221-23.

        The undisputed critical study on the subject, with a brief chapter on American examples of this genre, usually freedom boxes presented to dignitaries.

272 Bradbury, Frederick. GUIDE TO MARKS OF ORIGIN ON BRITISH AND IRISH SILVER PLATE FROM MID-16TH CENTURY TO THE YEAR 1959. 10th ed. Sheffield, Engl.: Northend, 1959. 93 p. Illus.

A pocket guidebook to the silver marks of Great Britain.

273 Buhler, Kathryn C. FRENCH, ENGLISH AND AMERICAN SILVER. Minneapolis, Minn.: Minneapolis Institute of Arts, 1956. 80 p. 66 illus.

A study of the relationship between the highest-quality silver produced in the three countries by a noted authority on American silver. Excellent illustrations make it easy to follow the informative text.

274 Carlson, Janice H. "Analysis of British and American Pewter by X-Ray Fluorescence Spectroscopy." WINTERTHUR PORTFOLIO 12 (1977): 65-85.

An explanation of the scientific attempts to determine compositional characteristics and to use them, when possible, for ascertaining place and time of manufacture. Study of some 1,300 pieces.

275 Clayton, Michael. THE COLLECTOR'S DICTIONARY OF THE SILVER AND GOLD OF GREAT BRITAIN AND NORTH AMERICA. New York: Country Life, 1971. 350 p. Illus. (some in color). Bibliog., pp. 345-49.

A dictionary that covers craftsmen, materials, techniques, and styles. Includes facsimiles of both British and American marks and has well-placed and clear illustrations.

276 Cotterell, Howard H. OLD PEWTER, ITS MAKERS AND MARKS IN ENGLAND, SCOTLAND AND IRELAND. London: Batsford, 1929. Reprint. Rutland, Vt.: Charles E. Tuttle Co., 1963. 432 p. Illus. Bibliog., p. 423.

An old but still valuable dictionary of pewterers and their marks, with historical background as an introduction.

277 Davis, Frank. FRENCH SILVER 1450-1825. New York: Frederick A. Praeger, 1970. 104 p. Illus. Bibliog., pp. 99-100.

A well-illustrated general history and guide to French silver of the period most relevant to the understanding of American developments. Clearly written.

278 Davis, John D. ENGLISH SILVER AT WILLIAMSBURG. Williamsburg, Va.: Colonial Williamsburg Foundation, 1976. viii, 254 p. Illus.

A beautifully illustrated catalog of one of the finest collections of English silver in this country. Each piece is described
and measured with a provenance provided and documented.
Descriptions of the usage of various pieces is often both
lengthy and useful. An appendix covers recent additions to
the collection. Excellent background for the understanding
of American silver.

279   Frederiks, Johan W. DUTCH SILVER. 4 vols. The Hague: Martinas
Nijhoff, 1952-1961. Vol. 1: xvi, 526 p. 382 plates. Vol. 2:
xxxiv, 211 p. 313 plates. Vol. 3: xii, 157 p. 332 plates. Vol.
4: xxxiv, 179 p. 334 plates.

A massive and very important background work for those interested in our early silver. Volume 1 covers the Renaissance
through the end of the eighteenth century and concentrates on
dishes, plaquettes, and tazze. Volume 2 covers wrought plate
of North and South Holland; volume 3, the wrought plate of
the Provences; and volume 4, ecclesiastical and secular plate.
Each volume has an index of masters, designs, and objects.

280   Gans, Moses H., and Duyvene de Wit-Klinkhamer, Theresa M. DUTCH
SILVER. London: Faber & Faber, 1961. 97 p. 144 plates. Bibliog.,
pp. 89-93.

A stylistic survey and discussion of technical influences. Includes a chapter on marks and one on value of the silver and
forgeries. Contains a thorough bibliography, a list of owners,
and excellent plates.

281   Grimwade, Arthur G. ROCOCO SILVER, 1727-65. London: Faber
& Faber, 1974. 96 p. Illus. Bibliog., pp. 68-69.

A brief but scholarly study of English silver during the rococo
era. The development of style, changes in technology, and
the different shapes and forms of objects.

282   Gyllensvard, Bo. T'ANG GOLD AND SILVER. London: K. Paul,
1957. 230 p. Illus.

A survey of the work in precious metals executed during the
important T'ang dynasty. Specific forms and decoration.

283   Helft, Jacques, ed. FRENCH MASTER GOLDSMITHS AND SILVER-
SMITHS FROM THE SEVENTEENTH TO THE NINETEENTH CENTURY.
New York: French and European Publications, 1966. 333 p. Illus.
Bibliog.

A collection of essays by authorities on French gold and silver. Includes facsimiles of the metalsmiths' marks. Introduces
innovations in forms and styles.

284 Hughes, Bernard, and Hughes, Therle. THREE CENTURES OF ENGLISH
DOMESTIC SILVER. New York: Wifred Funk, 1953. 248 p. Illus.

Chapters on candlesticks, spoons, punch bowls, and other categories of domestic items, excluding presentation pieces.
Clear advice on collecting and the identification of this work,
so often copied by American smiths.

285 Hughes, George B. SHEFFIELD SILVER PLATE. New York: Frederick
A. Praeger, 1970. 303 p. 269 illus. Bibliog., p. 267.

Discusses plating on steel as a process, explains various technical matters, and treats individual silver-plated objects by
type. Includes a section of notes on all of the illustrations.

286 Hughes, Graham. MODERN SILVER THROUGHOUT THE WORLD 1880-
1967. New York: Crown Publishers, 1967. 256 p. Illus. Bibliog.,
p. 255.

A popular survey of both European and American silver during
the late nineteenth and twentieth century to the date of writing. Traces styles and presents material on technical developments and a dictionary treatment of major silversmiths.

287 Jackson, Charles J. ENGLISH GOLDSMITHS AND THEIR MARKS.
2d ed. London: Macmillan Publishing Co., 1921. Reprint. New
York: Dover, 1964. 747 p. Illus.

The most comprehensive of the standard volumes on the gold
and silver of Great Britain. Background material on standards
for both metals and facsimiles of the marks.

288 Johnson, Ada M. HISPANIC SILVERWORK. New York: Hispanic
Society of America, 1944. 308 p. Illus. Bibliog., pp. 294-300.

A popular history of Spanish silver from the Gothic era to
1900. Includes a catalog of the society's fine collection and
introduces particularly Spanish stylistic developments.

289 Langdon, John. CANADIAN SILVERSMITHS 1700-1900. Toronto:
Stinehour, 1966. 145 p. Illus.

A careful history and checklist of Canadian silversmiths.
Marks are included, and illustrations are aimed at the beginning collector.

290 Michaelis, Ronald F. ANTIQUE PEWTER OF THE BRITISH ISLES.
London: Bell, 1955. Reprint. New York: Dover, 1971. 118 p.
Illus. Bibliog.

Individual chapters on decoration, history, forms, and marks, for the collector. Traces the development of style and how it relates to the major precious metal forms.

291   Moss, Morrie A. THE LILLIAN AND MORRIE MOSS COLLECTION OF PAUL STORR SILVER. Memphis: Privately printed, 1977. 279 p. 200 illus. (some in color).

This is the catalog of a major private collection, written by the collector.

292   Oman, Charles A., and Black, C. ENGLISH DOMESTIC SILVER. 7th ed. London: Black, 1968. xii, 240 p. 135 illus. Bibliog., pp. 233-34.

A valuable handbook which introduces the collector to styles and silvermakers. Revised edition has many new illustrations.

293   Strong, Donald E. GREEK AND ROMAN GOLD AND SILVER PLATE. Ithaca, N.Y.: Cornell University Press, 1966. 235 p. Illus. Bibliog.

A scholarly history and survey of the gold and silver work of classical antiquity, from early civilization through the fifth century of the Roman Empire. A thorough study of the use, supply and demand, and technology in reference to the handling of the precious metals in antiquity.

294   Wills, Geoffrey. SILVER FOR PLEASURE AND INVESTMENT. New York: Arco, 1969. 169 p. Illus. Bibliog., p. 170.

A collector's guide to English silver. Includes an index of silversmiths and their marks and a glossary of terms. Introduces the styles and new forms historically.

TEXTILES: GENERAL WORKS

295   Birrell, Verla L. THE TEXTILE ARTS. New York: Harper, 1959. 524 p. Illus. Bibliog., pp. 493-500.

A history of various textiles throughout the world to the present. Introduces various weaves and information about the development of looms. Also contains a glossary of technical terms.

296   Bridgeman, Harriet, and Drury, Elizabeth, eds. NEEDLEWORK: AN ILLUSTRATED HISTORY. New York and London: Paddington Press, 1978. 363 p. 389 illus. (110 in color). Bibliog.

A useful reference tool, with essays by eighteen experts on

the variety of needlework in different countries. A three-part
glossary--stitches, techniques, and miscellaneous--is quite
thorough, and the wide variety of illustrations range from
barely adequate to very good.

297 Editors of American Fabrics Magazine. AF ENCYCLOPEDIA OF TEX-
TILES. Englewood Cliffs, N.J.: Prentice-Hall, 1972. 636 p. Illus.

The history of textiles, the origin of various materials, and
the major technological developments associated with the textile industry. Includes basic terms and traces the introduction
of new ideas.

298 Flemming, Ernst R. AN ENCYCLOPEDIA OF TEXTILES. Rev. ed.
New York: Frederick A. Praeger, 1958. 30 p. 309 illus. (16 in
color).

A major picture book of textile art, covering both East and
West, up to the nineteenth century.

299 Glazier, Richard. HISTORIC TEXTILE FABRICS. New York: Charles
Scribner's Sons, 1923. 119 p. 83 plates. Bibliog., pp. 115-16.

An old but still useful solid treatment of woven textiles
throughout the world. Spans the ages from ancient Greek
civilization through the eighteenth century. Basic information
on techniques of decoration through printing and dyeing.

300 Hunter, George L. DECORATIVE TEXTILES. Philadelphia: J.B. Lippincott, 1918. 457 p. 580 illus. (27 in color). Bibliog., pp. 438-
47.

A very old but valuable standard history of textiles. Includes
material on lace, woven material, embroidery, printed material, and carpeting. Profusely illustrated and includes a glossary of textile-related terms. Used in interior decoration.

301 Jarry, Madeleine. WORLD TAPESTRY, FROM THEIR ORIGINS TO
THE PRESENT. New York: G.P. Putnam's Sons, 1969. 358 p.
Illus. Bibliog., pp. 349-54.

A good general survey of tapestry, from Egyptian civilization
to the twentieth century. Presents a separate chapter on technical processes and shows adaptations in method through different civilizations.

302 Jones, Mary E. A HISTORY OF WESTERN EMBROIDERY. New York:
Watson-Guptill, 1969. 159 p. 85 illus. (12 in color). Bibliog.,
p. 156.

A brief introduction to the techniques of embroidery is followed by individual chapters on embroidery in the various
countries of Europe and the United States. Includes a glossary of embroidery-related terms and a list of major museum
collections including embroidery.

303 Mayer, Christa M. MASTERPIECES OF WESTERN TEXTILES FROM THE
ART INSTITUTE. Chicago: Art Institute of Chicago, 1969. 224 p.
Illus. Bibliog.

A well-organized survey of Western textiles for the general
reader or collector. Introduces technical information and the
evolution of forms in textile construction.

304 Weibel, Adele C. TWO THOUSAND YEARS OF TEXTILES: THE
FIGURED TEXTILES OF EUROPE AND THE NEAR EAST. New York:
Pantheon, 1952. Reprint. New York: Hacker, 1972. 169 p. Illus.
Bibliog., pp. 165-67.

A carefully documented history that includes basic information
on both materials and techniques. The survey covers the
world's textiles from the prehistoric age to about 1800.

TEXTILES: COUNTRIES AND PERIODS

305 Beer, Alice B. TRADE GOODS, A STUDY OF INDIAN CHINTZ.
Washington, D.C.: Smithsonian Institution Press, 1970. 133 p. Illus.
Bibliog., pp. 125-29.

Surveys the textile products produced for the export market by
Indian chintz manufacturers and merchants, and relates the
work to European and American acceptance and developments.

306 Bolingbroke, Judith M. CAROLINIAN FABRICS. Leigh-on-Sea, Engl.:
F. Lewis, 1969. 20 p. 40 plates.

A study of the fabrics in use during the years from 1660-1685.
Important for understanding late seventeenth-century American
developments.

307 _____. WILLIAM AND MARY FABRICS. Leigh-on-Sea, Engl.: F.
Lewis, 1969. 20 p. 40 plates.

A study of the stylistic developments during the reign of William and Mary from 1688 to 1702.

308 Clouzot, Henri. PAINTED AND PRINTED FABRICS. New York:
Metropolitan Museum of Art, 1927. xvii, 108 p. 92 illus. (some in
color). Bibliog., pp. xv-xvii.

Provides a history of the major French factories that produced printed fabrics from 1760 to 1815. Also includes notes on early American efforts in such printing. Illustrations of the variety of printed fabrics.

309   Curry, David P. STITCHES IN TIME: SAMPLERS IN THE MUSEUM'S COLLECTION. Lawrence: University of Kansas Museum, 1975. 56 p. 34 illus. Bibliog.

Eighteenth- and nineteenth-century samplers from Europe, Latin America, and the United States. Historical background, complete, descriptive catalog entries, and discussion of the place of sampler making in the education of American women.

310   Digby, George W. ELIZABETHAN EMBROIDERY. New York: Thomas Yoseloff, 1964. 151 p. Illus. Bibliog., pp. 142-46.

A scholarly study of the variety of embroidery developments during the Elizabethan era. Both style and some technical matters are covered, with special attention to sources of design and decoration.

311   Dilley, Arthur U. ORIENTAL RUGS AND CARPETS. New York: Charles Scribner's Sons, 1931. xxii, 303 p. 79 illus. (some in color).

A thorough and comprehensive old study of the field. Beautiful high-quality illustrations help make this a useful source for the general reader and the collector of these rugs. Useful background for understanding American developments.

312   Franses, Jack. EUROPEAN AND ORIENTAL RUGS FOR PLEASURE AND INVESTMENT. New York: Arco, 1970. 176 p. Illus.

A general guidebook for the collector, with worldwide coverage. Based on general availability, it concentrates on and illustrates examples made during the last two centuries.

313   Gunsaulus, Helen C. JAPANESE TEXTILES. New York: Japan Society of New York, 1941. 94 p. Bibliog., pp. 93-94.

A collector's guide to the textiles of Japan from the fifth through the middle of the nineteenth century. Traces the evolution of objects as well as of style.

314   Haas, Louise K., and Haas, Robert B. QUILTS, COUNTERPANES, AND RELATED FABRICS. Santa Monica, Calif.: Privately printed, 1956. 10 illus.

The descriptive catalog of an exhibition of the authors' collection at the DeYoung Museum. Covers the various textile forms in both the eighteenth and the nineteenth centuries in America, Europe, and the Orient.

315   Horner, Mariana M. THE STORY OF SAMPLERS. Philadelphia: Philadelphia Museum of Art, 1971. 64 p. 54 illus.

History of samplers in America, England, Europe, and Mexico between 1662 and 1876, the years of greatest creativity and growth. Complete entries of all forty-eight works are provided, as well as comments on subjects, color, and other aesthetic questions.

316   Jones, Mary E. BRITISH AND AMERICAN TAPESTRIES. Hadleigh, Essex, Engl.: Tower Publications, 1953. 121 p.

Although only a small portion of this work covers the scant information on the New York ateliers, the rest serves as a good introduction to the English works which inspired them. High-quality illustrations include both English and American embroidered pictures.

317   _____. BRITISH SAMPLERS. Oxford, Engl.: Pen-in-Hand, 1948. 48 p. 37 plates.

A history and survey of British samplers from the time of the Tudor period through the era of decline in the twentieth century. Information about pattern books, stitches, and designs.

318   Jourdain, Margaret. THE HISTORY OF ENGLISH SECULAR EMBROIDERY. London: K. Paul, Trench, Trübner and Co., 1910. xv, 202 p. Illus.

An old but worthwhile study of nonvestment-related embroidery. Illustrates and discusses the use of embroidery on a wide variety of garments, coverings, and other objects.

319   Montgomery, Florence M. PRINTED TEXTILES: ENGLISH AND AMERICAN COTTONS AND LINENS 1700-1850. New York: Viking Press, 1970. 379 p. Illus. Bibliog., pp. 361-71.

The catalog consists of over 400 printed textiles in the Winterthur Museum collection. Dimensions, descriptions, and background information on each piece.

320   Morris, Barbara. VICTORIAN EMBROIDERY. New York: Universe, 1970. 238 p. Illus. Bibliog.

The emphasis of this volume is on English embroidery, but other European and American work is included. Appliqué, patchwork, whitework, and so on, are all included in this survey.

Interesting information on the Arts and Crafts Exhibiting Society.

321 Santangelo, Antonio. A TREASURY OF GREAT ITALIAN TEXTILES.
New York: Harry N. Abrams, 1964. 239 p. Illus. (some in color).
Bibliog., pp. 55-57.

A careful study of Italian developments in the field of textiles, from the Middle Ages to about 1800.

322 Schlosser, Ignace. THE BOOK OF RUGS: ORIENTAL AND EURO-
PEAN. New York: Crown Publishers, 1963. 318 p. Illus. Bibliog.,
pp. 307-9.

A popular survey and guide to carpets for the beginning collector. A brief historical text and basic background on technical material are followed by an illustrated catalog of rugs
made during the past two centuries.

323 Schuette, Marie, and Müller-Christensen, Sigrid. THE ART OF EM-
BROIDERY. London: Thames and Hudson, 1964. 336 p. Illus.
Bibliog.

A solid survey and guide to Western embroidery from late Roman times to the present. The handbook format presents a
brief background, including comparisons with Oriental work
and a descriptive catalog of quality pieces through the years.

324 Thornton, Peter. BAROQUE AND ROCOCO SILKS. New York: Taplinger, 1965. 209 p. Illus. Bibliog.

A serious study of the manufacture of silk from the mid-seventeenth century to 1770 in Western Europe. Careful descriptions of the plates.

325 Tilton, John K. TWO HUNDRED YEARS OF TEXTILE DESIGN. New
York: Scalamandre Museum of Textiles, 1956. 31 p. Illus.

Covers the range of colors, patterns, and materials in Britain,
France, and the United States in the eighteenth and nineteenth
centuries. Modest catalog with acceptable illustrations.

Chapter 6

GENERAL WORKS ON AMERICAN DECORATIVE ARTS

GENERAL STUDIES AND SURVEYS OF AMERICAN DECORATIVE ARTS

326 Ayres, James. AMERICAN ANTIQUES. London: Orbis, 1973. 113 p. Illus. Bibliog.

A general survey and study of American furniture and furnishings from about 1670 through 1920. Illustrated with a wide variety of pieces and contains modest bibliographic material.

327 Brazer, Esther S. EARLY AMERICAN DECORATION. Springfield, Mass.: Pond-Ekberg Co., 1940. xii, 273 p. Illus. (some in color).

Provides a brief historical chapter on decorative design and then discusses how various effects and types of decoration were created. Provides descriptive and technical information based on both written material and scientific analysis of objects.

328 Buckley, Charles E. AMERICAN ART OF THE COLONIES AND EARLY REPUBLIC. Chicago: Art Institute of Chicago, 1972. 84 p. 116 illus.

Essentially the catalog of an exhibition of American decorative art objects owned by Chicago area collectors. It is organized by location and period and concentrates on furniture and kitchen-related wares. Excellent catalog entries include provenance and make attributions to specific areas or craftsmen.

329 Card, Devere A. THE USE OF BURL IN AMERICA. Utica, N.Y.: Muson-Williams-Proctor Institute, 1971. 32 p. 35 illus.

The catalog of the collection of colonial American household objects made of wood. Emphasis on "treen" ware and its application to kitchen usage both for the storage and eating of food. Examines each cataloged object in comparison with objects of other materials and provides stylistic and historical data.

330 Christensen, Edwin. THE INDEX OF AMERICAN DESIGN. New York: Macmillan Publishing Co., 1950. xviii, 229 p. 378 illus. (many in color).

Information gathered from this large project of the Depression. WPA artists' watercolor renderings illustrate weather vanes, cigar-store Indians, warming pans, and hundreds of other objects made by American craftsmen.

331 Comstock, Helen. THE CONCISE ENCYCLOPEDIA OF AMERICAN ANTIQUES. 2 vols. New York: Hawthorn Books, 1958. 543 p. 352 illus. Bibliog.

Sixty-two short chapters on different aspects of the decorative and, in some cases, fine arts. Chapters on Windsor chairs, pewter, the craftsmanship of the Shakers, glass, hooked rugs, and so on, by important authorities in each field. Includes short bibliographies in each section and line drawings to supplement the plates.

332 DeJonge, Eric, ed. COUNTRY THINGS: FROM THE PAGES OF THE MAGAZINE ANTIQUES. Princeton, N.J.: Pyne Press, 1973. Var. pag. Illus.

Reprints of articles that have appeared in ANTIQUES, dealing with such decorative art subjects as southern provincial furniture, Ohio coverlets, American woodenware, and fifty-three others. Several articles deal with the collections at specific museums.

333 Downs, Joseph, and Winchester, Alice. A SELECTION OF AMERICAN INTERIORS 1640-1840 IN THE HENRY FRANCIS DU PONT WINTERTHUR MUSEUM, DELAWARE. New York: Antiques Magazine, 1951. 47 p. Illus. (some in color).

Various period rooms from the museum devoted to earlier American art and culture. Excellent quality illustrations of both high style and simple pieces.

334 Drepperd, Carl W. A DICTIONARY OF AMERICAN ANTIQUES. Garden City, N.Y.: Doubleday and Co., 1952. Reprint. New York: Award Books, 1962. viii, 404 p. Bibliog.

Primarily a picture book of American furniture and other objects.

335 _____. THE PRIMER OF AMERICAN ANTIQUES. Garden City, N.Y.: Doubleday, Doran and Co., 1944. xvi, 271 p. Illus.

An old but still useful handbook with seventy-two individual chapters on all aspects of material culture, from furniture and

hooked rugs to trade cards and cast iron mechanical banks.
General statements about each subject with line drawings to
indicate different stylistic periods or regional variations.

336 Dyer, Walter A. EARLY AMERICAN CRAFTSMEN. New York: Century Co., 1915. Reprint. New York: Burt Franklin, 1971. xv,
387 p. Illus. Bibliog., pp. 381-82.

The lives of the craftsmen and a discussion of the early developments in the rise of industrial arts. Illustrations of early
decorative art pieces. Major figures include Duncan Phyfe,
Samuel McIntire, Baron Stiegel, Paul Revere, and the Wil-
lards.

337 Eberlein, Harold D., and McClure, Abbott. THE PRACTICAL BOOK
OF AMERICAN ANTIQUES. Philadelphia: J.B. Lippincott Co.,
1927. iv, 390 p. Illus.

An early but well-written general introduction to the decorative arts of the colonial and early national period. Discusses
and illustrates the types and stylistic evolution of glassware,
pottery, silver, textiles, metalwork, and painted objects.

338 Fleming, E. McClung. "Early American Decorative Arts as Social
Documents." MISSISSIPPI VALLEY HISTORICAL REVIEW 45 (September
1958): 276-84.

A discussion of how household objects can be profitably studied
within the context of the broader society and can indicate
patterns of development.

339 Franco, Barbara. MASONIC SYMBOLS IN AMERICAN DECORATIVE
ARTS. Lexington, Ky.: Museum of Our National Heritage, 1976.
116 p. 117 illus. Bibliog.

An exotic but useful volume which outlines the history of the
organization in Europe and America, concentrating on the
years of its greatest attraction, 1775-1830, and the Victorian
era. Both ritual and domestic objects are discussed and illustrated with reference to both iconography and relevant philosophical and political influences.

340 Guild, Lurelle V. THE GEOGRAPHY OF AMERICAN ANTIQUES.
Garden City, N.Y.: Doubleday, Page and Co., 1935. xx, 283 p.
Illus. Bibliog., p. 278.

Emphasizes the most common elements of the furniture and
furnishings of the various colonies and, later, of the states.
Discusses forms and woods commonly used in each area. An
old but still useful study. Greatest amount of attention is
paid to furniture.

341 Harvard University. HARVARD TERCENTENARY EXHIBITION: FUR-
NITURE AND DECORATIVE ARTS OF THE PERIOD 1636–1836. Cambridge, Mass.: 1936. ix, 114 p. 70 illus.

> An illustrated exhibition catalog which provides a descriptive
> and historical note on 472 cataloged items. Also included is
> a biographical index of the craftsmen and original owners of
> the work. Covers a variety of early decorative arts.

342 Hasley Museum. TECHNOLOGICAL INNOVATION AND THE DEC-
ORATIVE ARTS. Wilmington, Del.: 1973. 80 p. 45 illus.

> The catalog of an exhibition of over 230 objects with catalog
> entries explaining how technological developments and mech-
> anization have affected the processes involved in creating the
> objects.

343 Hill, Ralph N., and Carlisle, Lilian B. THE STORY OF THE SHEL-
BURNE MUSEUM. Shelburne, Vt.: Shelburne Museum, 1960. 113 p.
Illus. (some in color).

> Although this serves as a history and guidebook to this large
> museum collection, it provides sufficient information on the
> types of objects illustrated to be useful to the general student
> of American decorative arts.

344 Hornung, Clarence P. TREASURY OF AMERICAN DESIGN. 2 vols.
New York: Harry N. Abrams, 1972. xxvii, 846 p. 2,901 illus.
(more than 800 in color).

> The author has taken the Depression-born Index of American
> Design project, and has provided both a text, and inclusion
> of all the renderings involved in the project. Includes Holger
> Cahill's original introduction to the project. Although the
> project was never completed in some parts of the country,
> this remains as an indispensable guide to the design traditions
> in American history.

345 Kettell, Russell H., ed. EARLY AMERICAN ROOMS, 1650–1858.
Portland, Maine: Southworth-Athoensen Press, 1936. Reprint. New
York: Dover, 1967. 200 p. 84 illus. (13 in color).

> A view and analysis of twelve period rooms from the early
> colonial period to the middle of the nineteenth century, from
> various parts of the country. A study in the history of taste.

346 Little, Nina F. COUNTRY ARTS IN EARLY AMERICAN HOMES.
New York: E.P. Dutton and Co., 1975. 221 p. 210 illus. (20 in
color).

> A study of rural decorative art objects in New England, and

their use in the actual setting. Covers the entire colonial
period and up to the middle of the nineteenth century.

347 McClinton, Katharine M. A HANDBOOK OF POPULAR ANTIQUES.
New York: Random House, 1946. xii, 244 p. Bibliog.

One of the best of the books for collectors, it provides a
reasonable introduction to the various antique objects of colonial and early federal America. Provides information of use
to the connoisseur.

348 R.W. Norton Art Gallery. AMERICAN SILVER AND PRESSED GLASS:
A COLLECTION IN THE R.W. NORTON ART GALLERY. Shreveport,
La.: 1967. 68 p. Illus. Bibliog., p. 67.

The catalog of a 1967 exhibition of the glass and silver holdings of the Norton Art Gallery. Broad nationwide coverage
with valuable identification of hallmarks.

349 Peterson, Harold L. AMERICANS AT HOME. New York: Charles
Scribner's Sons, 1971. 18 p. 205 plates.

A recent picture book of interiors of American homes, from
the colonial period to the late nineteenth century. Views of
both furniture and furnishings.

350 Phipps, Frances. COLLECTOR'S COMPLETE DICTIONARY OF AMERI-
CAN ANTIQUES. Garden City, N.Y.: Doubleday and Co., 1974.
640 p. 1,000 illus.

An illustrated dictionary which defines thousands of words relating to applied and decorative arts as they appeared between
the earliest colonial days and the mid-nineteenth century.

351 Pratt, Richard, and Pratt, Dorothy. THE TREASURY OF EARLY AMER-
ICAN HOMES. Rev. ed. New York: Hawthorn, 1959. 144 p. 200
color illus.

A handsomely illustrated picture book of interiors that cover
the colonial period through the mid-nineteenth century.

352 Press, Nancy N. THE HANDWROUGHT OBJECT, 1776-1976. Ithaca,
N.Y.: Herbert F. Johnson Museum of Art, Cornell University, 1976.
56 p. 91 illus. Bibliog.

Presents the continuity of objects in this country. Compares
cottage industry work with that of today's hobbyist. About
350 objects classified by natural substance, ceramics, fiber,
metal, and so on. Includes a list of contemporary craftsmen.

353   Quimby, Ian M.G. WINTERTHUR CONFERENCE REPORT 1973:
      TECHNOLOGICAL INNOVATION AND THE DECORATIVE ARTS.
      Charlottesville: University Press of Virginia, 1974. xiv, 373 p.
      Illus.

      These published papers discuss various technological processes
      and their effect on decorative arts: iron castings, pressed
      glass, calico, cylinder printing, and so on.

354   Raycraft, Donald R. EARLY AMERICAN FOLK AND COUNTRY AN-
      TIQUES. Rutland, Vt.: Charles E. Tuttle, 1971. 148 p. Illus. (24
      in color). Bibliog., pp. 137-38.

      Covers both the decorative art objects created away from the
      main centers of high-style activity and the indigenous folk
      objects of eighteenth- and nineteenth-century America.

355   Reif, Rita. TREASURE ROOMS OF AMERICA'S MANSIONS, MANORS,
      AND HOUSES. New York: Coward-McCann, 1970. 297 p. Illus.

      Primarily a picture book of important furniture and furnishings
      of the highest style and quality. Illustrates the fashion of
      representative periods.

356   Schwartz, Marvin D. AMERICAN INTERIORS, 1675-1885: A GUIDE
      TO THE PERIOD ROOMS IN THE BROOKLYN MUSEUM. New York:
      Brooklyn Museum, 1968. vi, 114 p. 83 illus. (19 in color).

      Discusses the use of the objects and arrangement and design
      of objects in each of the rooms, with information on materi-
      als, techniques, and style.

357   Stillinger, Elizabeth. THE "ANTIQUES" GUIDE TO DECORATIVE ARTS
      IN AMERICA, 1600-1875. New York: E.P. Dutton & Co., 1972.
      xv, 463 p. 626 illus. Bibliog., pp. 459-63.

      A comprehensive but general introduction to both English and
      American decorative arts in this country. Photographs of sig-
      nificant examples of work and line drawings highlight the fea-
      tures described in each period. Arranged by genres within
      each historical period.

358   Sweeney, John A. THE TREASURE HOUSE OF EARLY AMERICAN
      ROOMS. New York: Viking Press, 1963. 179 p. Illus.

      Captionized descriptions of the illustrations of the furnished
      rooms in the Henry F. du Pont Winterthur Museum.

359   Warren, David B. BAYOU BEND: AMERICAN FURNITURE, PAINT-
      INGS AND SILVER FROM THE BAYOU BEND COLLECTION. Houston:
      Museum of Fine Arts, 1975. 210 p. 374 illus. (18 in color). Several
      bibliogs.

Extensively illustrated catalog of the twenty-four period rooms
in the Bayou Bend collection. Illustrated works cover from
1650 to 1870 from the Atlantic cities to the Southwest. Silver and furniture are classified and grouped by form, and entries include references to similar works in other collections.
Biographies and bibliographies of individual craftsmen.

360 Winchester, Alice. HOW TO KNOW AMERICAN ANTIQUES. New
York: New American Library, 1951. 191 p. 300 line drawings.

Chapters on each medium plus lighting devices and fireplace
equipment. Craftsmen are discussed in connection with their
work in an intelligent and still useful survey.

STUDIES OF AMERICAN FOLK ART

It is not always easy to separate folk art from country pieces of decorative
arts, and many studies cover both forms. Material is included in this folk
section if it is primarily concerned with folk art rather than other forms.

361 Ames, Kenneth L. BEYOND NECESSITY: ART IN THE FOLK TRADI-
TION. Winterthur, Del.: Winterthur Museum, 1977. 131 p. 119
illus. (8 in color). Bibliog.

A philosophical treatment of the term "folk art" and an analysis of its production. Concerned with the furniture, pottery,
textiles, and metalwork produced by folk craftsmen in America.
The illustrations are all of objects in the Winterthur Museum
and are seen in their cultural context.

362 Andrews, Ruth. HOW TO KNOW AMERICAN FOLK ART. New York:
E.P. Dutton and Co., 1977. xix, 204 p. 158 illus. (37 in color).
Bibliogs.

Eleven illustrated essays by experts on such topics as "Redware
and Stoneware Folk Pottery," "American Country Furniture,"
and "American Quilts." Each essay has a brief bibliography
of major books.

363 Doty, Robert. AMERICAN FOLK ART IN OHIO COLLECTIONS. Akron, Ohio: Akron Art Institute, 1976. 96 p. 68 illus. (11 in color).

Examines the work in both private and public collections.
Describes the development of American folk art traditions and
traces them to Europe and sources. Examination of each entry
includes historical and descriptive information. Coverage of
quilts, pottery, weather vanes, whirligigs, and so on.

364 Kauffman, Henry J. PENNSYLVANIA DUTCH AMERICAN FOLK ART. Rev. ed. New York: Dover, 1964. 146 p. Illus. Bibliog., pp. 145–46.

Brief introductory remarks on various forms of folk (and non-folk) art as practiced by the Pennsylvania Germans, followed by a wide variety of captioned illustrations.

365 Lichten, Frances. FOLK ART OF RURAL PENNSYLVANIA. New York: Charles Scribner's Sons, 1946. xiv, 276 p. 389 illus. (32 in color).

A well-illustrated and carefully prepared pioneering study of the early crafts produced by the various settlers of the area. Captions are fully descriptive and useful, and the whole is a good guide to designs and local motifs. Thirteen chapters are each oriented to a particular material used by the craftsman-- wood, clay, wool, and so on.

366 Lipman, Jean, and Winchester, Alice. THE FLOWERING OF AMERICAN FOLK ART, 1776–1876. New York: Viking Press, 1974. 288 p. 410 illus. (110 in color). Bibliog., pp. 284–87.

The catalog of an important traveling exhibition of American decorative and functional arts in the folk tradition. The text describes the general conditions which helped produce the work and describes the role of the individual artists, when known.

367 Little, Nina F. THE ABBY ALDRICH ROCKEFELLER FOLK ART COLLECTION. Williamsburg, Va.: Colonial Williamsburg, 1957. xvi, 402 p. 105 color illus. Bibliog., pp. 393–94.

The catalog of a major collection of both paintings and useful objects made in the folk tradition. An excellent source of color illustrations of fine examples of work in each genre.

368 Lord, Priscilla S., and Foley, Daniel J. THE FOLK ARTS AND CRAFTS OF NEW ENGLAND. Philadelphia: Chilton Books, 1965. xix, 282 p. Over 500 illus. (14 in color). Bibliog., pp. 253–65.

A very general cultural history of the development of decorative arts in New England, covering both the work of the trained craftsman and the amateur. Discusses technical matters in a way that the general reader can absorb and provides an extensive bibliography for the serious student of the material.

369 Polley, Robert L., ed. AMERICA'S FOLK ART. New York: G.P. Putnam's Sons and Country Beautiful Foundation, 1968. 192 p. Illus. (62 in color).

A good introduction to the range of objects for daily living which were often created by the folk artist as well as the trained craftsman. This volume concentrates on the work of the former group.

370 Rumford, Beatrix T. FOLK ART IN AMERICA: A LIVING TRADITION. Atlanta: High Museum of Art, 1974. 96 p. 119 illus. (11 in color). Bibliog.

The catalog of an exhibition of 109 items from the Abby A. Rockefeller Folk Art Collection at Williamsburg, Virginia, which includes several examples of southern objects of everyday use. The catalog is classified by object type, and each work is described and illustrated. The essay explores the differences between northern and southern traditions.

371 Smith, Gordon M. AMERICAN FOLK ART FROM THE SHELBURNE MUSEUM. Buffalo, N.Y.: Albright-Knox Gallery, 1965. 36 p. 40 illus. (11 in color).

The catalog of a loan exhibition from a major museum of American craft objects. Some 115 catalog entries divided by object types: quilts, rugs, weather vanes. Attempts to date many undated objects.

372 Welsh, Peter C. AMERICAN FOLK ART: THE ART AND SPIRIT OF A PEOPLE. Washington, D.C.: Smithsonian Institution Press, 1965. Unpaged. 65 illus. (some in color). Bibliog.

A catalog of the collections of paintings, sculpture, and useful objects from the important Eleanor and Mabel Van Alstyne collection.

PERIOD STUDIES OF AMERICAN DECORATIVE ARTS

There is much overlap between the section on period studies and the section on geographical studies; a work on Pennsylvania Art Nouveau could have been placed in either section. Where the period seems more important than the location, period has been chosen, but it is admitted that the author has made a subjective judgement. In general, a period is defined as no more than one hundred years; anything longer is placed in the general category.

373 Bridenbaugh, Carl. THE COLONIAL CRAFTSMAN. New York: New York University Press, 1950. xii, 214 p. 17 illus.

This is the text of a series of lectures under the general heading of the book. Discusses the role and activities of both rural and urban craftsmen in colonial America, their manner of creation, and sales of their work. Fine cultural background.

General Works

374 Butler, Joseph T. AMERICAN ANTIQUES, 1800-1900: A COLLEC-
TOR'S HISTORY AND GUIDE. New York: Odyssey Press, 1965.
xxi, 203 p. 170 illus. (some in color). Bibliog., pp. 187-95.

Suitable for the novice in the field of decorative arts as well
as the collector, this volume treats each category--furniture,
glass, ceramics, textiles--in a cultural context and provides
clear, easy-to-read descriptive material.

375 Clark, Robert J., ed. THE ARTS AND CRAFTS MOVEMENT IN AMER-
ICA, 1876-1916. Princeton, N.J.: Princeton University Press, 1972.
190 p. 295 illus. Bibliog., pp. 187-90.

Individual essays on "Eastern Seaboard," "Chicago and the
Midwest," "Pacific Coast," "Arts and Crafts Book," and "Art
Pottery." Each was written by an authority on the field, and
all are well illustrated. The bibliography is very valuable for
further study of the era.

376 Colonial Williamsburg Foundation. THE WILLIAMSBURG COLLECTION
OF ANTIQUE FURNISHINGS. Williamsburg, Va.: 1973. 120 p.
Illus.

Important early American furniture, well illustrated at the colonial capitol of Virginia.

377 E.B. Crocker Art Gallery. THE EIGHTH BIENNIAL CRAFTS EXHIBI-
TION. Sacramento, Calif.: 1973. 76 p. 67 illus.

Over 200 items in glass, silver, pottery, and textiles show the
range of contemporary craft techniques and ideas. Catalog
entries are descriptive; very good plates.

378 Cunningham, Anna K. SCHUYLER MANSION: A CRITICAL CATA-
LOGUE OF THE FURNISHINGS AND DECORATIONS. Albany: New
York State Education Department, 1955. 141 p. Illus.

A complete itemization of the furniture and other objects in
the home of Philip Schuyler (1733-1804). Serves as a useful
tool for understanding how such a gentleman actually lived.

379 Davidson, Marshall B., ed. THE AMERICAN HERITAGE HISTORY OF
AMERICAN ANTIQUES FROM THE CIVIL WAR TO WORLD WAR I.
New York: American Heritage Publishing Co., 1969. 415 p. 646
illus. (many in color).

The third volume in a series, it contains many more "out-of-
the-home" objects. Discusses children's toys, greeting cards,
and so on, as well as furniture and painting. In addition to
the glossary of terms, there is a selection of advertisements
from the period.

380 _____ . THE AMERICAN HERITAGE HISTORY OF AMERICAN AN-
TIQUES FROM THE REVOLUTION TO THE CIVIL WAR. New York:
American Heritage Publishing Co., 1968. 416 p. 511 illus. (many in
color).

> Surveys American decorative arts, painting, and early photo-
> graphic attempts. Undocumented, but generally accurate. A
> glossary of terms and style charts of furniture are helpful tools.

381 _____ . THE AMERICAN HERITAGE HISTORY OF COLONIAL AN-
TIQUES. New York: American Heritage Publishing Co., 1967.
384 p. 580 illus. (many in color).

> A general survey of the furniture, household utensils, silver
> work, and painting of the colonial period of American history.
> Includes style charts of furniture and typical forms in silver.
> A glossary of terms is provided.

382 Fairbanks, Jonathan L., et al. PAUL REVERE'S BOSTON. Boston:
Museum of Fine Arts, 1975. 236 p. 172 illus. (37 in color).
Bibliog., pp. 216-18.

> A massive bicentennial exhibition and catalog that contains a
> great deal of information on late colonial ceramics, furniture,
> metalwork, and textiles. Good biographical essay on Revere,
> the craftsman and the patriot. Extensive bibliography.

383 Lavine, Sigmund A. HANDMADE IN AMERICA: THE HERITAGE OF
COLONIAL CRAFTSMEN. New York: Dodd, Mead and Co., 1968.
148 p. Illus. Bibliog.

> A simple overview of the role of colonial craftsmen in soci-
> ety, their way of making objects, and an examination of their
> selected standard works.

384 Maas, John. THE VICTORIAN HOME IN AMERICA. New York:
Hawthorn, 1972. 235 p. Illus. Bibliog.

> A witty yet scholarly look at Victorian America and the taste
> of the time. Illustrates both interiors and specific Victorian
> forms in the decorative arts.

385 McClinton, Katharine M. COLLECTING AMERICAN VICTORIAN AN-
TIQUES. New York: Charles Scribner's Sons, 1966. 288 p. Illus.
Bibliog., pp. 282-83.

> A well-written guide for the collector interested in Victorian
> Americana. Particularly useful in drawing distinctions between
> American and European objects.

386   McKean, Hugh F. THE ARTS OF LOUIS COMFORT TIFFANY AND
      HIS TIMES. Sarasota, Fla.: John and Mable Ringling Museum of Art,
      1975. 36 p. 79 illus. (18 in color).

      The catalog of an exhibition of the range and scope of Tiffany
      design in glass, jewelry, furniture, and painting. The eighty
      works are all in the McKean collection in Rollins College,
      Florida. Additional non-Tiffany contemporary work is also
      included.

387   Miller, Lillian B. THE DYE IS NOW CAST: THE ROAD TO AMERI-
      CAN INDEPENDENCE, 1774-1776. Washington, D.C.: National
      Portrait Gallery, 1975. 320 p. Illus.

      The catalog of a bicentennial exhibition which included six-
      teen period room arrangements. Each room setting included
      both paintings and decorative art objects of the place and
      time.

388   Morningstar, Connie. FLAPPER FURNITURE AND INTERIORS OF THE
      1920'S. Des Moines, Iowa: Wallace-Homestead, 1971. 123 p. Illus.

      A picture book of interiors of rooms of the 1920s. Furniture
      and general applied art objects.

389   Naylor, Gillian. THE ARTS AND CRAFTS MOVEMENT. Cambridge:
      MIT Press, 1971. 208 p. 101 illus. (some in color). Bibliog.,
      pp. 195-98.

      A study of the European movement including references to
      its influence in the United States. Particular attention is
      called to the meeting of Charles R. Ashbee with Frank Lloyd
      Wright.

390   Nordness, Lee. OBJECTS: U.S.A. New York: Viking Press, 1970.
      360 p. Illus.

      Contemporary craftsmen in enamel, ceramics, glass, metal,
      plastic, mosaic, wood, and textiles, and their work. Covers
      the range of decorative arts in mid-twentieth-century America
      and provides quotes by the artisans of their thoughts about
      their work.

391   Northend, Mary H. COLONIAL HOMES AND THEIR FURNISHINGS.
      Boston: Little Brown, 1912. 252 p. 117 plates.

      An old standard picture book of large, clear plates of New
      England interiors.

392   Reed, Gervais. THE AMERICAN CRAFTSMEN'S INVITATIONAL EXHI-
      BITION. Seattle: Henry Gallery, 1968. 56 p. 66 illus.

Glass, metalwork, and tapestries by fifteen contemporary craftsmen. The catalog of an invitational exhibition that helped spark the rebirth of interest in crafts on the West Coast.

393 Speenburgh, Gertrude. THE ARTS OF THE TIFFANYS. Chicago: Lightner Publishing Co., 1956. 119 p. Illus.

A history and study of the Tiffany family from Charles L. Tiffany through the existence of the current Tiffany and Company. Examines glass, metalwork, and related objects with attention to both artistic and historical material. Includes some anecdotal material and information geared to the enthusiastic collector.

394 Tracy, Berry B., and Gerdts, William H. CLASSICAL AMERICA, 1815-1845. Newark, N.J.: Newark Museum, 1963. 212 p. Illus. Bibliog., pp. 161-63.

Catalog of an exhibition of fine and decorative arts in the classical period is divided into two parts. The decorative arts portion provides information on the European background and discusses furniture, silver, ceramics, glass, wallpaper, textiles, lamps, stoves, and clocks. A fine documentation of a small but important period in our decorative arts history.

395 Tracy, Berry B.; Johnson, Marilynn; Schwartz, Marvin D.; and Boorsh, Suzanne. 19TH CENTURY AMERICA: FURNITURE AND OTHER DEC-ORATIVE ARTS. New York: Metropolitan Museum of Art, 1970. 256 p. 297 illus. (67 in color).

The major and well-organized catalog of the Metropolitan's 100th anniversary exhibition. Furniture, metals, glass, and so on, integrated into a well-written text by specialists in each area.

396 Triggs, Oscar L. CHAPTERS IN THE HISTORY OF THE ARTS AND CRAFTS MOVEMENT. Chicago: Bohemia Guild of the Industrial Art League, 1902. 198 p. Illus.

Primarily a discussion of the European development of the movement, but directed toward the reactivation of guild handi-craft in this country.

GEOGRAPHICAL STUDIES OF AMERICAN DECORATIVE ARTS

397 Adams, Ruth C. PENNSYLVANIA DUTCH ART. Cleveland: World Publishing, 1950. 64 p. Illus. (some in color).

An introduction to the scope and range of the decorative arts among the Pennsylvania Germans. Clear illustrations and an overview text.

398   Bacot, H. Parrott. SOUTHERN FURNITURE AND SILVER: THE FEDERAL PERIOD 1788-1830. Baton Rouge: Anglo-American Art Museum, Louisiana State University, 1968. 36 p. 36 illus.

The work of southern craftsmen in both Anglo-American and Franco-Spanish traditions. Includes twenty-seven cataloged pieces from the museum and local collections. Notes on known craftsmen and, unusually, on earlier restorations of the pieces under consideration.

399   Belknap, Henry W. ARTISTS AND CRAFTSMEN OF ESSEX COUNTY, MASSACHUSETTS. Salem, Mass.: Essex Institute, 1927. viii, 127 p. Illus.

Some concentration on the furniture of the area, with attention to other crafts as well. Records known information on the individuals and their period of activity.

400   Burroughs, Paul H. SOUTHERN ANTIQUES. Richmond, Va.: Garrett and Massie, 1931. xi, 191 p. Illus.

The furniture and furnishings of the Old South. Stylistic variations and similarities with the mainstream are developed and commentary is provided on each major piece illustrated.

401   Carpenter, Ralph E., Jr. THE ARTS AND CRAFTS OF NEWPORT, RHODE ISLAND, 1640-1820. Newport: Preservation Society of Newport County, 1954. xiii, 218 p. 139 illus.

Discusses furniture, silver, and some painting, and provides biographical material on the known craftsmen of the region. The bulk of the book is an illustrated catalog with descriptions and commentary on the various pieces.

402   Cummings, Abbott L., ed. RURAL HOUSEHOLD INVENTORIES: ESTABLISHING THE NAMES, USES, AND FURNISHINGS OF ROOMS IN THE COLONIAL NEW ENGLAND HOME, 1675-1775. Boston: Society for the Preservation of the New England Antiquities, 1964. xi, 306 p. 14 plates.

Divided into twenty-five-year sections, full inventories of the contents of homes are taken from auction and sales records.

403   Dow, George F. THE ARTS AND CRAFTS IN NEW ENGLAND, 1704-1775: GLEANINGS FROM BOSTON NEWSPAPERS RELATING TO PAINTING, ENGRAVING, SILVERSMITHS, PEWTERERS, CLOCKMAKERS,

FURNITURE, POTTERY, OLD HOUSES, COSTUME, TRADES, AND OCCUPATIONS, ETC. Topsfield, Mass.: Wayside Press, 1927. Reprint. New York: DaCapo Press, 1967. 326 p. 336 illus.

A collection of contemporary commentary, advertisements, and other useful information regarding activity in the decorative arts in New England.

404 Downs, Joseph. A HANDBOOK OF THE PENNSYLVANIA GERMAN GALLERIES IN THE AMERICAN WING. New York: Metropolitan Museum of Art, 1934. 22 p. Illus.

The modest catalog of the collection given by Emily de Forest, including furniture and furnishings. Itemization and illustration of the major pieces.

405 Downs, Joseph, and Phillips, John M. THE PRENTIS COLLECTION OF COLONIAL NEW ENGLAND FURNISHINGS. New York: New York Historical Society, 1951. 32 p. Illus. (some in color).

The catalog of a collection of New England furniture and furnishings of excellent quality.

406 Eaton, Allen H. HANDICRAFTS OF NEW ENGLAND. New York: Harper, 1949. 374 p. Illus.

An old standard of basic information on a variety of craft activities in colonial New England.

407 _____. HANDICRAFTS OF THE SOUTHERN HIGH LANDS. New York: Russell Sage Foundation, 1937. Reprint. New York: Dover, 1973. 370 p. 58 illus. 111 plates. Bibliog.

Discusses the origin and use of many everyday objects created in the rural South. Also discusses the revival of interest in them and their creation in the twentieth century. High-quality photographs.

408 Failey, Dean F.; Hefner, Robert J.; and Klaffey, Susan E. LONG ISLAND IS MY NATION: THE DECORATIVE ARTS & CRAFTSMEN, 1640-1830. Stony Brook, N.Y.: Museum of Stony Brook and Society for the Preservation of Long Island Antiquities, 1976. 308 p. 298 illus. Bibliographic essay.

More than 1,000 craftsmen are listed in the appendix of this major exhibition catalog. Chapters on seventeenth-century Dutch and English settlements and their traditions. Stylistic changes and mergers, and post-Revolutionary War growth and specialization. Special emphasis on metalsmiths and woodworking craftsmen. Maps and excellent reproductions.

409   Gordon, Carol E.   MADE IN UTICA.   Utica, N.Y.:   Munson-Williams
       Historical Society, 1976.   76 p.   80 illus.

       One of the three essays is devoted to the fine arts, but the
       majority of the discussion, illustrations, and catalog entries
       are concerned with decorative arts and crafts and manufactured
       objects from the city's past.   From the colonial period to
       1945.

410   Gottesman, Rita S[usswein]., comp.   THE ARTS AND CRAFTS IN NEW
       YORK.   Vol. 1, 1726-1776; 2, 1777-1779; 3, 1800-1804.   3 vols.
       New York: New York Historical Society, 1938, 1954, 1965.   Reprint
       3 vols. in 1.   DaCapo Press series in architecture and decorative art,
       vol. 35.   New York: DaCapo Press, 1970.   450 p.   Illus.

       Categories of crafts with entries under each heading.   A com-
       pilation of various newspaper advertisements and other news
       accounts culled from New York City's newspapers.   A sub-
       stantial analytical index is one of the great strengths of this
       approach and makes it a valuable reference tool.

411   Harris, Marleine R.   VIRGINIA ANTIQUES.   New York: Exposition
       Press, 1953.   183 p.   Illus.

       A collector's guide which concentrates on furniture, but also
       covers furnishings made and used in Virginia from the early
       colonial period through the nineteenth century.

412   Horowitz, Elinor L.   MOUNTAIN PEOPLE, MOUNTAIN CRAFTS.
       New York: J.B. Lippincott, 1974.   143 p.   196 illus.

       Emphasizes the processes utilized by Appalachian preindustrial
       craftsmen.   Provides a good overview of the conditions under
       which the objects are made and explores both folk craft and
       folk industry.

413   Isham, Norman M., and Brown, Albert F.   EARLY CONNECTICUT
       HOUSES.   Providence, R.I.:   Preston and Rounds, 1900.   Reprint.
       New York: Dover, 1965.   303 p.   188 illus.   Bibliog.

       Twenty-nine colonial houses are illustrated and discussed in
       terms of their organization and furnishings.   An old but im-
       pressive and thorough treatment of colonial interiors.

414   Jacobs, Muriel, and Ballard, Doris.   ANTIQUING IN NEW JERSEY
       AND BUCKS COUNTY, PENNSYLVANIA.   New Brunswick, N.J.:
       Rutgers University Press, 1978.   lxiv, 439 p.   Illus.   Bibliog.

       Brief essays on regional craftsmen followed by geographically
       organized lists of antique shows, dealers, restoration special-
       ists, and so on.

415   Leed, Gretel. NEW YORK CRAFTS 1700–1875. Ithaca, N.Y.:
       Ithaca College Museum of Art, 1967. 56 p. 26 illus.

       The catalog of some 350 items from the Ithaca area museums
       and collections. Ceramics, glass, furniture, needlework, and
       so on, arranged by craft. Brief introductory texts for each
       craft stress the evolution of style and technique from the co-
       lonial era through 1875.

416   Lerch, Lila. PENNSYLVANIA GERMAN ANTIQUES. Allentown,
       Pa.: Schlechler's, 1970. viii, 157 p. Illus.

       An introduction for collectors. Concentrates on the questions
       of design and decoration that make the work of the Pennsyl-
       vania Germans distinctive from mainstream objects.

417   Long, Deborah, and Trapp, Kenneth R. THE LADIES, GOD BLESS
       'EM: THE WOMAN'S ART MOVEMENT IN CINCINNATI IN THE
       NINETEENTH CENTURY. Cincinnati: Cincinnati Art Museum, 1976.
       70 p. 51 illus.

       Although concerned with all the organizations classified as
       women's art groups, it justifiably concentrates on those in-
       volved with the American pottery movement made famous in
       Cincinnati. Illustrations of objects are described and care-
       fully documented. Chronology of the groups and biographical
       notes.

418   Michael, George. THE TREASURY OF NEW ENGLAND ANTIQUES.
       New York: Hawthorn, 1969. xii, 210 p. Illus.

       A collector's guide, with particular attention paid to prime co-
       lonial pieces.

419   Morton, Robert. SOUTHERN ANTIQUES AND FOLK ART. Birming-
       ham, Ala.: Oxmoor House, 1976. 251 p. Illus. Bibliog., pp.
       242–44.

       An easy-to-read introduction to the unique styles and varia-
       tions that make southern objects unique. Illustrations docu-
       ment variety, and the bibliography is a sorely needed starting
       point in a neglected field.

420   Randall, Richard H., Jr. THE DECORATIVE ARTS OF NEW HAMP-
       SHIRE 1725–1825. Manchester, N.H.: Currier Gallery of Art, 1964.
       73 p. 106 illus.

       The catalog of a major exhibition of one hundred years of
       decorative arts in the state. Overwhelming emphasis on fur-
       niture, with a small amount of attention paid to glass, ceram-
       ics, and fine arts. Is clear and documented, with descriptive
       illustrations of most pieces.

421 Rice, A.W., and Stoudt, J.P. THE SHENANDOAH POTTERY. Strasburg, Va.: Shenandoah Publishing House, 1929. 277 p. 45 illus. (7 in color).

A history of the area potteries with emphasis on the important Bell pottery. The well-illustrated catalog contains the extensive Rice collection of over 2,000 pieces, of which about one hundred are pictured.

422 Schwartz, Barbara. NORTH CAROLINA CRAFTSMEN 1972. Raleigh: North Carolina Museum of Art, 1971. 25 p. Illus.

The catalog of an exhibition of over 130 works by eighty-five North Carolina craftsmen; objects in ceramics, glass, silver, leather, and textiles. A discussion of the role and scope of the contemporary craftsman and the special place in the local Carolina scene. Detailed catalog entries and good illustrations.

423 Smith, Elmer L. ARTS AND CRAFTS OF THE SHENANDOAH VALLEY. Witmer, Pa.: Shenandoah Valley Folklore Society, 1968. 43 p. Illus.

A picture book of the varieties of the local craft tradition in the Shenandoah Valley.

424 Steinfeldt, Cecilia, and Stover, Donald. EARLY TEXAN FURNITURE AND DECORATIVE ARTS. San Antonio, Tex.: Trinity University Press, 1973. 263 p. Illus.

The catalog of an important pioneering effort at getting together the various furniture and furnishings both used and made in Texas. Distinctive local features and types of objects are highlighted and provide the base for further examination.

425 Stoudt, John P. EARLY PENNSYLVANIA ARTS AND CRAFTS. New York: A.S. Barnes and Co., 1964. 364 p. 344 illus. (21 in color).

Covers some early painting and architecture but is essentially a cultural study of the society and the objects in use in daily life. Many of the illustrations show furniture and other crafts within the setting of the architecture of the period.

426 Tabakoff, Sheila K., et al. ARTS AND CRAFTS IN DETROIT, 1906–1976. THE MOVEMENT, THE SOCIETY, THE SCHOOL. Detroit: Detroit Institute of Arts, 1976. 296 p. 287 illus. (6 in color). Bibliog.

The catalog of an important exhibition that brings together the entire range of decorative and applied arts activities in the area. Particularly valuable for its discussion of pottery and metal developments with very important bibliography.

427 Van Hoesen, Walter H. CRAFTS AND CRAFTSMEN OF NEW JERSEY.
Cranbury, N.J.: Farleigh Dickenson University Press, 1973. 151 p.
Illus. Bibliog., pp. 242-43.

A good serious study of the development of decorative arts in
the state. Well illustrated, with a short but useful bibliography.

428 White, Margaret E. THE DECORATIVE ARTS OF EARLY NEW JERSEY.
Princeton, N.J.: Van Nostrand, 1964. 137 p. Illus. Bibliog.

A careful and scholarly study of New Jersey's production in
a variety of decorative arts media. Separates New Jersey
accomplishments from those of New York City and Philadelphia.

429 Wyckoff, Donald L. OHIO DESIGNER CRAFTSMEN. Columbus: Ohio
Arts Council, 1970. 41 p. 36 illus.

Represents the work and presents brief biographies of thirty-six
contemporary ceramists, metalsmiths, and weavers. Discusses
both the functional and the aesthetic value of the crafts.

STUDIES OF AFRO-AMERICAN, NATIVE-AMERICAN, AND SHAKER DECORATIVE ARTS

430 Andrews, Edward D. THE COMMUNITY INDUSTRIES OF THE SHAKERS.
Albany: New York State Museum, 1933. Reprint. Charlestown,
Mass.: Emporium Publications, 1972. 322 p. Illus. Bibliog.

The furniture, baskets, and other objects made by the members
of the Shaker communities. The pioneering study of their
work and its relationship to religious beliefs.

431 Batchelor, Elisabeth, et al. ART OF THE FIRST AMERICANS FROM
THE COLLECTION OF THE CINCINNATI ART MUSEUM. Cincinnati:
Cincinnati Art Museum, 1976. 104 p. 144 illus. (5 in color).
Bibliogs.

This is the catalog of Cincinnati's exhibition of over 1,000
objects of American Indian art. Baskets, beadwork, jewelry,
pottery, and textiles are all discussed, documented, and illustrated. Primarily an ethnographic rather than artistic point of
view, with emphasis on geographic influences on cultures and
problems of documentation and conservation.

432 Chase, Judith W. AFRO-AMERICAN ART AND CRAFT. New York:
Van Nostrand Reinhold, 1971. 142 p. Illus. Bibliog., pp. 138-39.

Traces the influence of African art to black American artists.

Some well-known, recently discovered, and anonymous artists
are both discussed and illustrated.

433   Coe, Ralph T. SACRED CIRCLES: TWO THOUSAND YEARS OF
NORTH AMERICAN INDIAN ART. Kansas City, Mo.: Nelson Gallery, Atkins Museum of Fine Arts, 1977. x, 252 p. Illus. Bibliog.

The catalog of an exhibition which includes hundreds of items
from both European and American collections. Divided into
six unique geographical sections, it broadly treats the major
American Indian art forms.

434   Dickey, Roland F. NEW MEXICO VILLAGE ARTS. Rev. ed. Albuquerque: University of New Mexico Press, 1970. xii, 264 p. Illus.
with drawings. Bibliog., pp. 254–58.

A sympathetic social and cultural history with description of
the crafts found in the homes of the villagers.

435   Dockstader, Frederick J. INDIAN ART IN AMERICA: THE ARTS AND
CRAFTS OF THE NORTH AMERICAN INDIAN. Greenwich, Conn.:
New York Graphic Society, 1966. 224 p. 248 illus. (many in color).
Bibliog., pp. 222–24.

A solid general survey of the various arts of the American
Indian with selections from prehistoric, historic, and contemporary American civilizations. Excellent quality color plates.

436   Feder, Norman. AMERICAN INDIAN ART. New York: Harry N.
Abrams, 1969. 445 p. Illus. (many in color). Bibliog., pp. 439–
44.

A geographically organized survey of the various Indian groups,
treating each one's productions and variety of forms.

437   _____. TWO HUNDRED YEARS OF NORTH AMERICAN INDIAN
ART. New York: Frederick A. Praeger, 1972. 128 p. 150 illus.
(8 in color). Bibliog., pp. 121–24.

The catalog of an exhibition held at the Whitney Museum of
American Art. Provides discussion and documentation of the
variety of art forms produced by both American and Canadian
tribes.

438   Friedman, Martin, ed. AMERICAN INDIAN ART: FORM AND TRA-
DITION. New York: E.P. Dutton, 1972. 154 p. Illus. (some in
color). Bibliog., pp. 148–51.

Many essays by specialized authorities on the different tribal
areas and their unique contributions. Includes a study of aesthetics and an essay on the relationship between the artist and
the artisan.

439 Maurer, Evan M. THE NATIVE AMERICAN HERITAGE. Chicago:
Art Institute of Chicago, 1977. 351 p. 566 illus. (33 in color).
Bibliog., pp. 345-51.

The catalog of a major exhibition of American Indian art held
at the Art Institute of Chicago. Arranged by geographical
region and profusely illustrated by representative pieces of a
wide range of functional and ceremonial objects.

440 Sprigg, June. BY SHAKER HANDS. THEIR ART AND THEIR WORLD.
New York: Alfred A. Knopf, 1975. xii, 212 p. Illus. Bibliog.,
pp. 209-12.

A text on the Shakers, their way of life, and their form of
manufacture of decorative arts objects. Some 250 drawings
of both their products and their tools.

441 Vlach, John M. THE AFRO-AMERICAN TRADITION IN DECORATIVE
ARTS. Cleveland: Cleveland Museum of Art, 1978. 175 p. Illus.

An exhibition catalog which traces the influence of various
African cultures on America and how those cultures have both
survived and adapted. Emphasis on basketry, pottery, quilting, and wood carving. Places the artistic output in a larger
historical and social context.

Chapter 7

AMERICAN CERAMICS

The relationship between porcelain and earthenware in America is similar to that between silver and pewter. In each case, the less expensive material was used for everyday ware, and the more expensive was used for show pieces and for use by the affluent.

Although this meant that far more earthenware was made than high-quality porcelain, it is also true that the earthenware was more easily destroyed or discarded. Thus we have very few examples and little information about earlier forms of earthenware.

In addition, many basic functional pottery forms endured throughout the years, making it harder to date earthenware than the style-adapted porcelain. Both geographic and period studies reflect these phenomena.

GENERAL STUDIES AND SURVEYS OF AMERICAN CERAMICS

442 Barber, Edwin A. CATALOGUE OF AMERICAN POTTERIES AND POR-
CELAINS. Philadelphia: Pennsylvania Museum and School of Industrial
Art, 1893. 43 p. Illus.

> The museum's catalog of the collection of ceramics formed by
> Barber. The text discusses both technical and aesthetic ques-
> tions.

443 _____. MARKS OF AMERICAN POTTERS. Philadelphia: Patterson &
White, 1904. Reprint. Southampton, N.Y.: Cracker Barrel Press, 1971.
174 p. Illus.

> A geographically divided catalog of American potters with
> more than 1,000 different marks, including different ones used
> by a firm over the years. A useful aid to scholar and con-
> noisseur alike.

444 _____. THE POTTERY AND PORCELAIN OF THE UNITED STATES.

New rev. ed. Watkins Glen, N.Y.: Century House, 1971. ix, 450 p. 222 illus. Bibliog., pp. 407-35.

Discussions of operations of American individuals and companies in terms of both geography and style. Particular attention is paid to Tucker porcelain, the first manufactured in this country. The section on ornamental tiles is valuable, as is the extensive updated bibliography.

445 Clement, Arthur W. NOTES ON AMERICAN CERAMICS: 1607-1943. Brooklyn: Brooklyn Museum, 1944. 63 p. 56 illus. Bibliog., pp. 35-36.

A guidebook to the museum's collection of American ceramic ware of several varieties, including decorative tiles. Covers the entire range of American production to the time of writing.

446 _____. OUR PIONEER POTTERS. New York: Privately printed, 1947. 94 p. 24 illus. Bibliog., pp. 89-91.

A small selective study of the subject, emphasizing the beginnings of each new development, whether New York stoneware or Tucker porcelain. Very well documented, the source of information for many later writers, and still worth reading for those interested in the pioneer efforts in American potteries. Discusses both craftsmen and the various firms.

447 Donhauser, Paul S. HISTORY OF AMERICAN CERAMICS: THE STUDIO POTTER. Dubuque, Iowa: Kendall/Hunt Publishing Co., 1978. xvi, 260 p. Illus. Bibliog., pp. 237-40.

Covers the colonial period, nineteenth-century traditional pottery, china painting, Art Nouveau, and the arts and crafts movements. Other chapters cover foreign influences during the twentieth century, the role of Alfred University's ceramics program, and contemporary developments. A wide variety of illustrations, useful appendixes, and a glossary of ceramic terms.

448 FORMS FROM THE EARTH: 1,000 YEARS OF POTTERY IN AMERICA. New York: Museum of Contemporary Crafts, 1962. 21 p. 25 illus.

Exhibition catalog of 299 items of the pre-Columbian period, the colonial years, and up through the first half of the twentieth century. Very little text.

449 Ketchum, William C., Jr. THE POTTERY AND PORCELAIN COLLECTOR'S HANDBOOK: A GUIDE TO EARLY AMERICAN CERAMICS FROM MAINE TO CALIFORNIA. New York: Funk and Wagnalls, 1974. xx, 204 p. Illus.

Although designated as a handbook for the collector, it serves quite well as an introduction to the techniques, stylistic changes, and history of ceramic work in this country. The appendix is a carefully selected list of potters and their period of activity, location, and type of ware produced.

450 Quimby, Ian M.G., ed. WINTERTHUR CONFERENCE REPORT, 1972: CERAMICS IN AMERICA. Charlottesville: University Press of Virginia, 1973. ix, 374 p. Illus.

A series of papers that explore American ceramics in light of archeological and connoisseurship evidence.

451 Ramsay, John. AMERICAN POTTERS AND POTTERY. New York: Tudor Publishing Co., 1947. xx, 304 p. 100 illus. Bibliog., pp. 244-51.

A good general survey which includes a chart and key to pottery forms, technical notes, an index of potters' marks, a check-list of potters by location, and a study of developments in the history of style and taste.

452 Spargo, John. EARLY AMERICAN POTTERY AND CHINA. Garden City, N.Y.: Garden City Publishing Co., 1948. xvii, 393 p. 64 illus. Bibliog., pp. 373-76.

A broad survey which remains valuable. Tables of marks and potters and descriptions of their work supplement chapters on the different periods, on classification by type, and on the unusual.

453 Stiles, Helen E. POTTERY IN THE UNITED STATES. New York: E.P. Dutton & Co., 1942. 329 p. Illus. Bibliog., pp. 317-24.

A somewhat chatty but useful survey of pottery, starting with an examination of early imports. The major pottery centers are examined and the various art ware sources are discussed. Separate chapters on brick and tile work.

454 Watkins, Lura W. EARLY NEW ENGLAND POTTERS AND THEIR WARES. Cambridge: Harvard University Press, 1950. x, 291 p. 136 illus. Bibliog., pp. 271-76.

A carefully written, scholarly study of the techniques and history of the potters, by location and by the work they produced. The peculiarities and distinctive characteristics of different potters are discussed and used as an aid in research.

PERIOD STUDIES OF AMERICAN CERAMICS

455 Barons, Richard I. AN EXHIBITION OF 18TH AND 19TH CENTURY AMERICAN FOLK ART. New Paltz: State University of New York at New Paltz, College Art Gallery, 1969. 35 p. 46 illus.

This catalog of an exhibition begins with an introduction to the subject of American folk pottery. Covers ceramic art of the entire eastern seaboard and includes descriptions of each of the sixty-three pieces in the exhibition.

456 Brand Library Art Center. BRAND V CERAMIC CONJUNCTION. Glendale, Calif.: 1975. 24 p. 16 illus.

An exhibition catalog with introductory material on fine art ceramics, a listing of the competition entries, and illustrations.

457 California, State University of, at San Francisco. Hayward Art Gallery. NUT ART. San Francisco: 1972. 35 p. 24 illus. Bibliog.

An examination of contemporary ceramic pieces by eighteen artists. The catalog includes personal statements by each artist, their photographs, and illustrations of both their studies and actual pieces.

458 California, University of, at Irvine. Art Gallery. ABSTRACT EXPRESSIONIST CERAMICS. Irvine, Calif.: 1955. 54 p. Illus. (8 in color).

The catalog of an exhibition of the ceramic work of ten American craftsmen. Includes such figures as Ken Price and Peter Voulkos.

459 Evans, Paul. ART POTTERY OF THE UNITED STATES: AN ENCYCLOPEDIA OF PRODUCERS AND THEIR MARKS. New York: Charles Scribner's Sons, 1974. 353 p. Illus. (8 in color). Marks.

Concentrates on the individual potter and his marks, with attention to both those who worked independently and those who worked for art pottery firms. Illustrations are oriented to suggesting opportunities for examination of the specific pieces.

460 Foley, Susan. A DECADE OF CERAMIC ART, 1962-1972: FROM THE COLLECTION OF PROFESSOR AND MRS. R. JOSEPH MONSEN. San Francisco: San Francisco Museum of Art, 1972. 60 p. 53 illus. (3 in color).

The catalog of a collection of contemporary American ceramic art. Illustrates changes from traditional pottery forms to a wider variety of forms.

461 Fort Wayne Museum of Art. FORT WAYNE INVITATIONAL CERAMICS EXHIBITION. Fort Wayne, Ind.: 1968. 19 p. 17 illus.

The catalog of a seventeen-artist exhibition. Includes biographical material on each ceramist and an illustration of a major piece.

462 Kovel, Ralph, and Kovel, Terry. THE KOVELS' COLLECTOR'S GUIDE TO AMERICAN ART POTTERY. New York: Crown Publishers, 1974. 378 p. 16 color illus.

A collector's handbook which is arranged by individual factory, throughout the country. Covers the period from 1870 to the end of the 1920s. Information on craftsmen, dates, specialty items, and pottery marks.

463 McKinnell, James, and Jonas, Abner. CLAY TODAY. Ames: New Gallery, Iowa State University, 1962. 20 p. 25 plates.

Introduction to ceramic work of the contemporary era and biographical information on each of some fifty artists represented in the exhibition.

464 Moore College of Art, Gallery. CLAY THINGS: EAST COAST INVITATIONAL. Philadelphia: 1974. 20 p. 9 illus.

The catalog of an invitational exhibition of nine important ceramists. A brief biography of each craftsman and a statement by each about his work.

465 Museum of Contemporary Crafts. CLAYWORKS: 20 AMERICANS. New York: 1971. 36 p. 25 illus.

The catalog of an exhibition of the work of twenty contemporary artists, including the biographies of each craftsman and itemizing ninety-seven pieces.

466 Nelson, Marion J. "Art Nouveau in American Ceramic." ART QUARTERLY 26, no. 4 (1963): 441-59.

Discusses the influence of European Art Nouveau, and its American manifestations in the mainstream of both the freehand and manufactured pottery of this country.

467 Noel-Hume, Ivor. POTTERY AND PORCELAIN IN COLONIAL WILLIAMSBURG'S ARCHAEOLOGICAL COLLECTIONS. Colonial Williamsburg Archaeological Series, no. 2. Williamsburg, Va.: Colonial Williamsburg, 1969. 46 p. 43 illus.

Itemizes and illustrates the variety of American and imported ceramic pieces unearthed at Williamsburg and dating from the seventeenth century.

468   Polak, Clark. BRAND IV CERAMIC CONJUNCTION. Glendale, Calif.: Brand Library Art Center, 1974. 8 p. 13 loose plates.

> This catalog concentrates on the sculptural objects made by the represented artists and discusses the interrelationship between sculpture and traditional ceramic technique.

469   Scripps College. NINETEENTH ANNUAL INVITATIONAL CERAMICS EXHIBITION. Claremont, Calif.: 1963. Unpaged. 34 illus.

> A brief exhibition catalog with illustration of a work by each of the invited ceramists.

470   Smith, Elmer L. POTTERY: A UTILITARIAN FOLK CRAFT. Lebanon, Pa.: Applied Arts Publishers, 1972. 32 p. Illus.

> A historical treatment of the major frontier-area potteries during the second half of the nineteenth century. Concerned with both earthenware and stoneware and illustrates representative pieces.

471   Smithsonian Institution. CERAMIC ARTS U.S.A. 1966. Washington, D.C.: 1966. 28 p. 100 illus.

> This exhibition catalog documents and illustrates one hundred pieces selected to indicate the range of ceramic activity in mid-century America.

472   Syracuse Museum of Fine Arts, American Ceramic Society. CONTEMPORARY AMERICAN CERAMICS. Syracuse, N.Y.: 1937. 18 p. 18 illus. (1 in color).

> The catalog of a traveling exhibition that presented 135 objects by fifty living American ceramists to a European audience.

473   Watkins, Ben. CERAMICS BY SIX. Boston: Society of Arts and Crafts, 1966. 6 p. 6 illus.

> Six contemporary artists who work in nontraditional ways and develop new forms.

474   Wooster, College of, Art Museum. FUNCTIONAL CERAMICS, 1974. Wooster, Ohio: 1974. 32 p. 21 illus.

> Twenty-one craftsmen have their work illustrated and discuss the aesthetics of functional creation. Contains biographical information and a brief exhibition record for each artist.

GEOGRAPHICAL STUDIES OF AMERICAN CERAMICS

475 Barret, Richard. BENNINGTON POTTERY & PORCELAIN: A GUIDE
TO IDENTIFICATION. New York: Bonanza Books, 1958. 348 p.
457 illus. (7 in color).

A brief history of the scope and range of ceramics produced
in Bennington, Vermont, during the nineteenth century. Profusely illustrated with examples of both functional and decorative objects with emphasis on production pieces.

476 Bivins, John. THE MORAVIAN POTTERS IN NORTH CAROLINA.
Chapel Hill: University of North Carolina Press, 1972. xiii, 300 p.
276 illus. Bibliog., pp. 289-90.

A detailed study of the history and output of the Moravian
pottery work in North Carolina. The activities and leadership
roles of the various masters are presented, and the different
products--candlesticks, pots, and Queensware--are discussed
and illustrated. Contains a good working glossary of items.

477 Branin, M. Lelyn. THE EARLY POTTERS AND POTTERIES OF MAINE.
Maine Heritage Series, no. 3. Middletown, Conn.: Wesleyan University Press, 1978. 262 p. 70 illus.

A brief background on pottery making is secondary to the
town-by-town survey of redware, stoneware, art pottery, and
so on, and the checklist of marks. The collector will find
this invaluable, and the historian and general reader will be
interested in the discussion of the impact of the Industrial Revolution on both the lives of the potters and the techniques for
pottery manufacture.

478 Clement, Arthur W. THE POTTERY AND PORCELAIN OF NEW JER-
SEY. Newark, N.J.: Newark Museum, 1947. 100 p. 52 illus.

Both the essay and catalog are divided by categories of pottery: redware, stoneware, moulded work, porcelain, and so
on. Catalog entries measure, describe, and date the pieces
and provide additional information as notes. Some 247 items
plus information about tools.

479 Crawford, Jean. JUGTOWN POTTERY: HISTORY AND DESIGN.
Winston-Salem, N.C.: John F. Blair, Publisher, 1964. 127 p. 25
illus. (12 in color). Bibliog., pp. 120-27.

A history of the Jugtown pottery and the shapes and designs
produced at that revival center. Good illustrations and a detailed bibliography of primary and secondary sources.

480　Everson Museum of Art of Syracuse and Onondaga County. 25TH CE-
RAMIC NATIONAL EXHIBITION, (1968-1970). Syracuse, N.Y.: 1968.
48 p. Illus.

The catalog of a major biennial exhibition of contemporary
ceramics. Itemization of 288 pieces and commentary by individual craftsmen.

481　Hawes, Lloyd E. DEDHAM POTTERY AND THE EARLIER ROBERTSON'S
CHELSEA POTTERIES. Dedham, Mass.: Dedham Historical Society,
1968. 52 p. 51 illus. Bibliog., p. 52.

Brief history of this important pottery center, and illustrations
of not only the major work, but of the factory and process as
well. Registration and potters' marks are illustrated.

482　James, Arthur E. THE POTTERS AND POTTERIES OF CHESTER COUN-
TY, PENNSYLVANIA. West Chester, Pa.: Chester County Historical
Society, 1945. 116 p. 20 illus. Map. List of potters, pp. 111-14.
Bibliog., pp. 115-16.

A brief history of the families involved in Chester County pottery activities. Information on both the use of various clays
and technilogical developments.

483　Ketchum, William C., Jr. EARLY POTTERS AND POTTERIES OF NEW
YORK STATE. New York: Funk and Wagnalls, 1970. x, 278 p.
Illus. Bibliog., pp. 254-69.

After an introduction to the art of the potter, a geographical
survey is the main body of the book. The work of potteries
in various parts of the state is examined, and a checklist of
New York State potters and their marks is provided. Bibliography is detailed and divided by region.

484　＿＿＿＿. THE POTTERY OF THE STATE. New York: Museum of American Folk Art, 1974. 14 p. Illus.

The history of the New York State pottery industry from the
seventeenth century to the end of the nineteenth. The catalog relates to both redware and stoneware, and illustrations
are from several geographical areas.

485　Loar, Peggy. INDIANA STONEWARE. Indianapolis: Indianapolis
Museum of Art, 1974. 48 p. 95 illus. Bibliog.

Traces the history of stoneware productions in Indiana from
1837 to 1974. Eighty-six works, including those by such contemporary figures as Karl Martz, are illustrated, described,
and provided with a provenance. Good general background
on American pottery making.

486   New Jersey State Museum. NEW JERSEY POTTERY TO 1840. Tren-
       ton: 1972. Unpaged. Illus. Bibliog.

       The catalog of an exhibition of the various New Jersey pot-
       teries with descriptions and illustrations of the variety of
       glazed redwares and stonewares. Discussion and illustration
       of the individual pieces.

487   Purviance, Louise; Purviance, Evan; and Schneider, Norris F. ZANES-
       VILLE ART POTTERY. Leon, Iowa: Mid-American Book Co., 1968.
       Unpaged. 23 color plates.

       Illustrations and discussion of the work of the major Zanesville
       potteries: S.A. Weller, J.B. Owens, and the important Rose-
       ville Pottery Company.

488   Rice, A.W., and Stoudt, J. THE SHENANDOAH POTTERY. Stras-
       burg, Va.: Shenandoah Publishing House, 1929. 277 p. 45 illus.
       (7 in color).

       A history of the area potteries with emphasis on the important
       Bell pottery. The well-illustrated catalog contains the exten-
       sive Rice collection of over 2,000 pieces of which about one
       hundred are pictured.

489   Rochester Museum and Science Center. CLAY IN THE HANDS OF
       THE POTTER; AN EXHIBITION OF POTTERY MANUFACTURED IN THE
       ROCHESTER AND GENESEE VALLEY REGION, C. 1793-1900. Roches-
       ter, N.Y.: 1974. 56 p. 57 illus. Bibliog., p. 56.

       Concentrates on the factory rather than the studio potter, pro-
       viding information about the various firms of the area, exam-
       ples of their work, and a history of regional stylistic evolu-
       tion. Illustrations, while not top quality, document provincial
       material seldom published elsewhere.

490   Spargo, John. POTTERS AND POTTERIES OF BENNINGTON. Boston:
       Houghton Mifflin, 1926. Reprint. New York: Dover, 1972. xvi,
       270 p. 49 illus. (8 in color).

       A well-respected older study of American ceramics through the
       work of the widely recognized work of the Bennington, Ver-
       mont, pottery center. Covers both the Norton and Fenton
       firms. Appendixes present data on Bennington clays. Illus-
       trations are from the author's own magnificent collection.

491   Wiltshire, William E. III. FOLK POTTERY OF THE SHENANDOAH
       VALLEY. New York: E.P. Dutton Co., 1975. 127 p. 60 color
       illus. 2 maps. Bibliog., p. 127.

       A brief history of the style of pottery and the potters in the

Shenandoah Valley, followed by large and useful color examples of the typical work of the region.

SPECIFIC CERAMIC TYPES IN AMERICA

492 Barber, Edwin A. ANGLO-AMERICAN POTTERY: OLD ENGLISH CHINA WITH AMERICAN VIEWS. 2d ed. Philadelphia: Patterson and White Co., 1901. 220 p. Illus.

A survey and description of the large amount of English china made for American markets. Covers the major firms' output of Liverpool and Staffordshire and contains information on printed ware.

493 _____. TULIP WARE OF THE PENNSYLVANIA-GERMAN POTTERS: AN HISTORICAL SKETCH OF THE ART OF SLIP-DECORATION IN THE UNITED STATES. Philadelphia: Pennsylvania Museum, 1903. Reprint. New York: Dover, 1975. 223 p. 94 illus.

The history of the manufacture and style of the tulip ware of this group, with attention paid to the methods and processes. A final chapter deals with non-Pennsylvania-Dutch workers in this medium.

494 Benjamin, Marcus. AMERICAN ART POTTERY. New York: Privately Printed, 1898. Reprint. Washington, D.C.: Privately Printed, 1907. 57 p. Illus.

An early firsthand account of visits to pottery centers in Boston, New Jersey, Ohio, and West Virginia. Provides a concise history of the art pottery industry from the last quarter of the nineteenth century.

495 Clarke, John M. THE SWISS INFLUENCE ON THE EARLY PENNSYL-VANIA SLIP DECORATED MAJOLICA. Albany, N.Y.: J.B. Lyon Co., 1908. 18 p. 8 illus.

An extremely old but valuable study in that the author separates the otherwise undocumented Swiss-inspired works from the superficially similar work derived from Germany. Interesting comparison of motifs with Swiss original work.

496 Earle, Alice. CHINA COLLECTING IN AMERICA. New York: Charles Scribner's Sons, 1892. 429 p. 66 figs.

A handbook for the collector which includes both American-made china and that made for the American market. Specific attention to patriotic subjects on china.

497 Greaser, Arlene, and Greaser, Paul H. HOMESPUN CERAMICS, A STUDY OF SPATTERWARE. 3d ed. Allentown, Pa.: Privately printed, 1967. 123 p. 250 illus.

Spatterware was widely used among the simple folk of New England and into the Midwest. Discusses the various stages in the development. Valuable for the wide range of illustrations, a clear indication of the taste of its users.

498 Guilland, Harold F. EARLY AMERICAN FOLK POTTERY. Philadelphia: Chilton Book Co., 1971. 322 p. Illus. (16 in color). Map. Bibliog., pp. 293-309.

Discusses the folk pottery of the country in general as background for the illustrations selected from the Index of American Design project of the federal government.

499 Henzke, Lucille. AMERICAN ART POTTERY. Camden, N.J.: Thomas Nelson and Sons, 1970. 336 p. Illus. (some in color).

Traces the art potteries in this country from the Fulper work of 1805 through those founded in the twentieth century. The work of Rookwood Pottery (1880-1960), Roseville Pottery (1892-1954), and Newcomb Pottery (1897-1940) are discussed in somewhat greater detail.

500 Hyde, J.A. Lloyd. ORIENTAL LOWESTOFT. New York: Charles Scribner's Sons, 1936. 161 p. 31 plates (1 in color).

The China trade work created for the American market. Explores the relationship of the East India companies with the Canton trading center.

501 Klamkin, Marian. AMERICAN PATRIOTIC AND POLITICAL CHINA. New York: Charles Scribner's Sons, 1972. 256 p. 342 illus.

The commemorative and contemporary designs and mottos that have been placed on ceramic ware have a long tradition that is explored in this study. Examples of propaganda, both serious and humorous, are illustrated.

502 Laidacker, Sam, ed. THE STANDARD CATALOGUE OF ANGLO-AMERICAN CHINA: FROM 1810 TO 1850. Scranton, Pa.: Privately printed, 1938. 91 p. 57 illus.

A survey and discussion of the major Staffordshire firms that made various decorated and printed ceramic ware for the American market. Illustrates and documents the variety of patterns, views, and potter's marks.

503   Leeper, Jeannette, and Schinsky, William. OVERGLAZE IMAGERY:
       CONE 019-016. Fullerton: Art Gallery, California State University,
       1977. 208 p. 181 illus. (41 in color). Bibliog.

       The first chapter, a solid history of painting on ceramics from
       the late Middle Ages through the late nineteenth century, is
       followed by a series of reprinted articles on the major devel-
       opments from the arts and crafts movement to date. The final
       chapter is concerned with the overglaze works of contemporary
       figures, particularly those active on the West Coast.

504   Low, John, and Low, J.C. ILLUSTRATED CATALOGUE OF ART TILES.
       Boston: C.A. Wellington and Co., 1881. 5 p. 26 plates.

       The catalog of John Low's art tiles. Discusses and illustrates
       both individual designs for fireplaces and sets for a variety of
       purposes.

505   McCauley, Robert H. LIVERPOOL TRANSFER DESIGNS ON ANGLO-
       AMERICAN POTTERY. Portland, Maine: Southworth-Anthoensen Press,
       1942. xxi, 150 p. 32 plates. 113 illus. Bibliog., p. 141.

       A list and description of each of 265 transfer designs used by
       Liverpool pottery makers on pieces made for the American
       market. Groups of patriotic and historical subjects are dis-
       cussed and many are illustrated.

506   Mudge, Jean. CHINESE EXPORT PORCELAIN FOR THE AMERICAN
       TRADE, 1785-1835. A Winterthur Series Book. Newark: University
       of Delaware Press, 1962. 284 p. 138 illus. Bibliog., pp. 235-49.

       A description of the ceramic trade emanating from Canton dis-
       tributing China ware to both America and Europe. Traces the
       history of the exportation to America and describes manufac-
       ture, design and decoration.

507   New York, University of, at Geneseo. College of Art and Sciences.
       RAKU INVITATIONAL. Geneseo, N.Y.: 1970. 28 p. 13 illus.

       A biographical treatment and photograph of each of the thir-
       teen ceramists working in this traditional ceramic medium.

508   R.W. Norton Art Gallery. THE AMERICAN PORCELAIN TRADITION:
       18TH, 19TH, AND 20TH CENTURIES. Shreveport, La.: 1972. 32 p.
       19 illus. (5 in color). Bibliog., pp. 29-30.

       A brief history of porcelain with particular attention to Amer-
       ican work. Concentrates on post-1830 objects borrowed from
       the major collections of the New Jersey State Museum.

509   Pitkin, Albert H. EARLY AMERICAN FOLK POTTERY: INCLUDING

THE HISTORY OF THE BENNINGTON POTTERY. Hartford, Conn.: Privately printed, 1918. 152 p. 26 illus.

A history of early American folk pottery in New England and the middle Atlantic states, with a large section devoted to the Bennington Pottery. Catalogs the Pitkin collection and illustrates some of the pottery marks.

510 Robacker, Earl F., and Robacker, Ada F. SPATTERWARE AND SPONGE: HARDY PERENNIALS OF CERAMICS. South Brunswick, N.J.: A.S. Barnes and Co., 1978. 167 p. Illus. Bibliog., pp. 159-62.

Although this ware is most commonly associated with Pennsylvania-Dutch origins, the authors show the longer and broader history of these decorated ceramic wares. Chapters on the various types and firms producing them, a compilation of marks, and a glossary of terms.

511 Schwartz, Marvin D., and Wolfe, Richard. HISTORY OF AMERICAN ART PORCELAIN. New York: Renaissance Editions, 1967. 93 p. 75 illus. (some in color). Bibliog., p. 93.

A background chapter on the history of porcelain is followed by a chronological study of developments in technique, and increasingly more important, in taste, and in style. Information on the illustrations is very specific.

512 Watkins, C. Malcolm. "North Devon Pottery and its Export to America in the 17th Century." U.S. NATIONAL MUSEUM BULLETIN 225 (1960): 17-59. Illus.

The history and documentation of one active segment of the trade between England and the colonies.

513 Webster, Donald B. DECORATED STONEWARE POTTERY OF NORTH AMERICA. Rutland, Vt.: Charles E. Tuttle, 1971. 232 p. 300 illus. Bibliog., pp. 229-30.

Arranged by subject matter, this survey of North American stonewares (primarily salt-glazed) discriminates among decoration, form, and origin. Historical and stylistic influences are also examined.

INDIVIDUAL CERAMISTS AND CERAMIC MANUFACTURERS

514 Altman, Violet, and Altman, Seymour. THE BOOK OF BUFFALO POTTERY. New York: Crown Publishers, Bonanza Books, 1969. 192 p. 378 illus. (8 in color). Bibliog., p. 187.

The history of the Buffalo, New York, pottery. Carefully and generously illustrated with examples of the scope and range of its production, including its basic staple, Deldare ware.

515   Arnest, Barbara M. VAN BRIGGLE POTTERY: THE EARLY YEARS. Colorado Springs: Colorado Springs Fine Arts Center, 1975. 72 p. 756 illus. (8 in color). Bibliog.

A solid and seminal study of the Van Briggles and their Colorado pottery from 1900 to 1912. The text is primarily a catalogue raisonné of their designs. Chronology of the pottery, biographies, bibliographies, and a list of public collections. Discussion of the unification of structure and decoration, and its relationship to Art Nouveau.

516   Barber, Daniel M., and Harmell, George R. "The Redware Pottery Factory of Alvin Wilcox at Mid 19th Century." HISTORICAL ARCHE-OLOGY 5, no. 1 (1971): 18-37.

History and discussion of the best documented of the earthware potteries in Ontario County during the middle of the nineteenth century (c. 1825-1862). Wilcox produced both lead-glazed ware and, later, drain tile.

517   Bohrod, Aaron. A POTTERY SKETCHBOOK. Madison: University of Wisconsin Press, 1959. 196 p. Illus.

A brief introduction to the artist is followed by drawings and illustrations of his designs on his pottery.

518   Breck, Joseph. A MEMORIAL EXHIBITION OF PORCELAIN AND STONEWARE BY ADELAIDE ALSOP ROBINEAU, 1865-1929. New York: Metropolitan Museum of Art, 1929. 24 p. 2 illus.

The catalog of a major retrospective exhibition of Robineau's work with a brief introduction to her life and influence on the revival of crafted ceramics. Itemizes seventy-one examples of her porcelain and stoneware.

519   Brown, Charles M. RETROSPECTIVE 1951-1969. Jacksonville, Fla.: Jacksonville Art Museum, 1969. 12 p. 12 illus.

The catalog of a modest Charles Brown retrospective exhibition. Itemizes ninety-three pieces exhibited.

520   Franco, Barbara. WHITE'S UTICA POTTERY. Utica, N.Y.: Munson-Williams-Proctor Institute, 1969. Unpaged. 10 illus.

The catalog of an exhibition devoted to the work of the White firm of Utica. Historical information and examples of the unique work.

521 Greer, Georgeanna H., and Black, Harding. THE MEYER FAMILY: MASTER POTTERS OF TEXAS. San Antonio, Tex.: San Antonio Museum Association, 1971. 97 p. Illus. (4 in color).

The history of the Meyer family pottery from its founding in 1887 to 1964. Describes and illustrates pieces from the different periods, reflecting changes in style and taste. Written to accompany an exhibition of Meyer work.

522 Grotell, Maija. MAIJA GROTELL. New York: Museum of Contemporary Crafts, 1968. 14 p. 11 illus.

Biographical information on the artist and a catalog list of her work is supplemented by her comments on her development and interests in her work.

523 Hood, Graham. BONNIN AND MORRIS OF PHILADELPHIA; THE FIRST AMERICAN PORCELAIN FACTORY, 1770-1772. Chapel Hill: University of North Carolina Press, published for the Institute of Early American History and Culture at Williamsburg, Va., 1972. xiii, 78 p. 56 illus.

A study and history of what appears to be the first American porcelain factory. Based on, and refers to, primary sources and outlines the production of the firm's short existence from 1770 to 1772.

524 Jones, Harvey L. STEVEN DESTAEBLER SCULPTURE. Oakland, Calif.: Oakland Museum Art Gallery, 1974. 32 p. 41 illus. (some in color).

The catalog of an exhibition of thirty-nine ceramic sculptures by a contemporary craftsman. Includes illustrations of the stages of development toward completion.

525 Kester, J. Bernard. CERAMICS—FORM AND TECHNIQUE. Los Angeles: University of California Art Galleries, 1970. 24 p. 31 illus.

The catalog of an exhibition of the work of Laura Andreson. A brief essay and entries on 133 items by the contemporary ceramist.

526 McVean, Albert F. "The Morganville Pottery." ANNUAL REPORT OF THE LEROY HISTORICAL SOCIETY—1972. (1972): 4-15.

Documents the existence, history, and variety of the products of the largest surviving pottery (1829-1900) in the New York upstate county of Genesee. The Morganville Pottery produced large quantities of earthenware flower pots and, after 1875, the new staple of drain tile.

527 Natzler, Gail R. NATZLER. Flagstaff, Ariz.: Craft and Folk Art Museum, 1977. 52 p. 18 illus. (8 in color). Bibliog.

The catalog of the work of Otto Natzler done since the death of his wife in 1971. Complete and descriptive catalog entries, biography, and good, detailed illustrations.

528 Natzler, Gertrud, and Natzler, Otto. CERAMICS: CATALOGUE OF THE COLLECTION OF MRS. LEONARD M. SPERRY AND A MONOGRAPH BY OTTO NATZLER. Los Angeles: Los Angeles County Museum of Art, 1968. 81 p. Plates (some in color).

The complete catalog of an important collection of Natzler ceramics with each work described, criticized, and explained by Otto Natzler. Individual essays provide autobiographical background, technical material, and the couple's ideas in ceramic form.

529 _____. THE CERAMIC WORK OF GERTRUD AND OTTO NATZLER: A RETROSPECTIVE EXHIBITION. Los Angeles: Los Angeles County Museum of Art, 1966. 49 p. 27 illus. (8 in color).

The retrospective exhibition catalog of the Natzlers' work during their years in the United States. Excellent reproductions.

530 Osgood, Cornelius. THE JUG, AND RELATED STONEWARE OF BENNINGTON. Rutland, Vt.: Charles E. Tuttle Co., 1971. 222 p. 31 illus. (8 in color). 38 figs. Bibliog., pp. 207-12.

A brief study and history of pottery and basic ceramic ware serves as background for a scholarly study of the work produced at the Norton Potteries firm in Bennington, Vermont.

531 Pear, Lillian M. THE PEWABIC POTTERY: A HISTORY OF ITS PRODUCTS AND ITS PEOPLE. Des Moines, Iowa: Wallace-Homestead Book Co., 1976. 295 p. Illus. (some in color). Bibliog., pp. 263-65.

A history of the small independent pottery founded by James Caulkins and Mary Perry in 1898 and continued by the latter until her death in 1961. Explains the role of both the founders and William Stratton, the architect, and husband of Perry. Particular attention is paid to the long-popular Pewabic tiles, used in many parts of the country.

532 Peck, Herbert. THE BOOK OF ROOKWOOD POTTERY. New York: Crown Publishers, 1968. viii, 184 p. Illus. (6 in color). Bibliog., p. 177.

A history of the Rookwood firm and its successors. The important managers are discussed and the changes in direction of pottery manufacturing are described. Additional material on

Rookwood marks and Rookwood in museum collections, and a note on the Zanesville competitors.

533   Pierson, Conway. CONWAY PIERSON. Santa Barbara: University of California at Santa Barbara, Art Gallery, 1967. 61 p. Illus. (4 in color).

A brief exhibition catalog which concentrates on the artist's recent work in both bronze and clay.

534   Poor, Henry V. A BOOK OF POTTERY: FROM MUD TO IMMOR-TALITY. Englewood Cliffs, N.J.: Prentice-Hall, 1958. 192 p. 50 illus. (5 in color). 61 figs. Bibliog., p. 187.

An autobiographical study by the muralist and ceramist. Presents his philosophy and attitude toward creating ceramic wares. Illustrations of his drawings and completed ceramic works. Also much technical information.

535   Rhodes, Daniel, and Natzler, Otto. FORM AND FIRE: NATZLER CERAMICS, 1939-1972. Washington, D.C.: Smithsonian Institution Press for the Renwick Gallery of the National Collection of Fine Arts, 1973. 120 p. Illus. (some in color). Bibliog., pp. 109-11.

A detailed major retrospective catalog of this important couple's ceramic work in the thirty plus years of their American experience. Biographical information, a catalog of 150 pieces, and information on locations of museum collections of their work.

536   Rippon, Ruth. RIPPON. Sacramento, Calif.: E.B. Crocker Art Gallery, 1971. 62 p. Illus. (11 in color).

The catalog of a full retrospective exhibition of almost two decades of the artist's drawings and ceramic pieces.

537   Slivka, Rose. PETER VOULKOS: A DIALOGUE WITH CLAY. Boston: New York Graphics Society, 1978. 184 p. 104 illus. (24 in color).

A study of one of the major ceramists of twentieth-century America who was partially responsible for the rebirth of interest in studio ceramics.

538   Snively, Robley D., and Snively, Mary E. POTTERY. Old Deerfield Series of Handicraft Manuals. Brattleboro, Vt.: Stephen Daye Press, 1940. 87 p. Illus.

Describes the technical and aesthetic processes of the potter and illustrates Edward Norman at work.

539   Wildenhain, Frans. FRANS WILDENHAIN RETROSPECTIVE. Bingham-
      ton, N.Y.: University Art Gallery, 1974. 44 p. 27 illus.

      Forty-year retrospective of an important twentieth-century ce-
      ramist. Itemizes 155 pieces in the exhibition, presents bio-
      graphical information, and presents a critical appraisal of his
      work by a variety of professionals.

540   Wildenhain, Marguerite. THE INVISIBLE CORE: A POTTER'S LIFE
      AND THOUGHTS. Palo Alto, Calif.: Pacific Books, 1973. 207 p.
      52 illus.

      An autobiographical essay and a total philosophical statement
      by a Bauhaus-disciplined craftsman and artist.

541   _____. POTTERY OF MARGUERITE WILDENHAIN: A SELECTION
      OF HER RECENT WORK. Raleigh: North Carolina Museum of Art,
      1968. 24 p. 18 illus.

      A brief biography and illustrations of her most recent work at
      the date of the exhibition.

INDIAN CERAMICS

542   Bunzel, Ruth L. THE PUEBLO POTTER: A STUDY IN CREATIVE IMAGI-
      NATION IN PRIMITIVE ART. New York: Columbia University Press,
      1929. Reprint. New York: Dover Publications, 1972. 134 p. 38
      illus. Bibliog., pp. 129-32.

      The designs, styles, and symbolism of the various American
      Pueblo Indian potters. Profusely illustrated in the appendixes,
      with designs. The whole story between each design is de-
      scribed and explained.

543   Chapman, Kenneth M. THE POTTERY OF SAN ILDEFONSO PUEBLO.
      Albuquerque: University of New Mexico Press, 1971. xvi, 260 p.
      174 illus. Bibliog., pp. 256-60.

      A careful study of the pottery of an important settled Indian
      village. Discusses style, technique, and the place of the
      pottery in the life of the individual and the community.

544   _____. THE POTTERY OF THE SANTO DOMINGO PUEBLO: A DE-
      TAILED STUDY OF ITS DECORATION. Santa Fe, N.Mex.: Labora-
      tory of Anthropology, 1936. 192 p. 34 figs. 79 plates. Bibliog.,
      p. 192.

      A detailed study of the decoration and design of this particu-
      lar Pueblo's wares. Some basic background information on
      technology and style is also provided.

545 _____. PUEBLO INDIAN POTTERY. 2 vols. Nice, France: C. Szwedzicki, 1936. Each vol. 16 p., 50 color plates.

A rich color picture book of the work of Pueblo Indian tribal pottery.

546 Collins, John E. A TRIBUTE TO LUCY M. LEWIS: ACOMA POTTER. Fullerton, Calif.: Museum of North Orange County, 1975. 75 p. Illus. (some in color). Bibliog., p. 73.

A brief biography of the Pueblo Indian potter with information on her designs, style, and technique.

547 Curry, Hilda J. NEGATIVE PAINTED POTTERY OF ANGEL MOUNDS SITE AND ITS DISTRIBUTION IN THE NEW WORLD. Indiana University Publications in Anthropology and Linguistics, Memoir no. 5. Baltimore: Waverly Press, 1950. 57 p. Illus.

The work indigenous to the Tennessee-Cumberland region of the United States is compared with examples from both the Southwest and Latin America. Traces the styles and explores and discusses the various forms.

548 Deetz, James. THE DYNAMICS OF STYLISTIC CHANGE IN ARIKARA CERAMICS. Illinois Studies in Anthropology, no. 4. Urbana: University of Illinois Press, 1965. 111 p. Illus. Bibliog., pp. 103-7.

An attempt at discovering the relationship between the ceramics produced in the eighteenth-century Arikara civilization and its social organization and structure.

549 Frank, Larry, and Harlow, Francis H. HISTORIC POTTERY OF THE PUEBLO INDIANS, 1600-1880. Boston: New York Graphic Society, 1974. 160 p. 198 illus. (32 in color). Bibliog., pp. 158-60.

A history and survey of the styles, types, and techniques of early Pueblo Indian pottery and a careful examination of almost 200 examples.

550 Goddard, Pliny E. POTTERY OF THE SOUTHWESTERN INDIANS. 1928. Reissue. New York: American Museum of Natural History, 1971. 30 p. Illus. Bibliog., pp. 12-13.

A description and analysis of Indian methodology in pottery construction. Also concerned with the various decorative designs and methods of application. Illustrations of both the potter at work and the finished forms.

551 Harlow, Francis H., and Young, John V. CONTEMPORARY PUEBLO INDIAN POTTERY. Santa Fe: Museum of New Mexico, 1965. 24 p. 13 illus. (5 in color).

Concerned with the Pueblo pottery usually sold by contemporary craftsmen. Explores sources of design and traces the technological methodology.

552 Holmes, William H. "Pottery of the Ancient Pueblos." In SMITHSONIAN INSTITUTION, BUREAU OF ETHNOLOGY, ANNUAL REPORT, vol. 4, pp. 257-360. Washington, D.C.: Smithsonian Institution, 1886. Illus.

A scholarly anthropological study of the methods, techniques, and variety of early Pueblo Indian pottery. Tries to place the work into the broader cultural spectrum.

553 Krevolin, Lewis. NAKED CLAY: 3000 YEARS OF UNADORNED POTTERY OF THE AMERICAN INDIAN. New York: Heye Foundation, Museum of the American Indian, 1972. 76 p. 107 illus. Bibliog., pp. 73-76.

The history and development of American Indian pottery making. Both technique and forms are discussed, and individual illustrated examples are itemized and discussed.

554 Lister, Robert H., and Lister, Florence C. THE EARL H. MORRIS MEMORIAL POTTERY COLLECTION: AN EXAMPLE OF TEN CENTURIES OF PREHISTORIC CERAMIC ART IN THE FOUR CORNERS COUNTRY OF SOUTHWESTERN UNITED STATES. Series in Anthropology, no. 16. Boulder: University of Colorado Press, 1969. ix, 94 p. 46 illus. (1 in color). Bibliog., p. 94.

The catalog of a major collection of this very early work in ceramic art. Carefully presented descriptive material on each item.

555 Marriott, Alice. MARIA: THE POTTER OF SAN ILDEFONSO. Civilization of the American Indian Series, vol. 27. Norman: University of Oklahoma Press, 1948. 294 p. Illus. Bibliog., pp. 291-94.

The biography and statements of Maria Martinez, the best known of the twentieth-century Pueblo potters. Describes her work and its relationship to her daily life.

556 Maxwell Museum of Anthropology. University of New Mexico. SEVEN FAMILIES IN PUEBLO POTTERY. Albuquerque: 1974. 112 p. Illus. (some in color).

The catalog of an exhibition of seven Pueblo Indian families of the American Southwest. Discusses their tradition over several generations and includes biographical chronology on each family.

557 Mera, H.P. STYLE TRENDS OF PUEBLO POTTERY. Memoirs of the Laboratory of Anthropology, vol. 3. Santa Fe, N.Mex.: Laboratory of Anthropology, 1939. 29 p. 67 plates. Figs. Bibliog., p. 29.

The basic text is concerned with Southwest American Indian pottery of the Pueblos from the sixteenth to the nineteenth centuries. Examines each illustrated work in great detail and discusses the evolution of both basic form and decorative patterns.

558 Morss, Noel. CLAY FIGURINES OF THE AMERICAN SOUTHWEST. Papers of the Peabody Museum of Archaeology and Ethnology, Harvard University, vol. 49, no. 1. Cambridge: Peabody Museum, 1954. x, 75 p. 31 illus. Figs.

An analysis and discussion of the place of clay figurines found in Utah in the cultural tradition of local early Indian populations. Attempts to place the importance of the objects in the appropriate setting and to understand their purpose.

559 Peterson, Susan. THE LIVING TRADITION OF MARIA MARTINEZ. Tokyo: Kodansha International, 1974. 300 p. 337 illus. (197 in color).

Not only discusses and illustrates the work of this famous San Ildefonso potter, but traces the work through five generations. Indicates the influence of Martinez on Pueblo pottery and of her culture on her. Excellent illustrations.

560 Putnam, F.W. "Pueblo Pottery." AMERICAN ART REVIEW, February 1881, pp. 150-54.

A very early illustrated article which compares late nineteenth-century examples of decorated Pueblo Indian pottery with earlier examples. Provides basic background information on technique.

561 Stiles, Helen G. POTTERY OF THE AMERICAN INDIANS. New York: E.P. Dutton and Co., 1939. 169 p. Illus. Bibliog., pp. 161-65.

A study of the Indian work in all of North America, it includes a section on the work found, for the most part, in the Southwest United States. Technical and stylistic material is presented in a journalistic fashion.

562 Tschopik, Harry, Jr. NAVAHO POTTERY MAKING. Papers of the Peabody Museum of Archaeology and Ethnology, Harvard University, vol. 17, no. 1. Cambridge: Peabody Museum, 1941. viii, 85 p. 16 illus. Bibliog., pp. 77-79.

An anthropologically oriented study based on field work, this work both describes the techniques of Navaho pottery making and presents commentary by practitioners of the craft. The author is also concerned with placing the pottery making tradition within a broader social context and thus compares the Navaho work with that of other Indian groups.

563 Wormington, Hannah M., and Neal, Arminta. THE STORY OF PUEBLO POTTERY. Denver: Denver Museum of Natural History, 1951. 61 p. Illus. Bibliog., p. 60.

A brief introduction to the history of Pueblo pottery from prehistorical times to the recent past. Illustrations are arranged chronologically rather than classified by type of object, but the range of forms is still defined to the reader.

Chapter 8
AMERICAN FURNITURE

Differences in furniture styles, from city to city and from city to country, are more traceable and dramatic than differences in any of the other decorative arts. High-style Philadelphia furniture is different from that made in Boston, and city-made objects are usually clearly distinguishable from country pieces.

Influences from abroad affected furniture styles more frequently than other forms, perhaps because furniture itself changed quite rapidly in Europe. In addition, the availability of European models, through various style books, helped form and change American taste.

Various sections of the furniture listings address period, geographic, and stylistic questions, including the revival styles which repeat each other through the years.

GENERAL STUDIES AND SURVEYS OF AMERICAN FURNITURE

564   Beck, Doreen. BOOK OF AMERICAN FURNITURE. Feltham, Engl.: Hamlyn, 1973. 96 p. 102 illus. (30 in color).

An illustrated basic survey of American furniture from 1650 to the middle of the twentieth century. Fine color plates.

565   Berry, Morris. EARLY AMERICAN FURNITURE INCLUDING MANY COLLECTOR'S PIECES OF RICH VENEER AND WITH INLAY. New York: American Art Association, 1930. 147 p. Illus.

The sale catalog of a major public auction of fine American furniture. Still used for the tracing of ownership of museum-quality pieces.

566   Bishop, Robert. HOW TO KNOW AMERICAN ANTIQUE FURNITURE. New York: E.P. Dutton and Co., 1973. 224 p. 300 illus. (12 in color). Bibliog.

A collector's guide covering the colonial period to 1915. Regional variations on basic styles and influences from English and European prototypes.

567 Bjerkoe, Ethel H. THE CABINET MAKERS OF AMERICA. Garden City, N.Y.: Doubleday and Co., 1957. xvii, 252 p. 32 illus. and line drawings. Bibliog., pp. 249–52.

A brief essay on the development of style and technique in furniture construction is followed by biographical entries on hundreds of known craftsmen. Discusses their work, when identified. Includes a useful glossary.

568 Butler, Joseph T. AMERICAN FURNITURE FROM THE FIRST COLO-NIES TO WORLD WAR I. London: Tribune Books, 1973. 144 p. Illus. (some in color). Bibliog.

A popular survey with good color illustrations that present much of the furniture within room interiors.

569 Comstock, Helen. AMERICAN FURNITURE: SEVENTEENTH, EIGH-TEENTH, AND NINETEENTH CENTURY STYLES. New York: Viking Press, 1962. 366 p. 655 illus. Bibliog., pp. 319–24.

The history of style in American furniture. Each chronologi-cal period has an introduction, charts summing up distinctive and new forms, characteristic designs, and new techniques. Many examples of work in each period are illustrated.

570 Cornelius, Charles O. EARLY AMERICAN FURNITURE. Century Co., 1926. xx, 278 p. 63 illus. Bibliog., pp. 263–68.

This is an overall survey of early furniture, discussing the evo-lution of styles with their regional application. The author also is concerned with early cabinetmakers and their role in society, and discusses the social status of the craftsmen.

571 Fales, Dean A. AMERICAN PAINTED FURNITURE, 1660–1880. New York: E.P. Dutton and Co., 1972. 298 p. 577 illus. (148 in color). Bibliog., pp. 289–93.

The major useful source on the history and development of this form. Divides painted furniture into three groups: plain painted furniture; painting used to imitate wood, marble, or other materials; and imaginative and fanciful painting.

572 Gaines, Edith, and Jenkins, Dorothy H. DICTIONARY OF ANTIQUE FURNITURE. Princeton, N.J.: Pyne Press, 1974. 80 p. Illus.

Reprint of a series of articles on American furniture which first appeared in WOMAN'S DAY magazine.

573 Gould, Mary E. EARLY AMERICAN WOODEN WARE. Springfield, Mass.: Pond Eckberg, 1942. Reprint. Rutland, Vt.: Charles E. Tuttle, 1962. xiv, 230 p. Illus.

Discussions on the construction and materials of these products of home industry. Provides information to enable identification. Excellent photographs include those of various kitchen utensils in addition to the wooden ware itself.

574 Gowans, Alan. IMAGES OF AMERICAN LIVING: FOUR CENTURIES OF ARCHITECTURE AND FURNITURE AS CULTURAL EXPRESSION. Philadelphia: J.B. Lippincott, 1964. 498 p. Illus. Bibliog.

Although most of our styles derive from England and Europe, our unique cultural situation modified the forms and styles. Traces that development and the relationships between the patrons and makers as well.

575 Halsey, R.T., and Cornelius, Charles O. A HANDBOOK OF THE AMERICAN WING. Rev. ed. New York: Metropolitan Museum of Art, 1938. xxiv, 312 p. Illus.

A discussion and description of the furniture in this important collection. Provides a history of each work and discussion as to the probable craftsman-creator.

576 Herman, Lloyd. PAINT ON WOOD: DECORATED AMERICAN FURNITURE SINCE THE 17TH CENTURY. Washington, D.C.: Smithsonian Institution Press, 1971. 36 p. 33 illus. (14 in color).

Discussion of the different techniques of decoration and what type of furniture was painted, and concentration on key pieces of both handmade and manufactured pieces. Catalog data on each item.

577 Kirk, John T. EARLY AMERICAN FURNITURE. New York: Alfred A. Knopf, 1970. xi, 209 p. 204 illus.

An unusual approach to the examination of American furniture, this volume has chapters on proportions and organization of furniture forms, the role of small details, and the interpretation of sources. The whole presents a connoisseurship education and provides tips for potential collectors.

578 Kovel, Ralph M., and Kovel, Terry H. AMERICAN COUNTRY FURNITURE, 1780-1875. New York: Crown Publishers, 1965. vii, 248 p. 691 illus. Bibliog., p. 232.

Illustrates the various developments and variations from the standard high styles in most of the basic furniture forms of the era. Short introductions to each section give a brief history of each form.

579　Entry deleted

580　Lockwood, Sarah M. ANTIQUES. Garden City, N.Y.: Doubleday, Doran and Co., 1936. 161 p. Illus. Bibliog., pp. 152-53.

An alphabetically arranged set of short essays on various periods and furniture forms and illustrated with line drawings. Filled with anecdotes and, often useful little facts, but very incomplete.

581　Margon, Lester. MASTERPIECES OF AMERICAN FURNITURE, 1620-1840. New York: Architectural Book Publishing Co., 1965. 256 p. Illus.

Individual quality works are illustrated and discussed, covering the range of American furniture from the colonial through the federal periods.

582　_____. MORE AMERICAN FURNITURE TREASURES, 1620-1840. New York: Architectural Book Publishing Co., 1971. 256 p. Illus. Bibliog., p. 95.

An anthology of major museum-quality pieces in photographs and measured drawings. Personal discussion of the pieces.

583　Miller, Edgar G., Jr. AMERICAN ANTIQUE FURNITURE. Baltimore: Lord Baltimore Press, 1937. Reprint. 2 vols. New York: Dover, 1967. li, 1,106 p. 2,115 illus.

Discusses everything from fakes to period styles, with many illustrations of each point. Over a dozen appendixes on such topics as hallmarks, auction sales, and furniture forms. Specific documentation and clear footnoting keep this quite old volume a standard, as well as a source of illustrations.

584　_____. THE STANDARD BOOK OF ANTIQUE FURNITURE. New York: Greystone Press, 1950. 856 p. Illus.

A one-volume abridgement of the massive AMERICAN ANTIQUE FURNITURE (see above).

585　Mooz, R. Peter. THE ART OF AMERICAN FURNITURE: A PORTFOLIO OF FURNITURE IN THE COLLECTIONS OF BOWDOIN COLLEGE

MUSEUM OF ART. Brunswick, Maine: Bowdoin College Museum of Art, 1974. 56 p. 43 illus.

Pieces of American furniture are compared with similar European types, covering the period from the sixteenth through the nineteenth centuries. Very fine illustrations accompany a fully documented set of catalog entries. Includes provenance.

586 Morse, Frances C. FURNITURE OF THE OLDEN TIME. New York: Macmillan Co., 1903. xvii, 371 p. 295 illus.

One of the pioneering studies of American furniture and European influences. Each chapter is devoted to a different furniture form, with special chapters on musical instruments, looking glasses, and so on.

587 Morse, John D., ed. COUNTRY CABINETWORK AND SIMPLE CITY FURNITURE. Charlottesville: University Press of Virginia, for the Henry Francis du Pont Winterthur Museum, 1970. xiv, 311 p. 57 illus. Bibliog.

A series of papers including two on specific families of furniture makers, the Dunlaps and Dominys; one on consumer taste; one on urban Massachusetts furniture; and others on topics related to technique and history. For the scholar.

588 Nagel, Charles. AMERICAN FURNITURE, 1650-1850. New York: Chanticleer Press, 1950. 110 p. 44 illus. Bibliog., p. 110.

A broadly stretched social and historical analysis of the period and a discussion of the place of furniture in its people's lives. Points out the relationship between furniture and the architecture as well. Excellent reproductions in this useful study.

589 Nutting, Wallace. FURNITURE TREASURY. Vols. 1 and 2. Framingham, Mass.: Old America Co., 1928. 5,000 illus.

A standard early reference which discusses and illustrates many pieces whose whereabouts are unknown. Volumes 1 and 2 are an illustrated history (with sources) of American furniture from the colonial period through the beginning of the nineteenth century. Some European material included.

590 _____. FURNITURE TREASURY. Vol. 3. Framingham, Mass.: Old America Co., 1933. 550 p. Illus. with line drawings by Ernest John Donnelly.

Supplements the text of volumes 1 and 2 (see above) with references to the 5,000 illustrations in the earlier work. Includes notes on collecting and a section on clocks, with an appendix of American clock makers.

591   Ormsbee, Thomas. FIELD GUIDE TO EARLY AMERICAN FURNITURE.
      Boston: Little Brown and Co., 1951. xxxix, 464 p. Illus. Bibliog.,
      pp. 463-64.

      A solid and substantial collector's guidebook to American co-
      lonial and nineteenth-century furniture. Many illustrations
      and references. Still useful for its insights and direct ap-
      proach.

592   _____. THE STORY OF AMERICAN FURNITURE. New York: Mac-
      millan Co., 1934. xxi, 276 p. 117 illus.

      A history of American furniture in an easy-to-read style, il-
      lustrated with both line drawings and plates.

593   Osburn, Burl N. MEASURED DRAWINGS OF EARLY AMERICAN FUR-
      NITURE. Milwaukee, Wis.: Brace Publishing Co., 1936. 94 p.
      Illus.

      After background information on the creators of periods of
      American furniture of the colonial and early federal periods
      is given, each section is devoted to a photograph of an ex-
      cellent piece of furniture, descriptive information about it
      and the style it represents, and a measured drawing of the
      piece.

594   Randall, Richard H., Jr. AMERICAN FURNITURE IN THE MUSEUM
      OF FINE ARTS, BOSTON. Boston: Museum of Fine Arts, 1965.
      273 p. 218 illus.

      The catalog of one of the major collections of American fur-
      niture from the colonial period through the nineteenth century.
      Each entry is described, documented, and illustrated.

595   Sack, Albert. FINE POINTS OF FURNITURE: EARLY AMERICAN.
      New York: Crown Publishers, 1950. xvi, 303 p. Illus.

      An interesting guide for the collector and connoisseur. Var-
      ious genres of furniture are examined and typical, better, and
      excellent examples of each are illustrated. The author ex-
      plains why proportions, woods, and so on, cause the selection
      of pieces in each category.

595a St. George, Robert Blair. THE WROUGHT COVENANT. Brockton,
      Mass.: Brockton Art Center, 1979. 13 p. 83 illus. Bibliog., pp.
      108-27.

      A study of furniture from the point of view of material culture.
      Provides source material and an extensive bibliography, both
      books and articles. Covers the area of southeastern New England
      from 1620 to 1700.

596 Singleton, Esther. THE FURNITURE OF OUR FOREFATHERS. Garden City, N.Y.: Doubleday, Page and Co., 1913. 664 p. Illus.

An old and chatty but valuable survey by geographical areas, including hundreds of drawings and excellent plates. Well indexed to maximize the value of useful, but scattered, tidbits of information.

597 Sironen, Marta K. A HISTORY OF AMERICAN FURNITURE. East Stroudsburg, Pa.: Touse Publishing Co., 1936. 150 p. Illus. (some in color).

An old and somewhat anecdotal survey, with carefully selected illustrations centered on the colonial period and the early nineteenth century.

597a Stickley, Gustav. CRAFTSMAN HOMES: ARCHITECTURE AND FUR-NISHINGS OF THE AMERICAN ARTS AND CRAFTS MOVEMENT. New York: Craftsman Publishing Co., 1909. Reprint. New York: Dover, 1979. 205 p. Illus.

A series of polemics in favor of Stickley's notion that the craftsman approach was the contemporary solution to planned design and furnishings.

598 Taylor, Henry H. KNOWING, COLLECTING AND RESTORING EARLY AMERICAN FURNITURE. Philadelphia: 1930. 156 p. 59 illus.

Clearly aimed at the beginning collector who has little ac-quaintanceship with the furniture field. Line drawings supple-ment both text and photographs, emphasizing basic forms and period styles.

599 Van Lennep, Gustave A. A GUIDE TO AMERICAN ANTIQUE FUR-NITURE. Philadelphia: Macrae Smith Co., 1937. ix, 95 p. Illus.

An old popular guidebook to early furniture. Interesting re-flection of the taste of the late 1930s.

600 Voss, Thomas M. ANTIQUE AMERICAN COUNTRY FURNITURE: A FIELD GUIDE. Philadelphia: J.B. Lippincott, 1978. 383 p. 145 illus. Bibliog., pp. 379-83.

A definition of antique country furniture is followed by an introduction to collecting. Treatment of questions of wood, paint, construction, and so on. The second half of this use-ful collector's handbook treats individual furniture forms and suggests how to examine them.

601 Weinhardt, Carl J. INDIANAPOLIS COLLECTS: AMERICAN FURNI-TURE 1700-1850. Indianapolis: Indianapolis Museum of Art, 1972. 32 p. 27 illus.

The chairs, tables, cabinetry, and accessories in Indianapolis collections. A brief history of American styles and adaptations from European and British models, with descriptive entries on ninety objects in the exhibition.

602 Williams, N. Lionel. COUNTRY FURNITURE OF EARLY AMERICA. Cranbury, N.J.: A.S. Barnes, 1970. 138 p. Illus.

Good illustrations of well-chosen examples of country furniture to 1850 taken from both private and museum collections. Information on construction details and period identification all geared toward the general, nonspecialist reader.

603 Winchester, Alice. "Early New England Furniture in the Shelburne Museum." CONNOISSEUR YEARBOOK, 1957, pp. 34-41.

Colonial and early nineteenth-century furniture in reconstructed settings. Contains and illustrates both country and stylish pieces.

604 Yarmon, Morton. EARLY AMERICAN ANTIQUE FURNITURE. Greenwich, Conn.: Fawcett Publications, 1952. 144 p. Illus.

A guide for the collector. Easy-to-follow text with illustrations of representative pieces.

GEOGRAPHICAL STUDIES OF FURNITURE MANUFACTURE

605 Ames, Kenneth L. "Grand Rapids Furniture at the Time of the Centennial." WINTERTHUR PORTFOLIO 10 (1975): 23-50.

Points out how three Grand Rapids firms that exhibit at the Centennial--Berkey and Gay; Phoenix; and Nelson, Matter and Co.--were to become giants of the furniture industry. Traces their early development and examines the kind of furniture they made.

606 Barnes, Jairua B., and Meals, Moscile T. AMERICAN FURNITURE IN THE WESTERN RESERVE 1680-1830. Cleveland: Western Reserve Historical Society, 1972. 133 p. Illus.

The catalog of a loan exhibition of furniture from the early days of settlement to the Jacksonian era. Includes both indigenous and imported objects.

607 Bissell, Charles S. ANTIQUE FURNITURE IN SUFFIELD, CONNECTICUT, 1670-1835. Hartford: Connecticut Historical Society, 1956. ix, 128 p. 60 illus.

A history of furniture making in and near this Connecticut town. Illustrated works of some of the seventy-two craftsmen

uncovered by the author show the diversity of their work and
their relation to the community. Some of the locally owned
pieces are attributed on the basis of known work.

608 Breeskin, Adelyn D., ed. BALTIMORE FURNITURE, THE WORK OF
BALTIMORE AND ANNAPOLIS CABINETMAKERS FROM 1760–1810.
Baltimore: Baltimore Museum of Art, 1947. 195 p. 125 illus.

Brief essays on the Hepplewhite-Sheridan and Chippendale period, and a thorough and detailed catalog of 125 pieces assigned to the area. Catalog entries also provide stylistic and
analytical as well as descriptive material.

609 Bulkeley, Houghton. CONTRIBUTIONS TO CONNECTICUT CABINET
MAKING. Hartford: Connecticut Historical Society, 1967. 97 p.
34 illus.

The collected articles of Bulkeley written for the society's bulletin from 1957 to 1966. Of particular interest are the articles on Aaron Roberts, John Wells, and the Norwich Cabinetmakers.

610 Burroughs, Paul H. SOUTHERN ANTIQUES. Richmond, Va.: Garett
and Massie, 1931. xi, 191 p. Illus.

Introductory chapters on the history of furniture making in the
five southern colonies, the woods used in the area and/or the
various historical periods. The bulk of the work is a descriptive catalog arranged by furniture type illustrated with large
clear plates.

611 Burton, E. Milby. CHARLESTON FURNITURE, 1700–1825. Charleston,
S.C.: Charleston Museum, 1955. ix, 150 p. 149 illus. Bibliog.,
pp. 143–45.

Some background history on the city precedes discussion of the
various types of furniture made there, by schools and on plan-
tations. The bulk of the volume is a biographical dictionary
of the individual craftsmen. Regional varations of traditional
models are discussed.

612 Catalano, Kathleen M. "Cabinetmaking in Philadelphia 1820–1840:
Transition from Craft to Industry." WINTERTHUR PORTFOLIO 13
(1979): 81–138.

A checklist of over 2,000 furniture craftsmen at work in Philadelphia between 1820 and 1840. An alphabetical listing including their specialties and the years they were listed in various directories. Background information on exports of Philadelphia furniture.

American Furniture

613 Connecticut Historical Society. GEORGE DUDLEY SEYMOUR'S FUR-
NITURE COLLECTION IN THE CONNECTICUT HISTORICAL SOCIETY.
Hartford: 1958. 141 p. Illus.

The catalog of the permanent collection of furniture, mostly
of Connecticut origin collected by Seymour. Includes references and the owner's comments about the circumstances under
which each piece was purchased and his opinions on quality
and restoration.

614 Dorman, Charles G. DELAWARE CABINETMAKERS AND ALLIED ARTI-
SANS 1655-1855. Wilmington: Historical Society of Delaware, 1960.
107 p. Illus.

An alphabetical biographical dictionary of craftsmen, including location, active dates, and any references to the individual. Draws upon indenture records and newspaper advertisements. Appended are several estate inventories of various
cabinetmakers.

615 Downs, Joseph, and Ralston, Ruth. NEW YORK STATE FURNITURE.
New York: Metropolitan Museum of Art, 1934. xxiii, 28 p. Illus.

The catalog of a loan exhibition which emphasized high quality and high-style pieces. Lists 256 items, including some
accessory pieces comments on unique qualities of the individual object, and makes some attributions.

616 Dundore, Roy H. PENNSYLVANIA GERMAN PAINTED FURNITURE.
Plymouth Meeting, Pa.: Keyser, 1946. 38 p. Illus.

The types of furniture and the unique forms of decorations
used on it, with background and discussion of Old World
sources.

617 Dunstan, William E. III. "The Colonial Cabinetmaker in Tidewater,
Virginia." VIRGINIA CAVALCADE 20, no. 4 (Summer 1970): 34-44.

Indicates that not all southern colonial furniture was imported
and illustrates several excellent examples of high-style work
made in the area.

618 Elder, William Voss III. BALTIMORE PAINTED FURNITURE, 1800-
1840. Baltimore: Baltimore Museum of Art, 1972. 132 p. 91 illus.
Bibliog., pp. 130-32.

An introductory essay on painted furniture in general and Baltimore work specifically. A massive and carefully documented
catalog, and a lengthy checklist of cabinetmakers and allied
tradesmen working in Baltimore from 1800 to 1840.

619 Fabian, Monroe. THE PENNSYLVANIA DECORATED CHEST. New

York: Universe Books, 1978. 230 p. 250 illus. (50 in color). Bibliog.

Analyzes the decorated chest in terms of use among the Pennsylvania Germans and questions of construction, woods, and hardware. The author gives pioneering information on the types of paint and discusses the popular design patterns, contrasting work found in various states. A substantial study of the genre.

620   Failey, Dean F. "The Furniture Tradition of Long Island's South Fork, 1640–1800." AMERICAN ART JOURNAL 11, no. 1 (January 1979): 49–64.

Explains and documents the ties between the Hampton area of Long Island and New England as a force which influenced furniture styles and design. Includes twenty illustrations of attributed or known South Fork pieces.

621   Fales, Dean A., Jr. ESSEX COUNTY FURNITURE: DOCUMENTED TREASURES FROM LOCAL COLLECTIONS, 1660–1860. A catalog of an exhibition held from 22 June to 12 October 1965. Salem, Mass.: Essex Institute, 1965. Unpaged. 76 illus.

A detailed loan exhibition catalog which includes descriptions, attributions, dates, and analysis of woods and paints. Lists special features and comments on the maker and references. Illustrates the production of a major center of furniture creation.

622   _____. THE FURNITURE OF HISTORIC DEERFIELD. New York: E.P. Dutton and Co., 1976. 294 p. 589 illus. (30 in color).

A full catalog of the New England colonial furniture at Deerfield. Complete in coverage of detail, giving all relevant information on each piece, including current condition and everything known about past restoration.

623   Fede, Helen M. WASHINGTON FURNITURE AT MOUNT VERNON. Mount Vernon, Va.: Mount Vernon Ladies Association of the Union, 1966. 72 p. 56 illus.

The catalog and guidebook to the furniture owned by the first president. Includes American–, British–, and European–made pieces.

624   Forman, Benno M. THE 17TH CENTURY CASE FURNITURE OF ESSEX COUNTY MASSACHUSETTS AND ITS MAKERS. Salem, Mass.: Privately printed, 1968. 160 p. Illus.

The high–quality furniture made in a major center of fine cabinetry, with emphasis on William and Mary pieces.

625 Gamon, Albert T. PENNSYLVANIA COUNTRY ANTIQUES. Englewood Cliffs, N.J.: Prentice-Hall, 1968. 189 p. Illus. Bibliog.,
pp. 185-86.

A guide to Pennsylvania rural furniture, aimed at the collector
rather than the scholar. Includes the work of the various isolated religious groups.

626 Greenlaw, Barry A. NEW ENGLAND FURNITURE AT WILLIAMSBURG.
Williamsburg, Va.: Williamsburg Foundation, 1974. viii, 195 p.
172 illus. (8 in color).

A well-illustrated and documented catalog of the important
collection at Williamsburg. Style, quality, and provenance
are discussed, and bibliographical references are provided.

627 Hancock, Harold B. "Furniture Craftsmen in Delaware Records."
WINTERTHUR PORTFOLIO 9 (1974): 175-212.

An alphabetical listing of Delaware furniture makers, specialties, place of work, available dates, and sources of identification. One appendix lists all known apprentices, and others
provide excerpts from the inventories of selected cabinetmakers.

628 Harris, Marleine R. VIRGINIA ANTIQUES. New York: Exposition
Press, 1953. viii, 183 p. 231 illus.

A chatty and somewhat anecdotal survey of the various furniture types found in early Virginia history. Categorized and
illustrated by types, beds, cupboards, tables, and so on.
Points out regional characteristics.

629 Hendrick, Robert E. "New York High-Style Furniture, 1750-1775."
BROOKLYN MUSEUM ANNUAL 8 (1966): 103-111.

Concentrates on the usually known or those pieces attributable
to the most prestigious cabinetmakers in late colonial America.

630 Hill, Anelia L. "American French Colonial Furniture." OLD FURNI-
TURE 8, no. 28 (September 1929): 33-38.

An illustrated discussion of the French influenced designs in
the vicinity of New Orleans during the colonial period. Important reference to Francois Seignouret of the old city.

631 Hopkins, Thomas S., and Cox, Walter S. COLONIAL FURNITURE OF
WEST NEW JERSEY. Haddonfield, N.J.: Historical Society of Haddonfield, 1936. 113 p. Illus.

A compilation of furniture identified as originating in the area.

632 Horner, William M., Jr. BLUE BOOK OF PHILADELPHIA FURNITURE.

Philadelphia: Privately printed, 1935. Reprint. New preface by Marina S. Carson, with corrections. New York: Highland House, 1978. 502 illus. (8 in color).

> The work of eighteen cabinetmakers, chairmakers, carvers, and joiners active in eighteenth-century Philadelphia. Over 500 illustrations of documented pieces and much useful information on their provenance.

633 Horton, Frank L., and Weekley, Carolyn J. THE SWISEGOOD SCHOOL OF CABINETMAKING. Winston-Salem, N.C.: Museum of Early Southern Decorative Arts, 1973. 50 p. 20 illus.

> A discussion of an important southern regional school of furniture making and a description and illustrations of the work of the various craftsmen.

634 Kane, Patricia E. FURNITURE OF THE NEW HAVEN COLONY: THE SEVENTEENTH CENTURY STYLE. New Haven, Conn.: New Haven Colony Historical Society, 1973. 93 p. 34 illus.

> The catalog of an exhibition which concentrates on early colonial developments and examines each of the illustrated objects in great detail. Careful descriptions, reasons for attributions, historical material on the owner family, and all physical information are provided.

635 Kettell, Russell Hawes. THE PINE FURNITURE OF EARLY NEW ENGLAND. Garden City, N.Y.: Doubleday, Doran and Co., 1929. xxiii, 618 p. Illus.

> Hundreds of illustrations of furniture built in this particular softwood. Includes a chapter on pine and one on construction techniques. The illustrated entries are divided into chapters on chests, tables, chairs, and so on.

636 Kihn, Phyllis. "Connecticut Cabinetmakers." CONNECTICUT HISTORICAL SOCIETY BULLETIN 32, no. 4 (October 1967): 97-144; (January 1968): 1-40.

> A biographical checklist of some 350 cabinetmakers and joiners with known work. Provides all available information on dates, location of business, professional and civic activities, and quotations from advertisements or record books. Includes a geographical index and a table of prices for cabinetwork in Hartford, Connecticut, in 1792.

637 Kirk, John T. CONNECTICUT FURNITURE: SEVENTEENTH AND EIGHTEENTH CENTURIES. Hartford, Conn.: Wadsworth Atheneum, 1967. xvi, 156 p. Illus. Bibliog., pp. 154-55.

> Traces the development of the various major furniture forms through their stylistic changes and explores sources of the styles in an exhibition of colonial work.

638   Koda, Paul. FREDERICK K. AND MARGARET R. BARBOUR'S FURNI-
       TURE COLLECTION. Hartford: Connecticut Historical Society, 1963.
       71 p. Illus.

       The very useful catalog of a collection of high-quality Con-
       necticut furniture. Each entry provides information on woods,
       dimensions, description, condition, history, and references,
       as well as good photographs.

639   _____. FREDERICK K. AND MARGARET R. BARBOUR'S FURNITURE
       COLLECTION: A SUPPLEMENT. Hartford: Connecticut Historical
       Society, 1970. 31 p. Illus.

       This supplement contains complete documentation of another
       fourteen major Connecticut pieces of furniture.

640   Lockwood, Luke V. THREE CENTURES OF CONNECTICUT FURNITURE
       1635-1935. Hartford: Tercentary Commission of the State of Connect-
       icut, 1935. 30 p. 40 plates.

       The catalog of 273 items in the 300th-year anniversary exhi-
       bition of Connecticut furniture. Illustrations of a wide vari-
       ety of clocks, chests, chairs, and tables.

641   Lynch, Ernest C. FURNITURE-ANTIQUES FOUND IN VIRGINIA.
       Milwaukee, Wis.: Bruce Publishing Co., 1954. 95 p. Illus.
       Bibliog., p. 93.

       The main portion of this volume is a collection of measured
       drawings of early furniture found in, and for the most part
       assumed to have been made in Virginia. A useful check for
       the connoisseur.

642   Lyon, Irving W. COLONIAL FURNITURE OF NEW ENGLAND. 3d
       ed. Boston: Houghton Mifflin, 1924. xii, 285 p. Illus.

       A history and survey of "domestic" furniture in New England
       homes in the seventeenth and eighteenth centuries. Includes
       both simple and high-style work, with reference to the intro-
       duction of new forms and ample illustrations.

643   McElroy, Cathryn J. "Furniture in Philadelphia: The First Fifty
       Years." WINTERTHUR PORTFOLIO 13 (1979): 61-80.

       Surveys Philadelphia wills and inventories filed in the years
       from 1682 to 1730. Specifies which of the wide variety of
       furniture forms were to be found in Philadelphia during the
       first half century of settlement.

644   Miller, V. Isabelle. FURNITURE BY NEW YORK CABINETMAKERS,

1650–1860. New York: Museum of the City of New York, 1956. 84 p. Illus.

The catalog of an important exhibition of the work of New York craftsmen. Descriptive entries, including the identity of the maker when known, and illustrations of many of the pieces. Bibliographical sources on well-known pieces are included.

645 Monahon, Eleanore B. "Providence Cabinetmakers." RHODE ISLAND HISTORY 23 (January 1964): 1–22.

Discusses colonial and nineteenth-century cabinetmaking and identifies the work of the more established craftsmen.

646 Morningstar, Connie V. EARLY UTAH FURNITURE. Logan: Utah State University Press, 1976. 93 p. Illus. Bibliog., pp. 40–41.

Background and material on the physical problems related to furniture making is followed by a directory of Utah cabinetmakers active before 1870. Sixty major pieces are illustrated and described.

647 Naeve, Milo M. THE WAY WEST: AMERICAN FURNITURE IN THE PIKES PEAK REGION, 1872–1972. Colorado Springs: Fine Arts Center, 1972. Unpaged. Illus.

The catalog of an exhibition covering one hundred years of furniture making in the area, from anonymous generalists to contemporary handcraftsmen.

648 Page, Addison F. KENTUCKY FURNITURE. Louisville, Ky.: J.A. Speed Art Museum, 1974. Unpaged. 86 illus.

An exhibition catalog of photographs, with descriptions, of late eighteenth- and nineteenth-century furniture made in Kentucky. Both known craftsmen and attributed pieces are included.

649 Page, John. LITCHFIELD COUNTY FURNITURE: 1730–1850. Litchfield, Conn.: Litchfield Historical Society, 1969. 124 p. 78 illus.

Attempts a definition of the local tradition in furniture making, and compares it to the urban mainstream. Lists known area cabinetmakers and provides biographical data. Catalog entries include stylistic analysis and background historical information.

650 Poesch, Jessie J. EARLY FURNITURE OF LOUISIANA, 1750–1830. New Orleans: Louisiana State Museum, 1972. xviii, 85 p. 73 illus. (1 in color).

The French-influenced furniture, made of rich woods, cataloged and carefully illustrated. The chairs, tables, and other pieces are discussed in terms of the particular interest in surface and linear patterns common in the area, in contrast to the more frequently studied eastern seaboard productions.

651 Rice, Norman S. NEW YORK FURNITURE BEFORE 1840. Albany, N.Y.: Albany Institute of History and Art, 1962. 63 p. Illus. Bibliog., pp. 62-63.

A selected catalog of the New York furniture in the museum, emphasizing quality pieces. Each piece is illustrated, described, and documented with particular reference to provenance. Contains both English- and Dutch-derived pieces.

652 Richards, Nancy E. "Furniture of the Lower Connecticut River Valley: The Hartford Area, 1785-1810." WINTERTHUR PORTFOLIO 4 (1968): 1-25.

Attempts to sort out some of the Hartford area cabinetmakers and to judge their influence. Follows several of the workmen from the early masters' shops to their own successes. New information about John Wells, John Porter, and Wood and Watson.

653 Robacker, Earl F. "The Paint-Decorated Furniture of the Pennsylvania Dutch." PENNSYLVANIA FOLKLIFE, Fall 1962, pp. 2-8.

Concentrates on the various designs and motifs used by the group, with reference to the historical origins of the decoration.

654 St. George, Robert B. "Style and Structure in the Joinery of Dedham and Medfield, Massachusetts, 1635-1685." WINTERTHUR PORTFOLIO 13 (1979): 1-46.

A study of a group of chests based on a linguistic approach. Identifies work by John Houghton and John Thurston. Includes substantial biographical information on the known furniture makers of Dedham and Medfield in the fifty-year period.

655 Schiffer, Margaret B. FURNITURE AND ITS MAKERS OF CHESTER COUNTY, PENNSYLVANIA. Philadelphia: University of Pennsylvania Press, 1966. 280 p. 168 illus. Bibliog., pp. 279-80.

A carefully researched and documented biographical survey of the furniture makers. Includes inventories of many of their works. Illustrations are also well documented and attributed.

656 Schild, Joan L. "Furniture Makers of Rochester, New York." NEW YORK HISTORY 37, no. 1 (1956): 97-106.

A survey of late colonial and nineteenth-century cabinetmakers and chairmakers in the environs of Rochester. Illustrations of both identified and attributed pieces.

657 Sikes, Jane E. THE FURNITURE MAKERS OF CINCINNATI, 1790-1849. Cincinnati, Ohio: Privately printed, 1978. 264 p. Illus. (some in color). Bibliog.

A brief and well-illustrated survey of Cincinnati furniture and an exhaustive checklist of more than 1,000 Cincinnati furniture makers and dealers. Based on primary research of newspapers, municipal records, and personal documents, and rich in information about the craftsmen during their sixty years of active work in the area.

658 Snyder, John J., Jr. PHILADELPHIA FURNITURE AND ITS MAKERS. New York: Universe, 1975. 160 p. 300 illus.

Traces the work of Philadelphia furniture makers during their years of greatest success and influence, in the eighteenth and early nineteenth centuries. Profusely illustrated with examples of many different types of forms.

659 Taylor, Lonn, and Warren, David B. TEXAS FURNITURE. Austin: University of Texas Press, 1975. Unpaged. 222 illus.

An introduction to and survey of the furniture makers active between 1840 and 1880 in the form of an exhibition cosponsored by the Museum of Fine Arts, Houston. Illustrations include tools used in furniture making.

660 Theus, W.H. SAVANNAH FURNITURE, 1735-1825. Savannah, Ga.: Privately printed, 1967. xi, 100 p. 23 illus.

Background history, a discussion of woods, and inventories of various houses help supplement the basic discussion of the types of furniture made in Savannah and a biographical dictionary of approximately fifty Savannah cabinetmakers. Also included is some information about New England furniture imported into Savannah.

661 Van Ravenswaay, Charles. "The Anglo-American Cabinetmakers of Missouri, 1800-1850." MISSOURI HISTORICAL SOCIETY BULLETIN 15 (April 1958).

Discusses both the furniture made by native craftsmen and the work imported through the fifty-year period. Includes a checklist of craftsmen working in St. Louis and discusses characteristics of their work.

662 Walters, Betty L. FURNITURE MAKERS OF INDIANA, 1793-1850. Indianapolis: Indiana Historical Society, 1977. 244 p. Illus.

A thorough survey of the early years of Indiana furniture making, including the work of both individual cabinetmakers and furniture firms. Biographical and stylistic information.

663 Watts, Melvin E. "New England Furniture in the Currier Collection." CURRIER GALLERY OF ART BULLETIN, July–September 1969, pp. 1–19.

Discussion and illustrations of the various pieces, primarily of Massachusetts and New Hampshire origin, in the collection.

664 White, Margaret E. EARLY FURNITURE MADE IN NEW JERSEY, 1690–1870. An Exhibition, October 10, 1958–January 11, 1959, The Newark Museum. Newark, N.J.: Newark Museum Association, 1958. 89 p. Illus. Bibliog., pp. 37–39.

Brief introductions to each era within the period are followed by catalog entries and illustrations of specific pieces within the stylistic era. Of great value is the biographical dictionary of hundreds of furniture makers who spent all or part of their careers in New Jersey.

665 Whitehill, Walter M., ed. BOSTON FURNITURE OF THE EIGHTEENTH CENTURY. Boston: Colonial Society of Massachusetts, 1974. xvi, 316 p. 174 illus. Bibliog., 303–5.

A collection of eight essays on such varying topics as "Boston Japanese Furniture," "Boston Blockfront Furniture," "Benjamin Frothingham," and "New England Timbers." Contains a checklist on Boston craftsmen and a useful bibliography on individual craftsmen.

666 Whitley, Edna T. A CHECKLIST OF KENTUCKY CABINETMAKERS FROM 1775–1859. Paris, Ky.: Privately printed, 1969. 155 p. 62 illus.

An alphabetical history of craftsmen with all available biographical information and location of major activity. Illustrated with examples of work reflecting both regional differences and influences from the major furniture centers.

667 Winchester, Alice, ed. SOUTHERN FURNITURE, 1640–1820. New York: Magazine Antiques, 1952. 64 p. 162 illus.

Essays by several authorities on various aspects of southern furniture, emphasizing the furniture of Charleston. Catalog entries accompanying the illustrations give dimensions, analyze woods, present origins, and explore other regional influences.

668 Winters, Robert E., Jr. NORTH CAROLINA FURNITURE 1700–1900. Raleigh: North Carolina Museum of History Associates, 1977. xiii, 77 p. 71 illus.

The catalog of an exhibition analyzing and exploring the evolution of the region's furniture styles over the 200-year period. Background essays on each era and catalog entries which locate, date, describe, and measure each work. Discussion of relevant material in a separate paragraph on each.

PERIOD STUDIES OF AMERICAN FURNITURE

669 Bishop, Robert C. AMERICAN FURNITURE, 1620-1720. Dearborn, Mich.: Greenfield Village and Henry Ford Museum, 1975. 32 p. Illus.

Surveys the period styles based on the illustrated pieces from the rooms in the collections of the two museums.

670 Bryant, Frederick J. WORKING DRAWINGS OF COLONIAL FURNITURE. Peoria, Ill.: Manual Arts Press, 1922. 54 p. Illus., including line drawings.

A guide for those who wish to duplicate antique furniture. Illustrated with examples of original pieces.

671 Downing, Alexander J. FURNITURE FOR THE VICTORIAN HOME. 1850. Reprint. Watkins Glen, N.Y.: American Life Foundation, Century House, 1968. 212 p. Illus.

A reprint, with added index, of this classic early treatise by Downing in which he lays out correct usage adapted from European models. Useful for understanding American taste at mid-nineteenth century.

672 Erving, Henry W. RANDOM NOTES ON COLONIAL FURNITURE. Hartford, Conn.: Privately printed, 1931. 60 p. Illus.

A personalized history by a collector and historian. Contains quotations from colonial writing and references to early records.

673 Freeman, Ruth, and Freeman, Graydon L. (Larry). VICTORIAN FURNITURE. Watkins Glen, N.Y.: Century House, 1950. 112 p. Illus.

An introductory handbook which explains and illustrates the various Victorian revivals and their manifestation in a variety of furniture forms.

674 Gilborn, Craig A. AMERICAN FURNITURE, 1660-1725. London: Hamlyn, 1972. 64 p. 52 illus.

A basic survey introduction to American furniture styles and their relationship to the mainstream of continental and English traditions. Regional differences are explored and illustrated.

675 Gottshall, Franklin H. SIMPLE COLONIAL FURNITURE. New York:
Brace Publishing Co., 1935. Reprint. New York: Bonanza Books,
1965. 124 p. Illus.

A book with high-quality plates of selected pieces of early
colonial furniture in a variety of forms.

676 Grotz, George. THE NEW ANTIQUES: KNOWING AND BUYING
VICTORIAN FURNITURE. Garden City, N.Y.: Doubleday and Co.,
1964. 224 p. Illus.

A popularly directed survey of American furniture covering
most of the nineteenth century and the first decade of the
twentieth century. Descriptions, classifications, and line
drawings of the various pieces.

677 Hanks, David. Introduction to VICTORIAN FURNITURE: TWO PAT-
TERN BOOKS. Philadelphia: Henry Carey Baird, 1868. Reprint.
Philadelphia: Athenaeum Library of Nineteenth Century America, 1977.
Unpaged. Illus.

Reprints of two important and rare nineteenth-century furniture
books: Baird's GOTHIC ALBUM and ALBUM OF FURNITURE.
Twenty-three and forty-eight plates, respectively, illustrate
the range and variety of Victorian taste in furniture.

678 Holloway, Edward S. THE PRACTICAL BOOK OF AMERICAN FURNI-
TURE AND DECORATION: COLONIAL AND FEDERAL. Philadelphia:
J.B. Lippincott Co., 1937. 191 p. 200 illus.

An early attempt at classifying and describing the work of
each period in terms of both appearances and influences.
Some background information on the period and constant references to specific changes from one period to the next.

679 Lockwood, Luke V. COLONIAL FURNITURE IN AMERICA. 2 vols.
New York: Charles Scribner's Sons, 1926. Vol. 1: xxiv, 398 p.
Vol. 2: xx, 354 p. 1,003 illus.

Chapters on each type of colonial furniture: tables, chairs,
cupboards, sideboards, and so on. General discussion of each
type, technical considerations, and many illustrations of varieties of each form. An extremely old, yet still valuable, re-
source.

680 Nutting, Wallace. FURNITURE OF THE PILGRIM CENTURY, 1620-
1720. Boston: Marshall Jones Co., 1921. ix, 587 p. 1,000 illus.

A massive pioneering study which provides both a commentary
on furniture types and describes and analyzes hundreds of specific individual pieces. Useful information about woods and

decoration. Still used for reference purposes and cited in all later studies.

681   Ormsbee, Thomas H. EARLY AMERICAN FURNITURE MAKERS: A SOCIAL AND BIOGRAPHICAL STUDY. New York: Thomas Y. Crowell Co., 1930. xviii, 183 p. 67 illus. Bibliog., pp. 177-79.

Chapters on the work and activity of the craftsmen during the seventeenth century: American Chippendales, Duncan Phyfe and his followers, and craftsmen who became involved in government and politics. A popular social history.

682   _____. FIELD GUIDE TO AMERICAN VICTORIAN FURNITURE. Boston: Little, Brown and Co., 1952. xxxii, 429 p. 283 illus. Bibliog., p. 429.

This is a guide for the collector. Line drawings of 283 different items show the range and depth of Victorian pieces. Chapters on the substyles of Victorian furniture; a discussion of woods and specialty items like cast-iron papier-mâché furniture.

683   Otto, Celia J. AMERICAN FURNITURE OF THE NINETEENTH CENTURY. New York: Viking Press, 1965. 229 p. 481 illus.

Chronological treatment of styles and of classes of objects: chairs, tables, mirrors, and so on, within chronology. A general encyclopedia of works.

684   Phipps, Frances. COLONIAL KITCHENS, THEIR FURNISHINGS, AND THEIR GARDENS. New York: Hawthorn Books, 1972. xxii, 346 p. Illus. Bibliog., pp. 327-36.

Very useful historical and cultural background for those interested in colonial decorative arts. The material contained is almost totally based on writings by early settlers and the diaries of travelers. A good balance to romantic restorations which assume too much about colonial furniture and furnishings.

685   Schwartz, Marvin D. AMERICAN FURNITURE OF THE COLONIAL PERIOD. New York: Metropolitan Museum of Art, 1976. xvi, 93 p. 80 illus. (some in color). Bibliog., p. 93.

An easy-to-follow primer on colonial furniture illustrated by carefully chosen examples from the museum's extensive collection. Divided into four periods: seventeenth century, William and Mary, Queen Anne, and Chippendale.

686   Shea, John G., and Wenger, Paul N. COLONIAL FURNITURE. Milwaukee: Bruce, 1935. 180 p. Illus. Bibliog.

Essentially a book of measured drawings of important and typical colonial pieces, with commentary.

687 Sigworth, Oliver F. THE FOUR STYLES OF A DECADE, 1740–1750. New York: New York Public Library, 1960. 33 p. Illus.

The catalog of an exhibition exploring the four great styles of the period: Chinese, Gothic, Palladian, and Rococo.

688 Wainwright, Nicholas B. COLONIAL GRANDEUR IN PHILADELPHIA: THE HOUSE AND FURNITURE OF GENERAL JOHN CADWALADER. Philadelphia: Historical Society of Pennsylvania, 1964. xii, 169 p. Illus.

The study and survey of this great eighteenth–century home present information on both English and American furniture, and their actual use in the home of the well–to–do.

689 Weil, Martin E. "A Cabinetmaker's Price Book." WINTERTHUR PORTFOLIO 13 (1979): 175–92.

A reproduction of a 1772 cabinetmaker's manuscript price book, which indicates that Philadelphia cabinetmakers attempted to fix prices to stabilize the market. Includes labor prices and antedates any known similar document.

AMERICAN FURNITURE STYLES

690 Bishop, Robert C. CENTURIES AND STYLES OF THE AMERICAN CHAIR, 1640–1970. New York: E.P. Dutton and Co., 1972. 516 p. Illus. Bibliog., pp. 508–10.

Covers both the traditional, including Wainscott and Windsor chairs, to the unusual chair tables of early America. Includes modern chairs to 1970. Illustrations of works in both private and public collections.

691 Comstock, Helen. THE LOOKING GLASS IN AMERICA, 1700–1825. New York: Viking Press, 1968. 128 p. 85 illus.

Surveys the ways the looking glass more a piece of furniture than glass, relates to the traditional period styles through illustrated examples. Includes a list of looking–glass makers and dealers.

692 Connecticut Historical Society. CONNECTICUT CHAIRS IN THE COLLECTION OF THE CONNECTICUT HISTORICAL SOCIETY. Hartford: 1956. 67 p. Illus.

A survey of the variety of chairs, Windsor, Queen Anne, Moravian, desk, and armchairs. Information on woods, decoration, and provenance.

693   Cooper, Wendy A. "American Chippendale Chairback Settees: Some Sources and Related Examples." AMERICAN ART JOURNAL 9, no. 2 (November 1977): 34–45.

Discussion of a form that appears to be uniquely American during the eighteenth century but which had English precedents. Traces their development and variety from the earliest late seventeenth-century example in maple through the later examples more commonly made of mahogany.

694   Corbin, Patricia. ALL ABOUT WICKER. New York: E.P. Dutton, 1978. 122 p. 131 illus. (24 in color).

A history of wicker furniture in America, from its rise in the Victorian era through its period of unpopularity through much of this century, and its recent revival. Emphasis on the Heywood-Wakefield Company and its imitators. Includes references to and illustrations from period literature.

695   Dreppard, Carl W. HANDBOOK OF ANTIQUE CHAIRS. New York: Doubleday and Co., 1948. 27 p. 489 illus.

Covers all of the types of chairs used in colonial through nineteenth-century America, whether domestic or imported. Contains a checklist of American chair makers from 1660 to 1850 and information about early advertising of chairs.

696   Dyer, Walter A., and Fraser, Esther S. THE ROCKING CHAIR, AN AMERICAN INSTITUTION. New York: Century Co., 1928. xiv, 127 p. 29 illus.

Discusses the origin, development, and acceptance of the rocking chair in this country, with a special section devoted to the Boston rocker. Includes information on their decorations and representative advertisements.

697   Erving, Henry W. THE HARTFORD CHEST. Hartford: Tercentenary Commission of the State of Connecticut, 1934. 12 p. Illus.

An analysis and description of the type of oak colonial chest known as the "Connecticut Chest" or the "Hartford Chest." Makes a case for the Hartford origins of the form.

698   Evans [Goyne], Nancy A. "The Bureau Table in America." WINTERTHUR PORTFOLIO 3 (1967): 25-36.

Discusses the bureau table as a popular form through the second half of the 1700s. Emphasis on the work of the Philadelphia cabinetmaker David Evans and several craftsmen in various colonies.

699 _____. "The Geneology of a Bookcase Desk." WINTERTHUR PORT-FOLIO 9 (1974): 213-22.

Traces the ownership of a walnut bookcase desk made by Job Coit in 1738. The piece is identified as the earliest documented block-front piece in America. Background information on Coit and his relationship with the colonial merchant, Daniel Henchman.

700 Iverson, Marion D. THE AMERICAN CHAIR, 1630-1890. New York: Hastings House, 1959. 241 p. 176 illus. Bibliog.

The author's coverage of chairs and their role in American style and life is thorough enough to enable us to see this form as a key to furniture styles of each period. Many contemporary quotations and information about ownership. Includes a good bibliography and a list of museums and historic houses in which furniture can be seen.

701 Kane, Patricia E. 300 YEARS OF AMERICAN SEATING FURNITURE. Boston: New York Graphic, 1976. 356 p. 402 illus. (18 in color).

Traces the chair and daybed through American history and points out regional variations and how cultural influences determine function. Based on the collection of furniture at Yale University.

702 Kenney, John T. THE HITCHCOCK CHAIR: THE STORY OF A CONNECTICUT YANKEE--L. HITCHCOCK OF HITCHCOCKSVILLE. New York: C.N. Potter, 1971. x, 339 p. Illus. Bibliog., pp. 333-34.

The Hitchcock chair was once very popular in the early nineteenth century. This volume examines the factory's work and the reason for the chair's popularity, and describes the restoration of the factory.

703 Kirk, John T. AMERICAN CHAIRS: QUEEN ANNE AND CHIPPEN-DALE. New York: Alfred A. Knopf, 1972. xi, 208 p. 251 illus.

Presents a regional approach to understanding and documenting the chair. A major part covers construction and design details and is followed by a well-illustrated catalog of specific pieces from each geographical area.

704 Lea, Zilla R., ed. THE ORNAMENTED CHAIR: ITS DEVELOPMENT

IN AMERICA, 1700–1890. Rutland, Vt.: Charles E. Tuttle Co., 1960. 173 p. Illus. (7 in color). Bibliog., pp. 165–67.

Seven chapters by various authors on the different periods in the history of this genre. Each section, on such topics as the Windsor chair and the rocking chair, is illustrated with several examples of such work. Although photographs are merely adequate, the details of important objects are very valuable.

705   Luther, Clair F. THE HADLEY CHEST. Hartford, Conn.: Case, Lockwood and Brainard Co., 1935. xxii, 144 p.

Discussion of this group of oak chests with their distinctive tulip and leaf pattern made in the Connecticut River Valley. From 1675 to about 1725.

706   MacDonald, William H. NINETEENTH CENTURY CHAIR MAKERS OF CENTRAL NEW JERSEY. Freehold, N.J.: Privately printed, 1960. 59 p.

Points out how much of this furniture has been incorrectly assigned to either New York or Philadelphia. A wide variety of styles by some rediscovered craftsmen.

707   Nutting, Wallace. AMERICAN WINDSORS. Framingham, Mass.: Old American Co., 1917. Reprint. Southampton, N.Y.: Cracker Barrel Press, 1972. 200 p. Illus.

An illustrated handbook of Windsor chairs, love seats, stools, and others, made between 1725 and 1825. A rich variety of types are described, dated, and evaluated as to scarcity and condition; commented upon in a lively and concise manner. Old but useful.

708   Ormsbee, Thomas H. THE WINDSOR CHAIR. New York: Deerfield Books, 1962. 223 p. 80 illus.

Although pointing out the English origins of the Windsor chair and including a small section on the English product, this is a study of the development of the type in America, a discussion of regional variations, and a checklist of American Windsor chair makers.

709   Van Way, Joseph S., and MacFarland, Anne S. A SELECTION OF 19TH CENTURY AMERICAN CHAIRS. Hartford, Conn.: Stowe-Day Foundation, 1973. 114 p. 38 illus. Bibliog.

A catalog, with excellent illustrations, of nineteenth-century chairs found in the Hartford area. Full catalog information and checklists of Hartford chair makers, cabinetmakers, and furniture businesses.

710   Walters, Betty L. THE KING OF DESKS: WOOTON'S PATENT SEC-
       RETARY. Washington, D.C.: Smithsonian Institution Press, 1969.
       32 p. Illus.

       A history and discussion of the once-famous Wooton folding
       design. Explores possible sources and describes the evolution
       of the form and the company until 1892. Photographs of ex-
       tant models, and newspaper and advertisement illustrations of
       others.

SPECIFIC AMERICAN FURNITURE FORMS

711   Albers, Marjorie K. OLD AMANA FURNITURE. Shenandoah, Iowa:
       Locust House, 1970. iii, 85 p. Illus.

       Discusses and illustrates the furniture made by and for the
       settlers of the Amana community of Iowa, a self-contained
       religious sect. Comments on the practicality and simplicity
       of the work.

712   Ames, Kenneth L. "Designed in France: Notes on the Transmission of
       French Style to America." WINTERTHUR PORTFOLIO 12 (1977):
       103-14.

       Discusses the sources of transmission of French-style furniture
       through the example of the Philadelphia firm of George Hen-
       kels. Emphasizes both the importance of Guilmard's designs
       and the fact that Americans probably copied specific imported
       pieces.

713   Andrews, Edward D., and Andrews, Faith. THE SHAKER FURNITURE:
       THE CRAFTSMANSHIP OF AN AMERICAN COMMUNAL SECT. New
       Haven: Yale University Press, 1937. xi, 133 p. 48 illus. Bibliog.,
       pp. 121-26.

       Chapters cover the cultural background of Shaker craftsman-
       ship, the purposes of the furniture, information about the
       craftsmen, and descriptions of the houses and shops. The ap-
       pendixes cover the chair industry of the group and notes on
       the construction of the pieces.

714   Ayres, James. "The American Chippendale Style." DISCOVERING
       ANTIQUES 43 (1971): 1028-32.

       A brief discussion of the American manifestation of the Chip-
       pendale style and some local variations. Illustrated with good
       color plates.

715   Conger, Clement E. "Chippendale Furniture in the Department of
       State Collection." AMERICAN ART JOURNAL 8 (May 1976): 84-98.

The work owned by and on loan to the Department of State and on display in the diplomatic reception room. Descriptions and illustration of key pieces and views of the furnished rooms.

716 Downs, Joseph. AMERICAN FURNITURE: QUEEN ANNE AND CHIPPENDALE PERIODS, IN THE HENRY FRANCIS DUPONT WINTERTHUR MUSEUM. New York: Macmillan Publishing Co., 1952. xlvi, unpaged. 401 illus. (many in color).

A descriptive catalog which provides stylistic, historical, and provenance material on almost 400 items of early American furniture. When known, the name of the craftsman and exact date are also provided.

717 _____. A PICTURE BOOK OF PHILADELPHIA CHIPPENDALE FURNITURE, 1750–1780. Philadelphia: Pennsylvania Museum of Art, 1931. 19 p. Plates.

A brief text followed by excellent-quality plates of major chairs, chests, and tables of the mid-eighteenth century in Philadelphia.

718 Elder, William V. III. MARYLAND QUEEN ANNE AND CHIPPENDALE FURNITURE OF THE EIGHTEENTH CENTURY. Baltimore: Baltimore Museum of Art, 1968. 128 p. 76 illus.

The catalog of the major exhibition of eighteenth-century furniture. Excellent plates and fully documented entries on each piece. Contains a list of Maryland cabinetmakers with references to advertisements.

719 Freeman, Graydon L. (Larry). FEDERAL-EMPIRE. Antique Furniture Handbooks Series, vol. 3. Watkins Glen, N.Y.: Century House, 1956. 80 p. Illus.

An illustrated handbook of furniture forms. A good introduction to the period.

720 Johnson, Theodore E. HANDS TO WORK AND HEARTS TO GOD: THE SHAKER TRADITION IN MAINE. Brunswick, Maine: Bowdoin College, 1969. Unpaged. 46 illus. Bibliog.

The catalog of a loan exhibition of Shaker furniture from the Sabbathday Lake community. Detailed entries and excellent-quality plates.

721 Kalec, Donald. "The Prairie School Furniture." PRAIRIE SCHOOL REVIEW 1, no.1 (1964): 5–15.

Shows how Prairie School architects supervised the furniture

selection and designed pieces in the spirit of their buildings.
Gives Frank Lloyd Wright a major place in the development
of their "total design" concept.

722 Madigan, Mary J. EASTLAKE-INFLUENCED AMERICAN FURNITURE,
1870-1890. Yonkers, N.Y.: Hudson River Museum, 1973. 66 p.
Illus. Bibliog., pp. 64-65.

Discusses the work of Charles L. Eastlake (1833-1906) and his
influence on American Victorian furniture. A well-researched
and illustrated exhibition catalog.

723 Meader, Robert F. ILLUSTRATED GUIDE TO SHAKER FURNITURE.
New York: Dover, 1972. ix, 128 p. Illus.

Information about the Shakers and their beliefs, illustrations
of the room settings from still-in-existence installations, and
a brief discussion of the utilization of various furniture forms.

724 Montgomery, Charles F. AMERICAN FURNITURE: THE FEDERAL PE-
RIOD, IN THE HENRY FRANCIS DUPONT WINTERTHUR MUSEUM.
New York: Viking Press, 1966. 497 p.

Discusses the development of the furniture styles, concentrating on the norm developed by skilled craftsmen in the cities.
Each work is described, variations that cause a local identification are pointed out, and a provenance is provided.

725 Ray, Marylyn. "A Reappraisal of Shaker Furniture and Society."
WINTERTHUR PORTFOLIO 8 (1973): 107-30.

A rejection of the common myth that Shaker furniture is the
embodiment of Shaker religious beliefs. States that much of
Shaker furniture was inspired by secular forms and ran contrary
to the tenets of the order. Lower standards of quality followed
the acceptance of producing for the marketplace.

726 Renwick Gallery. SHAKER: FURNITURE AND OBJECTS FROM THE
FAITH AND EDWARD DEMING ANDREWS COLLECTIONS. Washington, D.C.: Smithsonian Institution Press, 1973. 88 p. 40 illus.

An essay on the Shakers, a discussion of design in Shaker furniture, a conversation with Faith Andrews, the compiled writings of Andrews, and an exhibition catalog make up this volume for and by the family who are so closely identified with
Shaker art and life.

727 Shea, John G. THE AMERICAN SHAKERS AND THEIR FURNITURE.
New York: Van Nostrand Reinhold Co., 1971. xv, 208 p. Illus.

Chapters on the history of the Shakers, their general furniture design, construction, and finishing, are followed by illustrations of specific pieces with descriptive material and measured drawings.

728 Shepherd, Raymond V., Jr. "Cliveden and its Philadelphia-Chippendale Furniture: A Documented History." AMERICAN ART JOURNAL 8, no. 2 (November 1976): 2-16.

The history of the house and furnishings of the Chew family, who continuously owned it all until it went to the National Trust in 1972. Information about specific pieces of furniture and their quality.

729 Stewart, Patrick L. "The American Empire Style: Its Historical Background." AMERICAN ART JOURNAL 10, no. 2 (November 1978): 97-105.

A discussion of American furniture from 1812 through the Jacksonian era. Discusses the influences in the development of the style, especially that of Thomas Jefferson, and the relationship with France as a result of the War of 1812.

730 Zimmerman, Philip D. "A Methodological Study in the Identification of Some Important Philadelphia Chippendale Furniture." WINTERTHUR PORTFOLIO 13 (1979): 193-208.

A structural analysis examines the construction and documents related to two groupings of "Chippendale" chairs in attempting to make attributions. Makes a case for comparative study rather than for judgements based on the external similarity of pieces.

INDIVIDUAL FURNITURE MAKERS AND FURNITURE COMPANIES

731 Brady, Nancy H., ed. ROYCROFT HAND MADE FURNITURE. East Aurora, N.Y.: Roycrofters, 1912. Reprint. East Aurora, N.Y.: House of Hubbard, 1973. 61 p. Illus.

Useful for both scholar and collector in comparing pieces with the photographs of the original objects in the catalog. Measurements are included.

732 Burton, E. Milby. THOMAS ELFE, CHARLESTON CABINET MAKER. Charleston, S.C.: Charleston Museum, 1952. 34 p. Illus.

A biography and exploration of the work of an eighteenth-century (1719-1775) Charleston furniture maker. Illustrations of a variety of work known or attributed to his hand.

733   Caplan, Ralph. THE DESIGNS OF HERMAN MILLER. New York:
       Whitney Library of Design, 1976. 119 p. Illus. (8 in color).

       The growth and development of a major contemporary furniture
       company. History and explanation of the contributions of the
       company to the current design aesthetic. Ends on a pessimis-
       tic note with the expressed fear that Miller quality is being
       lost as the company adapts to the marketplace.

734   Catalano, Kathleen M. "Abraham Kimball (1798-1890), Salem Cabi-
       netmaker." AMERICAN ART JOURNAL 11, no. 2 (April 1979): 62-
       70.

       The work of a nineteenth-century cabinetmaker who produced
       chairs, tables, and many other items, in a successive variety
       of revival styles, until his retirement in 1845.

735   Cornelius, Charles O. FURNITURE MASTERPIECES OF DUNCAN
       PHYFE. Garden City, N.Y.: Doubleday, Page and Co., 1923. Re-
       print. New York: Dover, 1970. xii, 86 p. 66 illus.

       Biography and cultural history of his era, followed by a de-
       scription of his work, a detailed analysis of his style, and
       illustrations of his work in various forms.

736   Dreppard, Carl W. "Furniture Masterpieces by Jacob Bachman."
       LANCASTER COUNTY HISTORICAL SOCIETY PAPERS 49, no. 5
       (1945): 131-39.

       The substantial designs of an important Pennsylvania cabinet-
       maker.

737   Drexler, Arthur. CHARLES EAMES FURNITURE FROM THE DESIGN
       COLLECTION. New York: Museum of Modern Art, 1973. 56 p.
       85 illus. (1 in color).

       Complete descriptive and analytical entries for the furniture
       in the collection, with excellent illustrations. Discussion of
       the evolution of furniture design under mass production and
       Eames's place in that evolution. Special emphasis on the use
       of materials.

738   Dulaney, William L. "Wallace Nutting, Collector and Entrepreneur."
       WINTERTHUR PORTFOLIO 13 (1979): 47-60.

       A study of Nutting, the man, as writer, dealer, and furniture
       reproducer. Discusses his influence on the American furniture
       market and the value of his contributions to our understanding
       of colonial furniture.

739 Freeman, John Crosby. THE FORGOTTEN REBEL: GUSTAV STICKLEY AND HIS CRAFTSMAN MISSION FURNITURE. Watkins Glen, N.Y.: Century House, 1966. 112 p. Illus. Bibliog., pp. 110–11.

Several articles gathered to present a history of the work and a biography of the man who designed and originated the "mission" furniture of the early twentieth century. The relationship of Stickley to the general craftsman movement and to worldwide Art Nouveau is discussed in some detail.

740 Gillingham, Harrold E. "Benjamin Lehman, A Germantown Cabinetmaker." PENNSYLVANIA MAGAZINE 54, no. 4 (1930): 289–306.

An introduction to the life and work of a late eighteenth-century Pennsylvania cabinetmaker.

741 Golovin, Anne C. "Daniel Trotter: Eighteenth-Century Philadelphia Cabinetmaker." WINTERTHUR PORTFOLIO 6 (1970): 151–84.

A full reconstruction of Trotter's life and an attempt to attribute various pieces to his hand. Includes a full index of forms produced in his shop from which it is inferred that he worked in both simple and high-style furniture.

742 Hanks, David A. ISAAC E. SCOTT: REFORM FURNITURE IN CHICAGO. Chicago: Chicago School of Architecture Foundation, 1974. 31 p. 24 illus.

Biographical data on Scott, exploration of his relationship with the Glessner family, and discussion of the influences on his work, especially that of Eastlake. Also references to Scott's pottery and architectural designs.

743 Herman, Lloyd E. A MODERN CONSCIOUSNESS: D.J. DEPREE, FLORENCE KNOLL. Washington, D.C.: Smithsonian Institution Press, 1975. 32 p. Illus.

Biographies of the two individuals responsible for so much in the development of modern design in American furniture. Includes a small catalog of Knoll International and Herman Miller furniture, with information on designers, dimensions, and materials.

744 _____, ed. WOODENWORKS: FURNITURE OBJECTS BY FIVE CONTEMPORARY CRAFTSMEN. St. Paul: Minnesota Museum of Art and National Collection of Fine Arts, 1972. 48 p. Illus. Bibliog., pp. 47–48.

Biographical data, philosophical statements, and selected illustrations of work of George Nakashima, Sam Maloof, Wharton Esherick, Arthur E. Carpenter, and Wendell Castle.

745 Hill, John H. "Furniture Designs of Henry W. Jenkins & Sons, Co." WINTERTHUR PORTFOLIO 5 (1969): 154-87.

A brief introduction to the history of this important Baltimore firm and illustrations and discussion of major designs in several furniture forms.

746 Horner, William M., Jr. "Matthew Egerton, Jr., Cabinetmaker of New Jersey." ANTIQUARIAN 15, no. 6 (December 1930): 50-53, 114.

The successful cabinetmaker and joiner, and son of the founder of the Egerton family of New Brunswick, New Jersey. Attempts to place work, primarily the Kas and tall clock, within the proper context of the time and to develop the image of the individual.

747 Hummel, Charles F. WITH HAMMER IN HAND: THE DOMINY CRAFTSMEN OF EAST HAMPTON, NEW YORK. Winterthur, Del.: H.F. duPont Winterthur Museum, 1968. xiv, 424 p. 293 illus. Bibliog., pp. 407-14.

A history of a family of furniture makers, clock makers, and metalsmiths who worked in East Hampton from 1760 to 1840. Contains a massive and scholarly catalog of the family's tools and specific pieces of furniture and clocks. Useful for understanding American hand manufacture during the era.

748 Johnson, Marilynn A. "John Hewitt, Cabinetmaker." WINTERTHUR PORTFOLIO 4 (1968): 185-205.

The rise of the young son of a British cabinetmaker whose checkered career in New York and his importing furniture to the South ended in failure in New Jersey. An appendix on his work is based on a Hewitt account book of 1809-1812.

749 Jones, Edward V. "Charles-Honore Lannuier and Duncan Phyfe, Two Creative Geniuses of Federal New York." AMERICAN ART JOURNAL 9, no. 1 (May 1977): 4-14.

Explores the similarities and differences between the two furniture makers at work in New York. Illustrations comparing both known and attributed work of the two designers.

750 Koch, Robert. "Elbert Hubbard's Roycrofters as Artist-Craftsmen." WINTERTHUR PORTFOLIO 3 (1967): 67-82.

A discussion of the influences on Hubbard and his firm's production and a survey of the variety of their products. Stresses the importance of David Hunter.

751 McClelland, Nancy. DUNCAN PHYFE AND THE ENGLISH REGENCY, 1795-1830. New York: William R. Scott, 1939. xxix, 364 p. Illus. Bibliog., pp. 341-46.

An exhaustive study of the ideas and work of a major federal period craftsman, and the interrelation between high-style English developments and his adaptations.

752 Makinson, Randell L. GREENE & GREENE: FURNITURE AND RE-LATED DESIGNS. Santa Barbara, Calif.: Peregrine Smith, 1979. 162 p. Illus. Bibliog., pp. 153-54.

Traces the work of the Greene Brothers, the influences on their designs, and the relationship of their furniture designs to their architecture. Treats both their joint efforts and their later individual designs.

753 Nelson, George. THE HERMAN MILLER COLLECTION. Zeeland, Mich.: Herman Miller Furniture Co., 1950. 72 p. Illus.

The catalog of a noted furniture manufacturer, including the designs of Charles Eames, Isamu Noguchi, and Paul Laslo.

754 North Carolina Museum of History. THOMAS DAY, 19TH CENTURY NORTH CAROLINA CABINETMAKER. Raleigh, N.C.: 1975. 75 p. 50 illus.

The catalog of the first exhibition of the furniture and interior trim work by Day, a free black of the nineteenth century.

755 Parsons, Charles S. THE DUNLAPS AND THEIR FURNITURE. Manchester, N.Y.: Currier Gallery of Art, 1970. vi, 310 p. Illus. Bibliog.

An exhibition catalog which lays out the work of Major John Dunlap (1746-1792) and his relatives. A wide variety of beds, chests, desks, and chairs were made by some six to eight relatives, and pieces are each attributed to some member of the family.

756 Peirce, Donald C. "Mitchell and Rammelsberg: Cincinnati Furniture Manufacturers 1847-1881." WINTERTHUR PORTFOLIO 13 (1979): 209-29.

A study of the development of two independent cabinetmakers into a small partnership and eventually into a major factory with warehouses in four cities. Discusses the changes in taste and style of their wares.

757 Randall, Richard H., Jr. THE FURNITURE OF H.H. RICHARDSON. Boston: Museum of Fine Arts, 1962. 4 p. Illus.

The catalog of an exhibition of the furniture designed for his buildings.

758 _____. "George Bright, Cabinetmaker." ART QUARTERLY 27 (1964): 134-49.

The resurrection and reconstruction of the career of an eighteenth-century (1727-1805) Bostonian furniture maker considered important enough to have been arbiter in court cases involving other furniture makers. Documents some of his work.

759 _____. "Seymour Furniture Problems." MUSEUM OF FINE ARTS, BOSTON, BULLETIN 57, no. 310 (1959): 102-13.

The work of John Seymour and his son Thomas identified and separated.

760 Seitz, Albert F. "Furniture Making by the Slaugh Family of Lancaster, Pennsylvania." JOURNAL OF THE LANCASTER COUNTY HISTORIANS SOCIETY 73, no. 1 (1969): 1-25.

An illustrated survey of the carefully constructed pieces and a discussion of their sources.

761 Stoneman, Vernon C. JOHN AND THOMAS SEYMOUR: CABINETMAKERS IN BOSTON, 1794-1816. Boston: Special Publications, 1959. 393 p. 291 illus. Bibliog., pp. 392-93.

A major attempt to provide the history and analysis of the work in a perspective relating to their contemporaries, and to produce a catalog of their works. Each piece is described and illustrated.

762 Swan, Mabel. SAMUEL McINTIRE, CARVER, AND THE SANDERSONS, EARLY SALEM CABINET MAKERS. Salem, Mass.: Essex Institute, 1934. 44 p. Illus.

Samuel McIntire's carvings for the Sandersons' furniture is introduced among the correspondence and advertisements of the firm that form the substance of this volume.

763 Teitz, Richard S. THE FURNITURE OF WENDELL CASTLE. Wichita, Kans.: Wichita Art Museum, 1969. 16 p. 8 illus.

A modest catalog of the sculpturally oriented furniture of Castle, and a discussion of his use of fine woods, rather than a concern for technical processes. An interesting example of a craftsman fighting society's direction.

764 Triggs, Oscar L. ABOUT TOBEY HANDMADE FURNITURE. Chicago: Tobey Furniture Co., 1906. 26 p. Illus.

Although written as a promotional piece, this booklet is valuable for its illustrations of both craftsmen at work and of

individual pieces, as well as for the statements about the
aims of this important Chicago firm.

765 Waters, Deborah D. "Wares and Chairs." WINTERTHUR PORTFOLIO
13 (1979): 161-73.

Traces the history and stylistic consistency of four generations
of chair making by members of the Ware family of South Jersey. Heavy reliance on documentary evidence as to the family's activities in creating cane or rush seat ladder-back chairs.

Chapter 9

AMERICAN GLASS

In spite of its inherent fragility, early American glass has survived and is widely collected and recorded. Because so many are completely oriented to the collector, only a fraction of the hundreds of books and checklists on collecting specific forms such as bottles or flasks, or on various types such as pattern or engraved glass, have been included.

GENERAL STUDIES AND SURVEYS OF AMERICAN GLASS

766   Barber, Edwin A.   AMERICAN GLASSWARE.   Philadelphia: David McKay Co., 1900.   112 p.   Illus.

Chapters on early glassworks, on the identification of old glassware, on descriptions of some of the old firms, on representative designs, and so on.

767   Bergstom Art Center.   GLASS 1976.   Neenah, Wis.:   1976.   Unpaged. Illus.

Biographical and analytical material on nineteen contemporary glassworkers, with illustrations of their work.

768   Brooklyn Museum.   HANDBOOK OF AMERICAN GLASS INDUSTRIES. Brooklyn, N.Y.:   Brooklyn Museum Press, 1936.   117 p.   Illus.

A catalog and handbook compiled in conjunction with an exhibition of the American glass industry's products.   Illustrates contemporary glass of the day from a wide variety of firms.

769   Davidson, Marshall.   EARLY AMERICAN GLASS: A PICTURE BOOK. New York: Metropolitan Museum of Art, 1940.   24 p.   Illus.

A primer on American glass with clear text and good illustration.

770   Davis, Pearce. THE DEVELOPMENT OF THE AMERICAN GLASS IN-
DUSTRY. Harvard Economic Series. New York: Russell and Russell,
1970. xiv, 316 p. Bibliog., pp. 295-305.

Concerned with both the development of manufacturing and
trade. A thorough and well-documented study, including information on technological developments and the effects of
foreign competition.

771   Hartley, Julia M. OLD AMERICAN GLASS: THE MILLS COLLEC-
TION AT TEXAS CHRISTIAN UNIVERSITY. Fort Worth: Texas Christian University Press, 1975. 279 p. 34 illus. (16 in color).

The well-documented and finely illustrated catalog of a major
collection of American art, blown, cut, and pressed glass.

772   Hubbard, Clarence T. "Home Utensils in Glass." ANTIQUES JOUR-
NAL 21 (June 1966): 14-16.

A brief article that points out the range of practical objects
made in glass in addition to the widely collected bottles and
vases. Candleholders and other items are discussed and illustrated.

773   JOURNAL OF GLASS STUDIES. Corning, N.Y.: Corning Museum of
Glass, 1959-- . Annual.

Although this journal treats the subject of glass throughout the
world and historically, many of its articles are concerned with
developments in the United States.

774   Knittle, Rhea M. EARLY AMERICAN GLASS. New York: Century
Co., 1927. Reprint. Garden City, N.Y.: Garden City Publishing
Co., 1948. 496 p. Illus. Bibliog., pp. 449-53.

A well-written general history of American glass from the colonial era through the middle of the nineteenth century. After
the first chapter provides a background for the understanding
of glass, its properties, and the techniques used in its creation, individual chapters trace the developments and cover
each important firm.

775   Lanmon, Dwight P.; Brill, Robert H.; and Reilly, George J. "Some
Blown 'Three-Mold' Suspicions Confirmed." JOURNAL OF GLASS
STUDIES 15 (1973): 143-73.

A major analytical, technical, and scientific study in evalua-
tion of suspected forgeries of earlier, much-sought-after Mutzer
glass. Includes a catalog of objects related to the Mutzer
group.

776   Lee, Ruth W. ANTIQUE FAKES AND REPRODUCTIONS. Northboro,
      Mass.: Privately printed, 1950. xviii, 117 p. 166 illus.

      American glass is the vehicle for this book, the best of those
      which contrast real with fake decorative art objects. Fakes
      are not only discussed, but illustrations match real and phony
      objects. An education in itself.

777   Lindsey, Bessie M. AMERICAN HISTORICAL GLASS. Rutland, Vt.:
      Charles E. Tuttle Co., 1966. xxviii, 541 p. 532 illus.

      An easy-to-follow popular survey of American glass from the
      colonial period through the date of publication. Large pres-
      entation and commemorative pieces are highlighted throughout
      both text and illustrations.

778   McClinton, Katharine M. AMERICAN GLASS. American Arts Library.
      Cleveland: World Publishing Co., 1950. 64 p. Illus. Bibliog.,
      p. 64.

      A popular survey of American glass from the colonial period
      into the twentieth century. Clearly written and with good
      illustrations.

779   McKearin, George S., and McKearin, Helen. AMERICAN GLASS.
      Rev. ed. New York: Crown Publishers, 1971. xvi, 634 p. 2,000
      illus. 1,000 drawings. Bibliog., pp. 615-617.

      Revised and brought up-to-date, this remains the major one-
      volume study of the subject. Chapters 1 through 3 provide
      a historical overview of the field and its early history in this
      country. Other chapters are devoted to the history and products
      of major glass-producing companies, and a few deal with spe-
      cific products: pictorial and historical flasks, pattern molded
      bottles, fancy wares, and others.

780   _____. TWO HUNDRED YEARS OF AMERICAN BLOWN GLASS. 6th
      ed. New York: Crown Publishers, 1966. 382 p. 105 illus. (18 in
      color). Bibliog.

      Carefully researched chapters on the periods in the history of
      American blown glass through the middle of the twentieth cen-
      tury. The plates are fully described, the important generic
      qualities are discussed, and each provenance, when known, is
      provided.

781   McKearin, Helen. EARLY AMERICAN GLASS. New York: Parke-
      Bernet Galleries, 1940. 112 p. Illus.

      The sale catalog of this important collection of South Jersey,
      New York State, New England, and Midwest glass belonging
      to Mrs. Frederick S. Fish.

782   McQuade, Arthur J. ILLUSTRATED GUIDE--EARLY AMERICAN GLASS. Portland, Maine: Portland Lithographic Co., 1969. 71 p. Illus.

        A handbook for the collector; includes a number of European items.

783   Marsh, Tracy H. THE AMERICAN STORY RECORDED IN GLASS. Minneapolis: Privately printed, 1962. xxix, 450 p. 410 illus. Bibliog., pp. 441-42.

        Takes many selected topics throughout American history that have been the inspiration for making glass objects decorated with symbols and messages of the events. Text is overly anecdotal and illustrations are of poor quality, but the volume does present the wide variety of commemorative work, especially on bottles, flasks, and plates.

784   Maust, Don, ed. BOTTLE AND GLASS HANDBOOK. Uniontown, Pa.: E.G. Warman, 1956. 158 p. Illus.

        A popular guide for collectors. Includes a brief history of American glassmaking and highlights variety of colors and shapes.

785   Northend, Mary H. AMERICAN GLASS. New York: Dodd, Mead and Co., 1927. xviii, 209 p. Illus.

        An old but still useful survey of the history of glassmaking in America from Jamestown through the early twentieth century. Individual chapters on the various glass objects: cups, plates, table glass, candlesticks and lamps.

786   Papert, Emma. THE ILLUSTRATED GUIDE TO AMERICAN GLASS. New York: Hawthorn Books, 1972. ix, 289 p. 266 illus. Bibliog., pp. 267-71.

        Provides a history of the American glass craft, European influences, and cultural forces that shaped it. Changes in forms, styles, and technology are discussed and examples of work in each era are illustrated. Of interest to the general reader and collector.

787   Revi, Albert C. SPINNING WHEEL'S COLLECTABLE GLASS. Hanover, Pa.: Spinning Wheel, 1974. 160 p. Illus.

        A collection of articles from thirty years of the magazine SPINNING WHEEL. Includes articles on art, blown, cut, Deco, and modern glass.

788 Schwartz, Marvin D. COLLECTOR'S GUIDE TO ANTIQUE AMERICAN GLASS. Garden City, N.Y.: Doubleday and Co., 1969. 150 p. Illus.

> Presents material on glass and techniques in general and European background as a basis for examining the variety of American glass technique and products. Covers the colonial period through the early twentieth century.

789 Smith, Ray W. "Ancient Influences in American Glass." NEW ENGLAND GALAXY, Winter 1965, pp. 44–51.

> Discusses both form and technology. Comparative illustrations help point out the relationship between American works and their antecedents.

790 Spillman, Jane S. "American Glass, An Overview." GLASS ART 4, no. 1 (January 1976): 12–19.

> An easy-to-follow article-length survey of American glass from Jamestown through the revival of glassblowing at the Toledo Museum in 1963. Introduces the major styles, forms, and companies.

791 _____. "Glasses with American Views." JOURNAL OF GLASS STUDIES 19 (1977): 134–46.

> Discusses three groups of glasses: those with views of Philadelphia; Americo-Bohemian type; and several miscellaneous ones. Explores the question of whether they were made in Europe or the United States.

792 Van Tassel, Valentine. AMERICAN GLASS. New York: M. Barrows and Co., 1950. 191 p. 74 illus.

> A popular guide for beginning collectors of glass, this volume nonetheless includes carefully written information on techniques and decoration of glassmaking, covering the early years through the beginning of the twentieth century.

793 Watkins, Lura W. AMERICAN GLASS AND GLASS MAKING. New York: Chanticleer Press, 1950. 104 p. 55 color illus. Line drawings. Bibliog.

> A clearly written history of glassmaking in the United States from Jamestown to the present. Excellent illustrations are a balance to the sometimes technically difficult text. A good introduction to the field. Also lists major public collections of American glass.

GEOGRAPHICAL STUDIES OF GLASS MANUFACTURE

794 Baker, Henry. "Archeological Investigations at Fort Cooper, Inverness, Florida." BUREAU OF HISTORIC SITES AND PROPERTIES, BULLETIN 5 (1976): 21-45.

A discussion of the findings in a nineteenth-century trash dump. Bottle fragments, window glass, and various other glass pieces. Suggests that highly developed glass manufacturing existed in the area.

795 Bining, William. "The Glass Industry of Western Pennsylvania, 1797-1857." WESTERN PENNSYLVANIA HISTORICAL MAGAZINE 19 (December 1936): 255-268.

Concentrates on the large glass houses around Pittsburgh, through the great era of mechanical glass production.

796 Bishop, James W. THE GLASS INDUSTRY OF ALLEGANY COUNTY, MARYLAND. Cumberland, Md.: Privately printed, 1968. 94 p. Illus. Bibliog.

Traces the history of glass manufacture in the area and compares individual pieces to mainstream examples. Good illustrations and careful reliance on documentary evidence.

797 Bole, Robert D., and Walton, Edward H., Jr. THE GLASSBORO STORY, 1779-1964. York, Pa.: Maple Press Co., 1964. xii, 337 p. Illus.

The town and immediate vicinity of Glassboro as a center of glass manufacturing since the time of the Revolution. Discusses the way glass was made and examines the styles.

798 Bond, Marcelle. THE BEAUTY OF ALBANY GLASS, 1893-1902. Berne, Ind.: Publishers Printing House, 1977. 125 p. Illus.

A history of glassmaking in Albany, Indiana, and the place of its production in the larger glass arena. Illustrations of a few identifiable pieces.

799 Brothers, A. Stanley. "Early Glassmaking in California." GLASS INDUSTRY 33 (May 1952): 253-70.

A succinct survey on nineteenth-century attempts at developing glassmaking in various parts of the state. Illustrates some of the products of the area and discusses the problems encountered in developing the industry.

800 Brown, James A., ed. THE ZIMMERMAN SITE--REPORT ON EXCAVATIONS AT THE GRAND VILLAGE OF KASKASKIA, LA SALLE

COUNTY, ILLINOIS. Springfield: Illinois State Museum, 1961.
86 p. Illus.

An archeological report on findings at an old Indian site,
which contains information on glass beads used in trade there.

801 Cresthull, Paul. "Bottle Rim Types Found in Maryland." MARYLAND
ARCHEOLOGY 4, no. 2 (September 1968): 38-54; 5, no. 1 (March
1969): 19-28.

A thorough analysis and identification of rims, which enable
both collector and scholar to judge probable creators of most
Maryland-area bottles. Illustrations provide suitable comparisons.

802 DiBartolomeo, Robert E. "19th Century Eastern Ohio Glass Factories."
SPINNING WHEEL 27, no. 8 (October 1971): 16-19; 27, no. 9
(November 1971): 24-28.

The rise of mechanical devices helped the growth of the glass
industry in the area of Bridgeport, Ohio. Illustrations of some
documented work from the area and notes on their importance.

803 Dunn, Jean W. "Glass--Lancaster and Lockport, N.Y." ADVEN-
TURES IN WESTERN NEW YORK HISTORY 17, no. 1 (1971): 1-20.

A general historical overview of the rise, development, and
decline of glass manufacturing in western New York. Illustrations of several local products.

804 Evers, Jo. STANDARD CUT GLASS VALUE GUIDE. Paducah, Ky.:
Collector Books, 1975. 155 p. Illus.

Two thousand illustrations of American cut glass, referenced
by design and manufacturer. A collector's guide.

805 Harrington, Jean C. A TRYAL OF GLASSE: THE STORY OF GLASS-
MAKING AT JAMESTOWN. Richmond, Va.: Dietz Press, 1972.
55 p. Illus.

Documents the existence of glassblowing manufacture as early
as the first decade of the sixteenth century. Reconstructs the
probable range of work produced during the brief period of
the colonies' existence. A revision of his GLASSMAKING
AT JAMESTOWN--AMERICA'S FIRST INDUSTRY (1952).

806 Innes, Lowell. EARLY GLASS OF THE PITTSBURGH DISTRICT. Pittsburgh, Pa.: Carnegie Museum, 1949. 56 p. Illus.

The catalog of the first major exhibition of nineteenth-century
Pittsburgh glass. Traces the changes of style and production

American Glass

in relation to both taste and technology. Good illustrations.

807 _____. "New Hampshire Glass Exhibition at the Currier." NA-
TIONAL ANTIQUES REVIEW 2 (March 1971): 24-30.

An illustrated article that reviews the New Hampshire glass
exhibited at the Currier Gallery of Art. Discusses the major
nineteenth-century firms.

808 _____. PITTSBURGH GLASS 1797-1891: A HISTORY AND GUIDE
FOR COLLECTORS. Boston: Houghton Mifflin Co., 1976. xix,
522 p. 524 illus. (12 in color). Bibliog., pp. 489-94.

Traces the early developments in preblown glass at the end of
the eighteenth century through the various developments to
art glass at the end of the nineteenth, when nine individual
Pittsburgh firms merged with others and became the United
States Glass Company. Part 1 covers history and part 2 presents chapters on the various types and patterns of glass:
Many useful illustrations. An appendix lists important patents.

809 Jefferson, Josephine. WHEELING GLASS. Mt. Vernon, Ohio: Guide
Publishing Co., 1947. 86 p. 16 illus.

Traces and discusses the 125 years of glass manufacture in the
town of Wheeling. Also useful in understanding early glassmaking in general. Careful documentation.

810 Johnson, Virgil S. MILLVILLE GLASS: THE EARLY DAYS. Millville,
N.J.: Delaware Bay Trading Co., 1971. 128 p. Illus.

The history of the glass industry in the area, with illustrations
of both identified and attributable pieces.

811 Keyes, Fenton. "The Springs: Glass Houses and Bottles of Saratoga
Springs, N.Y." NEW YORK HISTORY 38, no. 2 (1957): 212-23.

The history of the glass industry in the area, with illustrations
of representative types of glass objects created there.

812 Lanman, Dwight P. "The Baltimore Glass Trade, 1780-1820." WIN-
TERTHUR PORTFOLIO 5 (1969): 15-48.

A discussion of the development of a glass industry during the
difficult years of strong British domination and competition.
Illustrates documented pieces from Baltimore.

813 Lippert, Catherine. GREENTOWN GLASS. Indianapolis, Ind.: Indianapolis Museum of Art, 1975. 43 p. Illus. Bibliog.

146

An exhibition catalog covering the work of the late nineteenth-century firms active in the Greentown, Indiana, area.
History of the Indiana Tumbler and Goblet Company, National
Glass Company, and others. Illustrations of a variety of conventional and specialty colored glass.

814   Lyman, Susan E. "The Albany Glass Works and Some of Their Records." NEW YORK HISTORICAL SOCIETY QUARTERLY BULLETIN
26, no. 3 (July 1942): 55-61.

An illustrated article that outlines the history of glassmaking
in the Albany area and documents the extent of the Albany
Glass Works' activity.

815   Measell, Brenda, and Measell, James. A GUIDE TO REPRODUCTIONS
OF GREENTOWN GLASS. Tulsa, Okla.: Delos L. Hill, 1974.
37 p. Illus.

Provides sources of illustrations of this popular glassware. Includes some illustrations of typical pieces.

816   Murray, Melvin L. HISTORY OF FOSTORIA, OHIO GLASS 1887-
1920. Fostoria, Ohio: Privately printed, 1977. 57 p. Illus.
Bibliog.

A brief history of one of the small Ohio factories whose work
is known only to glass buffs. Illustrates the typical Fostoria
products and explains the reason for its decline.

817   Pepper, Adeline. THE GLASS GAFFERS OF NEW JERSEY AND THEIR
CREATIONS, 1739-1970. New York: Charles Scribner's Sons, 1971.
320 p. 237 illus. (19 in color). Bibliog., pp. 316-20.

Discusses the history of glassblowing in New Jersey, a major
center for that form, and provides information on individual
companies and the various types of glass products. Some data
on cut glass are included.

818   Pyne Press. PENNSYLVANIA GLASSWARE, 1870-1904. Princeton,
N.J.: 1972. 156 p. Illus. Bibliog.

The editors of Pyne Press pulled together the gamut of Pennsylvania glass objects, from flasks and tankards to stemware and
cut-glass bowls. Profusely illustrated and includes plates from
catalogs of major firms and line drawings. Contains a list of
holdings in major collections.

819   Righter, Miriam. IOWA CITY GLASS. Iowa City, Iowa: Privately
printed, 1963. 55 p. Illus. Bibliog.

An introduction to the little-known work of the Iowa City
Flint Glass Manufacturing Company. Based on organized documentation and illustrates the products they made.

820 Rosenblum, Beatrice. HANDBOOK GUIDE TO ORANGE COUNTY
BOTTLES. Middletown, N.Y.: T. Emmett Henderson, 1974. 228 p.
Illus.

Careful research and study produced a well-organized and useful collector's guidebook.

821 Schneider, Norris F. ZANESVILLE GLASS. Zanesville, Ohio: Privately printed, 1956. 28 p.

A compilation of several articles on Zanesville glass found in
the Zanesville SUNDAY TIMES SIGNAL between July and
September 1956.

822 Smith, Dudley C. "Sand and Firewood." CATALYST 50, no. 7
(September 1965): 198–202.

Describes glassmaking in New Jersey. Illustrations of identified pieces.

823 Smith, Miles A. "Zanesville Glass." JOURNAL OF GLASS STUDIES
2 (1960): 113–23.

A technical and visual analysis of the glass produced in early
nineteenth-century Zanesville. Emphasizes the use of the
molds and questions of color and size.

824 Toulouse, Julian H. "The Bottle Makers of the Pacific Northwest."
WESTERN COLLECTOR 8, no. 7 (July 1970): 32–37; 8, no. 8 (August 1970): 32–37.

A brief general history of bottle manufacture in the area with
illustrations of the more common types.

825 Wall, A.J. "Proposals for Establishing a Glass Works in the City of
New York in 1752." NEW YORK HISTORICAL SOCIETY QUARTERLY
BULLETIN 10, no. 2 (April 1926): 95–99.

Explores how boosterism and manufacturing combined to develop the glass industry as early as the middle of the eighteenth century. Puts the effort in historical perspective.

826 White, Margaret. "Glass Makers of New Jersey." NEW JERSEY
HISTORICAL SOCIETY, PROCEEDINGS 73, no. 3 (July 1955): 209–
13.

A brief history of glassmaking in the state first identified with a large-scale industry and many small firms. Illustrations of some of the identified south Jersey type of glass.

827   Wilson, Kenneth M. GLASS IN NEW ENGLAND. Sturbridge, Mass.: Old Sturbridge Village, 1969. 47 p. Illus.

A brief introduction to glassmaking from the colonial period through the nineteenth century. One of a series of guides based on the pieces in the Old Sturbridge Village collection.

828   _____. NEW ENGLAND GLASS AND GLASSMAKING. New York: Thomas Y. Crowell Co., 1972. 401 p. 365 illus. Bibliog., pp. 385-86.

A detailed scholarly study of the history and development of the glass industry in New England. Historical roots are traced and individual chapters on window, bottle, and flint glasshouses provide documentation on developments in each area. Individual firms are covered. A chronological list of New England glasshouses and products is also provided.

SPECIFIC PERIODS

829   Anderton, Johana G. THE GLASS RAINBOW--DEPRESSION GLASS, ITS ORIGINS AND PATTERNS. North Kansas City, Mo.: Trojan Press, 1969. 112 p. Illus.

An introduction to Depression-period glass for the beginning collector. Categorized by types, patterns, and colors.

830   Bird, George O. "A Note on Some Design Relationships in Nineteenth Century American Glass." JOURNAL OF GLASS STUDIES 5 (1963): 133-36.

Is interested in and attempts to document the relationships between certain utilitarian glass objects and counterparts in ceramic. Emphasis on works relating to Meissen porcelain.

831   Conway, Darlyne. DEPRESSION ERA GLASS HANDBOOK AND PRICING GUIDE. San Angelo, Tex.: Educator Books, 1971. 168 p. Illus.

A collector's guidebook for identifying and pricing the popular Depression-era type of glass. Illustrations and descriptive information are useful.

832   Florence, Gene. THE COLLECTORS ENCYCLOPEDIA OF DEPRESSION GLASS. 3d ed. Paducah, Ky.: Collectors Books, 1977. 208 p. Approx. 1,800 illus.

Illustrates and lists the work of the various firms producing
the cheaply made glass which has become so popular among
collectors. Classifications include size, colors, and patterns.

833   GLASS ART MAGAZINE 1 (December 1973): 4–46.

The entire December issue is devoted to the history and illustration of contemporary glassworkers and their products.

834   Horton, Christine. "Cut Glass--1880–1915." AMERICAN ANTIQUES
4, no. 5 (May 1976): 34–40.

Discusses developments in the manufacture of cut glass during
the period of its widest popularity and greatest success. Historical material on individual firms and some illustrations.

835   Klamkin, Marian. THE COLLECTORS GUIDE TO DEPRESSION GLASS.
New York: Hawthorn Books, 1973. 225 p. Illus. Bibliog., p. 214.

Essentially for the collector and interested layman, this volume documents the history and manufacture of machine-made
inexpensive table and gift ware of the 1920s through World
War II. Discussion on the work of several major firms, varieties of products, and various collector-related chapters.

836   _____. THE DEPRESSION GLASS COLLECTOR'S PRICE GUIDE. New
York: Hawthorn Books, 1974. xii, 102 p. Illus.

Prices of thousands of Depression-glass objects, arranged by
objects, size and color.

837   Lee, Ruth W. NINETEENTH CENTURY ART GLASS. New York:
M. Barrows and Co., 1952. 128 p. 42 illus.

An introduction to art glass, concentrating on the end of the
nineteenth century. Each chapter is devoted to a particular
kind, Amberina, Burmese, Pomona, and others, as created
and often copied by the various rival firms. Discusses variations and changes in taste in an easy-flowing conversational
text.

838   _____. VICTORIAN GLASS: SPECIALTIES OF THE NINETEENTH
CENTURY. Northboro, Mass.: Privately printed, 1944. xxix, 608 p.
Illus.

A handbook survey of American pressed and patterned glass
oriented to the collector.

839   Lorrain, Dessamae. "An Archeologists Guide to Nineteenth Century
American Glass." HISTORICAL ARCHEOLOGY 11, no. 1 (1968):
35–44.

Where American glass was manufactured and the early technology of its creation.

840 Myers, Jeol P. "New American Glass." CRAFT HORIZONS 36, no. 4 (August 1976): 36-41.

Trends in hand glasswork, both traditional and sculptural.

841 Revi, Albert C. AMERICAN ART NOUVEAU GLASS. Camden, N.J.: Thomas Nelson and Sons, 1968. 476 p. 561 illus. (some in color). Bibliog., pp. 463-64.

The introduction provides a brief overview of the influences and sources of Art Nouveau. Individual chapters cover the history, work, and specific qualities of the major firms of Tiffany Glass Company, Douglas Nash Corporation, Steuben Glass Works, and others. Each appendix is a catalog of a major manufacturer of glass. Excellent descriptive entries for the many illustrations.

842 Stout, Sandra M. DEPRESSION GLASS PRICE GUIDE. Des Moines, Iowa: Wallace-Homestead Book Co., 1972. 191 p. Illus.

A collector's handbook to shapes, sizes, and prices.

843 Toledo Museum of Art. AMERICAN GLASS NOW. Toledo: 1972. 64 p. 44 illus. (8 in color).

An exhibition of 171 contemporary glass objects, both utilitarian and purely sculptural. Excellent illustrations of many of the works accompany the informational catalog entries. Biographies of the craftsmen and a statement of purpose by Robert Phillips and Paul Smith.

844 Weatherman, Hazel M. COLORED GLASSWARE OF THE DEPRESSION ERA. Springfield, Mo.: Glass Books, 1970. 239 p. Illus.

A collector's guide to types and patterns. A supplement, "Price Trends," indicates 1970 values and the differences in appeal of various pieces.

845 _____. COLORED GLASSWARE OF THE DEPRESSION ERA: BOOK 2. Springfield, Mo.: Privately printed, 1974. 400 p. Illus.

The second part of a comprehensive collector's guide to the inexpensive Depression-period glass much sought after contemporary collectors. Reference to appeal of the various colors and sizes of pieces.

846 Wisconsin, University of. DIRECTIONS IN CONTEMPORARY GLASS

1976: NATIONAL GLASS INVITATIONAL III. Madison: 1976.
16 p. Illus.

Biographical information on each of the glass workers, discussion of their approaches, and illustrations of exhibited work.

SPECIFIC TYPES OF GLASS

847 Barret, Richard C. BLOWN AND PRESSED GLASS. Bennington, Vt.: Privately printed, 1966. 30 p. Illus. (some in color).

A guidebook for collectors. Good color plates.

848 _____. IDENTIFICATION OF AMERICAN ART GLASS. Manchester, Vt.: Forward's Color Productions, 1964. 30 p. Illus. (some in color).

Illustrations of art glass objects in the collection of the Bennington Museum. A guide for collectors.

849 _____. POPULAR AMERICAN RUBY-STAINED PATTERN GLASS. Bennington, Vt.: Privately printed, 1968. 31 p. Color plates.

A guide to the popular red or ruby pattern glass collected by Mr. and Mrs. C. Kenneth Vincent. Very good color plates.

850 Belknap, E. McCamly. MILK GLASS. New York: Crown Publishers, 1959. xiv, 327 p. Illus. Bibliog., p. xiv.

An illustrated guide for collectors, with an introduction by George S. McKearin, describing the developments in glass manufacture in America.

851 Boger, Bill, and Boger, Louise. AMERICAN BRILLIANT CUT GLASS. New York: Crown Publishers, 1977. 183 p. Illus.

A thorough, popular survey of the widely made late nineteenth- and early twentieth-century glass. Good illustrations.

852 Consentino, Geraldine, and Stewart, Regina. CARNIVAL GLASS: A GUIDE FOR THE BEGINNING COLLECTOR. New York: Golden Press, 1976. 128 p. Illus.

Informs the aspiring collector about the history of carnival glass and illustrates examples of favorite forms, sizes, and colors. Tips on pricing and scarcity.

853 Daniel, Dorothy. CUT AND ENGRAVED GLASS. New York: M. Barrows and Co., 1950. 441 p. 165 illus. Bibliog.

Covers all glass decorated by moving wheel, dividing American products into three periods: Stiegel, national, and Brilliant (late 1880s on). Each type of glass form is discussed and illustrated with photographs, line drawings, and catalog cuts.

854 Darr, Patrick T. A GUIDE TO ART AND PATTERN GLASS. Springfield, Mass.: Pilgrim House, 1960. 120 p. Illus.

A popular collector's guide, listing companies, patterns, color, and so on.

855 DiBartolomeo, Robert, ed. AMERICAN GLASS FROM THE PAGES OF ANTIQUES II. PRESSED AND CUT. Princeton, N.J.: Pyne Press, 1974. 216 p. Illus.

A series of articles culled from the magazine ANTIQUES, all dealing with pressed and cut glass.

856 Doubles, Malcolm R. PATTERN GLASS CHECKLIST. Richmond, Va.: Privately printed, 1959. 100 p.

A collector's guide, with all known patterns by the identifiable manufacturers.

857 Ehrhardt, Alpha L. CUT GLASS PRICE GUIDE TO 1500 PIECES. Kansas City, Mo.: Heart of America, 1973. 120 p. Illus. Bibliog.

Illustrates 1,500 pieces of American cut glass and establishes current prices for the collector.

858 Fitzpatrick, Paul. "American Cut Glass at the 1876 Centennial." ANTIQUES JOURNAL 30, no. 12 (December 1975): 20-23 +.

Cut glass was very popular by the time of the Centennial and major manufacturers exhibited their wares. The author documents which work was actually shown and illustrates select pieces.

859 Freeman, Larry [Graydon La Verne]. IRIDESCENT GLASS. Watkins Glen, N.Y.: Century House, 1956. 128 p. Illus.

After a brief introduction to the method of producing iridescent glass, chapters are devoted to several major firms associated with the manufacture. Discusses stylistic and technical differences and contains some information of interest to collectors.

860 Hartung, Marion T. OPALESCENT PATTERN GLASS. Des Moines, Iowa: Wallace-Homestead, 1971. 112 p.

A collector's guide and checklist.

861   House, Caurtman G. RELATIVE VALUES OF EARLY AMERICAN PAT-
       TERNED GLASS; A CHECKLIST WITH PRICES COVERING MORE THAN
       7,000 FORMS IN THE 200 MOST POPULAR DESIGNS OF AMERICAN
       PRESSED GLASS. Albion, N.Y.: Eddy Press, 1944. 155 p.

       Still useful for the number of identified forms at that date to
       check prices against.

862   Kamm, Minnie E. TWO HUNDRED PATTERN GLASS PITCHERS. De-
       troit: Motschall Co., 1952. 188 p. Illus.

       Line drawings of American pattern glass pitchers. Aimed at
       the specialized collector.

863   Kamm, Minnie E., and Wood, Serry. THE KAMM-WOOD ENCY-
       CLOPEDIA OF ANTIQUE PATTERN GLASS. 2 vols. Watkins Glen,
       N.Y.: Century House, 1961. 670 p. Illus.

       A handbook of American pattern glass of the nineteenth cen-
       tury. Good illustrations of a variety of popular patterns.
       Consolidates eight pattern glass-pitcher books by the authors.

864   Klamkin, Marian. THE COLLECTORS GUIDE TO CARNIVAL GLASS.
       New York: Hawthorn, 1976. 230 p. Illus. (32 in color).

       The inexpensive colored glass available through carnivals in
       America are classified and illustrated.

865   Lee, Ruth W. EARLY AMERICAN PRESSED GLASS. 19th ed. North-
       boro, Mass.: Privately printed, 1946. xxix, 666 p. 190 illus.

       An old volume, with some omissions, but the most encyclope-
       dic coverage of the subject. Every conceivable type of ob-
       ject or set has been included and most are illustrated. Pro-
       vides standardized names for the available pressed-glass pat-
       terns in the era, 1840-80, and the means of identifying them.

866   Metz, Alice H. EARLY AMERICAN PATTERN GLASS. 2 vols. West-
       field, N.Y.: Guide Publishing Co., 1958. 243 p. Illus.

       A collector's guide to the identification and pricing of some
       1,500 individual patterns. Provides terminology, references
       to standard texts, and indexing, in addition to photographs of
       the various patterns.

867   Pearson, J. Michael, and Pearson, Dorothy T. AMERICAN CUT
       GLASS FOR THE DISCRIMINATING COLLECTOR. 2 vols. New York:
       Vantage Press, 1965, 1969. Vol. 1: 204 p. 600 illus. Vol. 2:
       190 p. Illus.

The collector is presented with descriptions and illustrations of a wide variety of patterns and forms by major and minor glass firms.

868   _____. ENCYCLOPEDIA OF AMERICAN CUT AND ENGRAVED GLASS, 1880-1917. Vol. 1: GEOMETRIC CONCEPTIONS. Miami Beach, Fla.: Privately printed, 1975. 272 p. Illus.

This volume is concerned with geometric patterning. Information about firms, varieties of glass, and standard and unusual patterns.

869   _____. ENCYCLOPEDIA OF AMERICAN CUT AND ENGRAVED GLASS, 1800-1917. Vol. 2: REALISTIC PATTERNS. Miami Beach, Fla.: Privately printed, 1977. 172 p. Illus.

A supplement to volume 1 (see above), and concerned with items other than geometric forms, especially the delicate, engraved glass of the late nineteenth century.

870   Presznick, Rose M. CARNIVAL AND IRIDESCENT GLASS PRICE GUIDE. Lodi, Ohio: Privately printed, 1966. 96 p. Illus.

A listing of known companies and prices by size, shape, and color. Out-of-date prices, but useful organization and illustrations.

871   _____. CARNIVAL AND IRIDESCENT GLASS WITH PRICE GUIDE-BOOK II. Lodi, Ohio: Privately printed, 1960. 79 p. Illus.

Additional items classified, priced, and illustrated.

872   Revi, Albert C[hristian]. AMERICAN CUT AND ENGRAVED GLASS. Camden, N.J.: Thomas Nelson and Sons, 1965. xix, 497 p. 205 illus. Bibliog., p. 471.

Traces the history of cut glassware in America, describing the products of the known companies. Explores stylistic developments from early imitative work, through the great era at the end of the nineteenth century, to the decline in the second quarter of the twentieth century. Chapters are devoted to each cut-glass manufacturing region. Line drawings supplement photographs of actual works.

873   _____. AMERICAN PRESSED GLASS AND FIGURE BOTTLES. New York: Thomas Nelson and Sons, 1964. xi, 446 p. Illus. Bibliog., p. 413.

Historical material on the development of the pressed-glass

industry in this country is followed by sections on each documented glass company active in the field. The varieties of
each firm's work are outlined and illustrated. Documentation
on designs and patents is provided, and a special chapter is
concerned with figure bottles in America.

874 _____. "Introduction." In CUT GLASS CATALOG (1881-1921).
New York: Dorflinger and Sons, 1921. Reprint. Introduction by
Albert C. Revi. Hanover, Pa.: Everybody's Press, 1970. Unpaged.
45 plates.

A reprint of the catalog illustrating the work of this important
manufacturer of cut glass, covering the years 1881-1921.

875 Rose, James H. THE STORY OF AMERICAN PRESSED GLASS OF THE
LACY PERIOD. 1825-1850. Corning, N.Y.: Corning Museum of
Glass, 1954. 163 p. 31 illus.

A catalog of an exhibition which provided a comprehensive
survey of both the styles and designs of the brief period during which this glass was in vogue. Contains 942 catalog entries, each described with measurements provided. A small
section on European Lacy glass is included in the catalog.

876 Schwartz, Marvin D., comp. AMERICAN GLASS FROM THE PAGES
OF ANTIQUES. Vol. 1: BLOWN AND MOLDED. Princeton, N.J.:
Pyne Press, 1974. 224 p. Illus.

Selected articles on American glass taken from the magazine
ANTIQUES.

877 Seigfried, Ellen. AMERICAN BLOWN GLASS, 1765-1865. Athens:
Ohio University, 1966. 12 p. Illus.

The catalog of an exhibition of the important collection of
blown glass owned by Earl and Ellen Seigfried.

878 Steuben Glass. A SELECTION OF ENGRAVED CRYSTAL. New York:
1961. Unpaged. 39 illus.

Thirty-nine clear and excellent plates of major pieces of the
firm's engraved crystal. Includes a selection of biographical
sketches of artists and designers whose work is illustrated.

879 Warman, Edwin G. AMERICAN CUT GLASS. 1954. Reissue. Uniontown, Pa.: Privately printed, 1970. 118 p. Illus.

Illustrates and classifies the cut-glass patterns of the era from
1895 to 1915. Includes information on all the major manufacturers of cut glass.

880 Wiener, Herbert, and Lipkowitz, Freda. RARITIES IN AMERICAN CUT GLASS. Houston: Collectors House of Books, 1975. 294 p. Illus.

An illustrated guidebook for collectors. Covers the works of both the major and little-known producers around the turn of the century.

881 Willey, Harold E. HEISEY'S CUT HANDMADE GLASSWARE. Newark, Ohio: Privately printed, 1974. 147 p. Illus.

A collector's guide to one part of this firm's extremely popular output.

GLASS FORMS

882 Adams, John P. BOTTLE COLLECTING IN NEW ENGLAND--A GUIDE TO DIGGING, IDENTIFICATION, AND PRICING. Somersworth: New Hampshire Publishing Co., 1969. 120 p. Illus.

A collector's guidebook. Though the prices are quickly out-of-date, they serve as a guide to the relative scarcity of the various forms.

883 Archer, Margaret, and Archer, Douglas. GLASS CANDLESTICKS. Paducah, Ky.: Collector Books, 1975. 100 p. Illus.

A history and survey of variations of a once popular form. Illustrates and discusses the work of attributed and identified items.

884 Baldwin, Joseph K. A COLLECTOR'S GUIDE TO PATENT AND PROPRIETARY MEDICINE BOTTLES OF THE NINETEENTH CENTURY. New York: Thomas Nelson and Sons, 1970. 540 p. Line drawings.

Illustrates the wide range of shapes and subjects of the decoration on these widely available bottles. The line drawings are useful for identification purposes.

885 Bradley, Stephen H.; Ryan, C.S.; and Ryan, R.R. HEISEY STEMWARE. Newark, Ohio: Spencer Walker Press, 1976. 238 p. Illus.

A collectors guide to the popular glassware of the Heisey firm.

886 Brooks Memorial Art Gallery. THE LATE HIRAM NORCROSS COLLECTION OF CHESTNUT BOTTLES. Memphis: 1966. 23 p. Plates.

The catalog of an exhibition of this unusually specific collection. Good illustrations document the diversity of the form.

887   Butler, Joseph T. CANDLE-HOLDERS IN AMERICA, 1650–1900. New York: Crown Publishers, 1967. xiv, 178 p. 136 illus. Bibliog., pp. 170–72.

> A guide to the candleholders in common usage, whether American or European. Useful as a general work on material culture or for the serious collector.

888   Cloak, Evelyn C. GLASS PAPERWEIGHTS OF THE BERGSTROM ART CENTER. New York: Crown Publishers, 1969. 196 p. Color illus. Bibliog., pp. 173–90.

> A catalog of the glass paperweights of many countries; the section on American work is particularly well illustrated. Contains an extremely detailed bibliography.

889   Freeman, Larry (Graydon La Verne). GRAND OLD AMERICAN BOTTLES. Watkins Glen, N.Y.: Century House, 1964. 808 p. Illus.

> Oriented to the collector, this volume contains innumerable descriptive listings of bottles covering the entire range of American history. Illustrates representative types of designs and imagery.

890   Goodell, Donald. THE AMERICAN BOTTLE COLLECTOR'S PRICE GUIDE. Rutland, Vt.: Charles E. Tuttle Co., 1973. 144 p. Illus.

> The best organized and consistently accurate of the many "collectors guides" relating to American bottles. Although prices are quickly out-of-date, the guide is still useful for looking up the various companies, shapes, and sizes.

891   Kendrick, Grace. THE MOUTH BLOWN BOTTLE. Kallon, Nev.: Privately printed, 1967. viii, 200 p. Illus. Bibliog., pp. 195–96.

> The bottle, in all its varieties of size, shape, and color, is classified, discussed historically, and illustrated. For the specialist collector.

892   Ketchum, William C., Jr. A TREASURY OF AMERICAN BOTTLES. New York: Bobbs-Merrill Co., 1975. 224 p. 174 illus. (52 in color).

> The history of American glass from the early seventeenth century into the twentieth century. Detailed discussion of the bottle styles used for a wide variety of beverages, medicines, and foods.

893   Lechler, Doris, and O'Neill, Virginia. A COLLECTOR'S GUIDE TO CHILDREN'S GLASS DISHES. Nashville: T. Nelson, 1976. Unpaged. 200 illus.

Discusses and illustrates the popular glass dishes of the late nineteenth and early twentieth centuries.

894 Lee, Ruth W., and Rose, James H. AMERICAN GLASS CUP PLATES. Rev. ed. Northboro, Mass.: Privately printed, 1971. xviii, 445 p. 131 illus.

After a brief introduction to these cups plates, an exhaustive history of stylistic change and a checklist is provided for each period. Colors and dimensions for the objects created by each company are provided. A rigorous but down-to-earth treatment of the subject.

895 McKearin, Helen. THE STORY OF AMERICAN HISTORICAL FLASKS. Corning, N.Y.: Corning Museum of Glass, 1953. 70 p. Illus.

The pocket-sized catalog of an exhibition of a popular glass form of the middle of the nineteenth century. Discusses and illustrates such popular subjects as George Washington and other historical figures, Masonic symbols, and patriotic imagery.

896 McMurray, Charles. COLLECTOR'S GUIDE OF FLASKS AND BOTTLES. Dayton, Ohio: Privately printed, 1927. 170 p. Illus.

One of the early guides by a dedicated collector. Illustrates and explores the variety of shapes, sizes, and decorations of this basic American form.

897 Melvin, Jean S. AMERICAN GLASS PAPER WEIGHTS AND THEIR MAKERS. New York: Thomas Nelson and Sons, 1970. 287 p. Illus.

The most accurate and comprehensive survey of these widely collected glass items. Abundant illustrations show the range of design of the form.

898 Neal, L.W., and Neal, D.B. PRESSED GLASS SALT DISHES OF THE LACY PERIOD, 1825-1850. Philadelphia: Privately printed, 1962. Unpaged. 465 illus.

Essentially a set of large line drawings, done to scale, of hundreds of examples of these objects. Covers both identified American pieces and unidentified and unknown European ones. Classified by design for easy reference and indicates color as well. A valuable reference tool on a neglected field of glass.

899 Neustadt, Egon. THE LAMPS OF TIFFANY. New York: Fairfield Press, 1970. 224 p. 300 illus. (234 in color).

Based on the collection of the Neustadt Museum of Tiffany

American Glass

Art; documents the scope and variety of the designs and colors in the Tiffany lamps. Many excellent color plates.

900 Owens, Richard. CARNIVAL GLASS TUMBLERS. La Habra, Calif.: Privately printed, 1973. 128 p. 240 illus.

A collector's guide to popular forms of carnival glass.

901 Putnam, H.G. BOTTLE IDENTIFICATION. Jamestown, Calif.: Privately printed, 1965. Unpaged. Illus.

A survey of the commercial bottles of the second half of the nineteenth century in the United States. Some illustrations of representative types.

902 Rose, James H. "18th Century Enameled Beakers with English Inscriptions." JOURNAL OF GLASS STUDIES 1 (1959): 94–102.

Discusses the difficulty of classifying peasant enamel glass and makes a case that these pieces are American rather than European in origin. Also addresses the question of the market for these works.

903 Thompson, J.H. BITTERS BOTTLES. Watkins Glen, N.Y.: Century House, 1947. 100 p. Illus.

Illustrated checklist with notes on relative availability of items on the marketplace. Index of patent bottles. A poorly designed work, but useful.

904 Van Rensselaer, Stephen. EARLY AMERICAN BOTTLES AND FLASKS. Petersborough, N.H.: Transcript Printing Co., 1926. Reprint (2 vols. in 1). Ann Arbor, Mich.: John Edwards, 1975. Vol. 1: xi, 244 p. Illus. Vol. 2: 314 p. Illus.

The first part of this pioneering study presents us with a history of the creation and manufacture of glass in the United States. The second part is essentially an illustrated checklist of types of bottles and flasks. Illustrates variations on both well-known types and each period, including unusual pieces.

905 Walbridge, William S. AMERICAN BOTTLES OLD AND NEW. Toledo: Owens Bottle Co., 1920. 113 p. Illus.

A brief introductory chapter on early developments in glass manufacture in America is followed by a survey of the range and scope of flask and bottle making until about 1860. The subsequent half of the book is devoted to a history and description of the Owen Bottle Machine and other technological developments in glassmaking and manufacture.

906 Watson, Richard. BITTERS BOTTLES. New York: Thomas Nelson and Sons, 1965. 304 p. Illus.

Aimed at the bottle collector. Lists and illustrates the works of all known producers of bitters bottles, tracking shapes, sizes, and colors.

907 Wilson, Bill, and Wilson, Betty. SPIRIT BOTTLES OF THE OLD WEST. Santa Rosa, Calif.: Privately printed, 1967. 181 p. Illus. Bibliog.

Spirit bottles in a variety of sizes, shapes, and colors have been collected for many years, and this compact illustrated collector's guide places them for easy reference.

INDIVIDUAL GLASSMAKERS AND GLASS COMPANIES

908 Allison, Grace. KEMPLE GLASS WORKS, 1945-1970. Costa Mesa, Calif.: Rainbow Review Glass Journal, 1977. 14 p. Illus.

The production and history of a contemporary western firm.

909 Amayo, Mario. TIFFANY GLASS. New York: Walker and Co., 1967. 84 p. Illus. (2 in color).

A brief but well-written history of Tiffany glass with biographical material included. Oriented to the collector, but a useful primer for anyone wishing to learn about the artist and his work.

910 Amherst College. THE ART OF SIDNEY WAUGH. Amherst, Mass.: 1964. Unpaged. Illus.

An exhibition catalog which discusses and illustrates the work of a major glass designer. Biographical information.

911 Avila, George C. THE PAIRPOINT GLASS STORY. Mattapoisett, Mass.: Reynolds-DeWalt Printing Co., 1968. xiv, 238 p. 227 illus. (8 in color).

Outlines the growth and history of this Massachusetts firm. Includes hundreds of illustrations of the full range of their products during almost one hundred years of manufacture.

912 Bakewell, Mary E. "The Bakewell Glass Factory." CARNEGIE MAGAZINE 21 (July 1947): 35-40.

Written by a member of one of the great Pittsburgh glass dynasties, it provides a brief history of the firm.

913 Bennett, Harold, and Bennett, Judy. THE CAMBRIDGE GLASS BOOK. Des Moines, Iowa: Wallace-Homestead, 1970. 96 p. Illus. (some in color).

> A history and appreciation of Cambridge glass, with description and illustrations of specific pieces. Checklist of forms and colors.

914 _____, eds. CATALOGUE OF TABLE GLASSWARE, LAMPS, BARWARE AND NOVELTIES MANUFACTURED BY THE CAMBRIDGE GLASS COMPANY. Cambridge, Ohio: Cambridge Glass Co., 1909. Reprint. Cambridge, Ohio: Cambridge Glass Museum, 1976. 106 p. Illus.

> This reprinted catalog illustrates the hundreds of items produced by this important manufacturer of common household glass. Useful for both the collector and scholar who wish to identify or attribute works of the period.

915 Bing, Samuel. ARTISTIC AMERICA: TIFFANY GLASS, AND ART NOUVEAU. Cambridge: MIT Press, 1970. xiv, 260 p. Illus. (some in color).

> The greatest part of this work is translated from his LA CULTURE ARTISTIQUE EN AMERIQUE (1970). Individual essays on the three subjects in the title.

916 Bones, Frances. THE BOOK OF DUNCAN GLASS. Des Moines, Iowa: Wallace-Homestead Book Co., 1973. 117 p. Illus.

> A brief history of the Duncan Company and its successor firms, from the founding in 1865 through the closing in 1956. Both black and white and color illustrations of major pieces and descriptions of each item. The second half of the book is a reprint of the DUNCAN AND MILLER CATALOG of about 1900. The only real source for identification purposes.

917 BOSTON AND SANDWICH GLASS CO., BOSTON. Boston: 1874. Reprint. Wellesley Hills, Mass.: Lee Publications, 1968. Unpaged. Illus.

> A photograph reproduction of the richly illustrated 1874 catalog of the company's products.

918 Buechner, Thomas S. FREDERICK CARDER--HIS LIFE AND WORK. Corning, N.Y.: Corning Museum of Glass, 1952. 23 p. Illus.

> An exhibition catalog which presents Carder's work for his own Steuben glass firm until 1935 and the work of his subsequent association with Corning. Biographical material and good illustrations.

919   Chipman, Frank W. THE ROMANCE OF OLD SANDWICH GLASS.
      Sandwich, Mass.: Sandwich Publishing Co., 1932. 158 p. Illus.

      The rise, success, and end of Deming Jarves's Sandwich glass
      factory, a major glass producer for over sixty years. Chapters
      on molds, patterns, types, and colored glass. Discusses some
      collections and provides a dictionary of 158 "authenticated
      patterns and types of old Sandwich Glass."

920   Clarke, Mary S. THE GLASS PHOENIX. New York: Viking Press,
      1969. 272 p.

      A historical novel based on the famous Boston and Sandwich
      Glass Company.

921   Cudd, Viola N. HEISEY GLASSWARE. Brenham, Tex.: Hermann
      Print Shop, 1969. 242 p. 195 illus.

      A popular guidebook and checklist to a wide sampling of the
      prodigious Heisey output.

922   Daniel, Dorothy. "The First Glasshouse West of the Alleghenies."
      WESTERN PENNSYLVANIA HISTORICAL MAGAZINE 32 (September-
      December 1949): 97-113.

      The founding and history of the Pittsburgh Glass Works on the
      Monongahela River. Suggests a date of founding as 1795.

923   [DeKay, Charles.] THE ART WORK OF LOUIS C. TIFFANY. New
      York: Doubleday Page, 1914. xxxii, 91 p. Illus. (some in color).

      A commissioned biography and study of the man and his paint-
      ing, glass, and ceramic ware. Lacks some of the information
      subsequently discovered by research, but has the immediacy of
      personal contact with the artist and those close to him.

924   Delaplaine, Edward S. JOHN FREDERICK AMELUNG, MARYLAND
      GLASSMAKER. Frederick, Md.: Frederick Newspost, 1971. 16 p.
      Illus.

      A general introduction to the life and work of the pioneering
      glassmaker of New Bremen, Maryland. Illustrations of known
      pieces.

925   Ericson, Eric E. A GUIDE TO COLORED STEUBEN GLASS 1903-1933.
      Loveland, Colo.: Lithographic Press, 1963. 113 p. Illus.

      A well-illustrated guide for the collector. Introduces various
      Carder specialties and presents information on colors and sizes.

926   Evans, Wendy. "Dominick Labino." CRAFTS 10 (September-October 1974): 36-39.

Explores the pioneering and contemporary work of one of the principal glassmaking specialists of modern times. Illustrates the evolution of his work into more contemporary forms.

927   Everhart Museum. DORFLINGER GLASS. Scranton, Pa.: 1960. 20 p. Illus.

The catalog of an exhibition of the work of the Dorflinger firm. Individual works have complete descriptive entries.

928   Farrar, Estelle S. H.P. SINCLAIRE, JR. GLASSMAKER. 2 vols. Garden City, N.Y.: Privately printed, 1974, 1975. Vol. 1: vii, 152 p. Illus. Bibliog., pp. 145-46. Vol. 2: viii, 119 p. Illus. (some in color). Bibliog., p. 114.

The two-volume history of Sinclaire's glass and company. Traces the development of his engraved glass and discusses his place in the evolution of the Corning glass industry. Includes hundreds of line drawings of various shaped objects and their measurements.

929   Fauster, Carl U. "Libbey Color-Cased Glass, Circa 1920." GLASS 1, no. 2 (January-February 1973): 30-34.

An introduction to the twentieth-century glass concept of color casing as adapted by Libbey. Illustrates the rich effects of the process.

930   _____. "Libbey Cut Glass Exhibit: St. Louis World's Fair 1904." JOURNAL OF GLASS STUDIES 19 (1977): 160-68.

Discusses the collection sponsored by the St. Louis firm of Mermod and Jaccard, a major dealer in Libbey glass. Also explains the rise of interest in cut glass and illustrates some major examples.

931   Field, Anne E. ON THE TRAIL OF STODDARD GLASS. Dublin, N.H.: Wm. L. Bauhan, 1975. 110 p. 40 plates. Bibliog.

Discusses the major New Hampshire glasshouses of the nineteenth century (1842-1873), South Stoddard Glass, New Granite Glass Works, and others, and identifies their work for the collector.

932   Foley, Jasena R. "The Ontario Glass Manufacturing Company." JOURNAL OF GLASS STUDIES 6 (1964): 136-47.

The founding in 1810, subsequent evolution, and final decay

of the New York company in 1847 are recorded, and an
analysis of the reasons for failure are provided. Includes illustrations of a few pieces of glass clearly identified with the
firm.

933 Gardner, Paul V. THE GLASS OF FREDERICK CARDER. New York:
Crown Publishers, 1971. vi, 373 p. 389 illus. (84 in color).
Bibliog., pp. 363-64.

The life and work of the founder of the Steuben Glass Works.
Individual chapters on the special color technique for which
the designer was known, on architectural glass, and on his
use of the lost wax process. Over half the volume is an illustrated catalog with hundreds of line drawings included.
The comprehensive work on Carder's contributions to American
glass.

934 Gardner, Paul V., and Plaut, James S. STEUBEN: SEVENTY YEARS
OF AMERICAN GLASSMAKING. New York: Praeger, 1974. 172 p.
96 illus. (16 in color).

The catalog of an exhibition organized by the Toledo Museum,
divided into two main parts: the Carder years (1903-1932)
and the Houghton years (1933-1973). The catalog includes
dimensions, name and mark of designer, and a descriptive paragraph. Useful analysis of the relation of each piece to larger
trends in the decorative arts.

935 Hart, Joey. "The Dorflinger Glass Story." ANTIQUES JOURNAL
23 (May 1968): 8-13.

A general article introducing the reader to one of the major
turn-of-the-century manufacturers of fine cut glass. Illustrations of museum-quality pieces.

936 Heiges, George L. HENRY WILLIAM STIEGEL AND HIS ASSOCIATES;
A STORY OF EARLY AMERICAN INDUSTRY. Manheim, Pa.: N.p.,
1948. 227 p. Illus.

The history of the pioneering glass manufacturer known as
Baron Stiegel, who developed one of the earliest glass industries, yet died penniless.

937 Herrick, Ruth. GREENTOWN GLASS. Grand Rapids, Mich.: Privately printed, 1959. 40 p. 36 plates. Bibliog., pp. 37-40.

The history of the Indiana Tumbler and Goblet Company of
Greentown, Indiana (1894-1903), and the work produced there.
Also covers reproductions and imitations. Each section deals
with one of the successful patterns or colors. Many small but
useable illustrations. Valuable for the collector of this glassware.

938   Hotchkiss, John F. CARDER'S STEUBEN GLASS: HANDBOOK AND
       PRICE GUIDE. Pittsford, N.Y.: Hotchkiss House, 1972. 119 p.
       Illus.

       This collector's handbook provides information on the identifi-
       cation and classification of Carder's Steuben glass from 1903
       to 1932, the year the catalog was originally printed. In-
       cludes the retail price and estimated 1971 current values.
       The latter is out-of-date, but the guide and illustrations are
       still useful.

939   Hume, Ivor N. "Archaelogical Excavations on the Site of John Fred-
       erick Amelung's New Bremen Glass Manufactory 1962-1963." JOUR-
       NAL OF GLASS STUDIES 18 (1976): 137-214.

       A major scholarly report of the process, discoveries, and con-
       clusions concerning Amelung's factory and its production. De-
       tailed documentation of the fregments of objects found there,
       and analysis of origins.

940   Hunter, Frederick W. STIEGEL GLASS. New York: Dover, 1950.
       xxii, 308 p. 169 illus. (16 in color).

       Includes biographical material on Steigel (1729-1785), a de-
       scription and discussion of his work and techniques, and illus-
       trations of his pitchers, glasses, bottles, and other forms.

941   Illinois Glass Company. ILLUSTRATED CATALOGUE AND PRICE LIST.
       Chicago: 1903. Reprint. Watkins Glen, N.Y.: Century House,
       1968. Unpaged. Illus.

       Useful reprint of the catalog illustrates the specific types and
       styles of the firm's production.

942   Irwin, Frederick T. THE STORY OF SANDWICH GLASS AND GLASS
       WORKERS. Manchester, N.H.: Granite State Press, 1926. 99 p.
       Illus.

       A brief history of the firm with chapters on pressed, cut, en-
       graved, and painted glass produced there. Includes informa-
       tion on the major figures associated with the company.

943   Jarves, Deming. REMINISCENCES OF GLASSMAKING. New York:
       Hurd and Houghton, 1865. iv, 116 p. Illus.

       Autobiography and reminiscences of an important founder of
       the major New England glassmaking operation, Boston and
       Sandwich Glass Company.

944   Keefe, John W. LIBBEY GLASS: A TRADITION OF 150 YEARS,
       1818-1968. Toledo: Toledo Museum of Art, 1968. 69 p. Illus.
       Bibliog., p. 69.

The catalog of an exhibition of 224 items of the New England Glass Company and its successors. A history of the firm is given, followed by a chapter on techniques of creating blown, pressed, cut, and engraved glass. A well-documented and beautifully photographed exhibition catalog.

945 Koch, Robert. LOUIS C. TIFFANY, REBEL IN GLASS. New York: Crown Publishers, 1964. 246 p. Illus. (some in color). Bibliog., pp. 222-33.

The standard modern biography of the artist-designer. Supersedes the one DeKay wrote during Tiffany's lifetime (see no. 923). The development of his career and study of his work is combined with a biographical narrative. Contains many photographs and documentary evidence of his career.

946 _____. LOUIS C. TIFFANY'S ART GLASS. New York: Crown Publishers, 1977. ix, 134 p. 128 illus. (some in color). Bibliog., pp. 41-42.

Includes selected statements by Tiffany, sections on various art glass products, and a carefully organized catalog of selected and representative work. A good introduction to Tiffany's work in glass.

947 _____. LOUIS C. TIFFANY'S GLASS-BRONZES-LAMPS. New York: Crown Publishers, 1971. 208 p. Illus.

A guide for collectors. Greater concentration on the glass and illustrates a number of otherwise unpublished pieces.

948 Kramer, LeRoy. JOHANN BALTASAR KRAMER: PIONEER AMERICAN GLASS BLOWER. Chicago: Privately printed, 1934. 62 p. Illus.

Although primarily a genealogical record of the Kramer family, there is some useful material on the first Kramer, his work, and his association with both Stiegel and Amelung.

949 Krause, Gail. THE ENCYCLOPEDIA OF DUNCAN GLASS. Hicksville, N.Y.: Exposition Press, 1976. 223 p. Illus.

Guide to the production and style changes of some ninety years of handmade production beginning in 1865. Illustrates a wide variety of the firm's products.

950 Lanahan, Jack. FREDERICK CARDER AND HIS STEUBEN GLASS, 1903-1933. West Nyack, N.Y.: Dexter Press, 1968. 35 p. Colored plates.

A popular history of the life and work of the founder and

principal designer of the Steuben glassworks. Good plates illustrate Carder's love of color.

951 Lane, Lyman. A RARE COLLECTION OF KEENE AND STODDARD GLASS. Manchester, Vt.: Forward's Color Productions, 1970. 44 p. 20 color illus.

Documented and carefully described works of the New Hampshire firm of Keene and Stoddard. Good-quality color illustrations with text on the back of each.

952 Lanmon, Dwight P., and Palmer, Arlene M. "John Frederick Amelung and the New Bremen Glass Manufacturing." JOURNAL OF GLASS STUDIES 18 (1976): 13-136.

A careful and scholarly biography of Amelung and a criticism of his contributions to glassmaking. Includes a detailed descriptive and analytical catalog, and an appendix documenting Amelung's land transactions in New Bremen area.

953 Lee, Ruth W. SANDWICH GLASS: HISTORY OF THE BOSTON AND SANDWICH GLASS COMPANY. Northboro, Mass.: Privately printed, 1947. xxvii, 590 p. 227 illus.

A continuous narrative of the history of the company is followed by chapters on individual glass forms made by the company. The descriptive text provides information about taste and scarcity of forms. Continuous references to the book's many illustrations.

954 Lewis, Albert. "The Gifts of the Gods, an Interview with Paul Marioni." GLASS 6, no. 2 (October 1978): 24-41.

Examines the decorative pieces, the stained glass, and the functional objects of a young experimental glassmaker in San Francisco. Dialogue with the artist on the sources and inspirations of his methods and imagery.

955 Libbey Glass Co. THE LIBBEY GLASS COMPANY, CUT GLASS. Toledo: 1896. Reprint. Toledo: Antique and Historic Glass Foundation, 1968. 25 p. Illus.

This catalog is devoted to the cut glass produced by the Libbey Glass Company at the end of the nineteenth century.

956 Littleton, Harvey. "Littleton Remembers." GLASS ART 4, no. 1 (January 1976): 20-31.

The founder of the American renaissance in glassmaking traces the history of his involvement and the steps in developing interest in and support for the craft in this country.

957 Lohmann, Watson M. WHITNEY GLASS WORKS, ILLUSTRATED CAT-
ALOG AND PRICE LIST, WITH HISTORICAL NOTES, 1900-1918. Pit-
man, N.J.: Privately printed, 1972. 64 p. Illus. Bibliog., p. 28.

An introduction to the history and works of an early twentieth-century descendant in the original glassblowing area of
Glassboro, N.J. Includes a reprint of the firm's 1904 catalog.

958 McLaughlin, Warner. "A History of the Bedford Crown Glass Works
at Bedford, Clinton County, N.Y." NEW YORK HISTORY 26
(1945): 368-76.

A brief historical documentation of a little-known glassmaking
center.

959 Measell, James. GLASS WAS HIS LIFE: THE STORY OF JACOB
ROSENTHAL. Greentown, Ind.: National Greentown Glass Association, 1976. 17 p. Illus.

The life and work of a glass chemist who worked for the Indiana Tumbler and Goblet Company and invented a "chocolate
glass."

960 Miller, Everett R., and Miller, Addie R. THE NEW MARTINSVILLE
GLASS STORY. Marietta, Ohio: Richardson Publishing Co., 1972.
62 p. 550 illus. (some in color).

The history of a small but important nineteenth-century Ohio
firm, with illustrations of known products and primary documentation.

961 Miller, Robert W. MARY GREGORY AND HER GLASS. Des Moines,
Iowa: Wallace-Homestead, 1972. 32 p. 34 illus. (color).

Discusses and illustrates Mary Gregory's work for the Boston
and Sandwich Glass Company during the decade from 1870 to
1880.

962 Oland, Dwight D. "The New Bremen Glass Manufactory." MARY-
LAND HISTORICAL MAGAZINE 68 (Fall 1973): 255-72.

A well-written general article describing the history and work
of the expatriate pioneer glassmaker. Illustrates some of the
major engraved presentation pieces.

963 Padgett, Leonard E. PAIRPOINT GLASS. Clinton, Md.: Privately
printed, 1968. 23 p. Illus.

A pioneering study and introduction to the history and work of
the Massachusetts-based Pairpoint Company from 1869 until its

American Glass

end in 1958. Illustrations of pieces attributable to the firm.

964 Palmer, Arlene. THE BALTIMORE GLASS WORKS. Baltimore: Maryland Archeological Society, 1971. Unpaged. Illus.

The history of the founding and early developments of the Baltimore Glass Works. Discusses both products and technology involved in the glassmaking process.

965 _____. THE WISTERBURGH GLASSWORKS: THE BEGINNING OF JERSEY GLASSMAKING. Alloway, N.J.: Alloway Township Bicentennial Committee, 1976. 38 p. Illus.

A general history of Wister's experiments in glassmaking in the area, with reference to the glass of the times. Illustrated with examples from the period.

966 Pattinson, Lillian G. "The Union Glass Company of Somerville, Massachusetts." NATIONAL EARLY AMERICAN GLASS CLUB, BULLETIN 60 (December 1961): 4-7.

Introduction to the almost unknown work of a smaller Massachusetts company.

967 Plaut, James S. STEUBEN GLASS. 3d ed. New York: Dover, 1972. xi, 111 p. 72 illus.

A picture book with excellent photographs of many of Steuben's best-known pieces of the past forty-five years. Includes a brief commentary on the processes at Steuben and a list of major exhibitions of the firm's glass.

968 Rockwell, Robert F. FREDERICK CARDER AND HIS STEUBEN GLASS, 1903-1933. West Nyack, N.Y.: Dexter Press, 1966. 32 p. Illus.

An account of the origin, development, and end of the Steuben Glass Company under the direction of Carder. Illustrates and discusses the color creations and special forms for which the firm became famous.

969 Rogers, Millard F., Jr. "A Glass Recipe Book of the New England Glass Company." JOURNAL OF GLASS STUDIES 7 (1965): 107-13.

The actual formula and description for preparation of glass from one of the great and successful nineteenth-century American glass manufacturers.

970 _____. THE NEW ENGLAND GLASS COMPANY, 1818-1888. Toledo: Toledo Museum of Art, 1963. 80 p. Illus. Bibliog., p. 80.

The catalog of the first major exhibition of the production of
the New England Glass Company, with 273 items listed, described, and documented. Many are illustrated and a useful,
though brief, history of the company is provided.

971 Smith, Don E. FINDLAY PATTERN GLASS. Fostoria, Ohio: Privately
printed, 1970. x, 132 p. Illus.

A brief history of a local glassmaking manufactory. Includes
information and illustrations of its products. Based on primary
archival research of the community.

972 Spillman, Jane S. "Robert L. Hewes, Glass Manufacturer." JOUR-
NAL OF GLASS STUDIES 12 (1970): 140-48.

Traces Hewes's various attempts to develop glass manufacturing
on a solid footing in New Hampshire, Boston, and East Hartford, Connecticut.

973 Spillman, Jane S., and Farrar, Estelle S. THE CUT AND ENGRAVED
GLASS OF CORNING, 1868-1940. Corning, New York: Corning
Museum of Glass, 1977. 104 p. 123 illus. Bibliog.

This exhibition catalogs the bowls, vases, and other cut and
engraved glass objects made in Corning during its years of
greatest activity. The text provides technical background on
production, discusses the historical material, and lists both the
craftsmen and firms involved in glass production. The single
most important study in the field.

974 Steuben Glass. STEUBEN CRYSTAL. New York: 1956. Unpaged.
38 illus.

A handsome set of plates of some of the finest designer and
presentation pieces produced by the firm. Of particular interest are the pieces designed by such artists as Matisse and
Tchelitchew.

975 Stout, Sandra M. THE COMPLETE BOOK OF McKEE GLASS. North
Kansas City, Mo.: Trojan Press, 1972. 456 p. 150 illus.

A classified catalog of the production of a firm noted for Depression-era practical wares, which were created to compete
with ceramic industry products. Illustrations help the collector identify probable McKee pieces.

976 Swan, Frank H. THE PORTLAND GLASS COMPANY. Providence,
R.I.: Roger Williams Press, 1939. Revised and enlarged by Marion
Dana. Des Moines, Iowa: Wallace-Homestead, 1974. 106 p. Illus.

A good general history of the company. Provides selected
items from its range of glass products without being a total
catalog.

977 Torgersen, Dorothy, and Tozour, Rachel. "Cape May Glass Company."
CAPE MAY COUNTY MAGAZINE OF HISTORY AND GENEOLOGY
5, no. 6 (June 1960): 239-52.

History and documentation of a once flourishing glass company.
Illustrations of surviving pieces.

978 Watkins, Lura W. CAMBRIDGE GLASS, 1818-1888. Rev. ed. Boston: Little, Brown, 1953. xxi, 199 p. Illus.

Valuable guide to this often ignored glass production. Orig-
inally considered indispensable, it remains the standard volume
on the New England Glass Company.

979 _____. "Pressed Glass of the New England Glass Company--An Early
Catalogue at the Corning Museum." JOURNAL OF GLASS STUDIES
12 (1970): 149-64.

An old illustrated catalog of the New England Glass Company
presents an opportunity to see the variety of pressed-glass
products made by the firm.

980 Waugh, Sidney. STEUBEN GLASS. New York: Steuben Glass, 1947.
45 p. Illus.

Brief introductions to the variety of traditional techniques used
by the firm. The rest of the volume is devoted to large,
high-quality reproductions of representative pieces designed
and produced by Steuben craftsmen.

981 Weatherman, Hazel M. FOSTORIA: ITS FIRST 50 YEARS. Springfield, Mo.: Privately printed, 1972. 320 p. 450 illus. (8 in color).

The output of the West Virginia firm during the late 1880s
through the early 1940s. Illustration of 450 patterns.

982 Weinstein, Joel. "A Conversation with Harvey Littleton." GLASS
ART 1, no. 4 (August 1973): 42-47.

The leader of the American revival in glassmaking talks about
his work and the state of the art.

983 Welker, Mary; Welker, Lyle; Welker, Lynn. THE CAMBRIDGE GLASS
COMPANY CATALOG. New Concord, Ohio: Privately printed,
1970. 120 p. Illus.

Useful for both collectors and scholars.

984 Williams, Lenore W. SANDWICH GLASS. Bridgeport, Conn.: Park City Engraving Co., 1922. 113 p. 26 plates.

A technically oriented handbook for collectors to help identify and classify Sandwich glass. Includes a brief history of the Sandwich Glass Works, and provides a note on reproductions of the original glass.

985 Wilson, Kenneth M. "The Glastenbury Glass Factory Company." JOURNAL OF GLASS STUDIES 5 (1963): 117-32.

A report of the excavation of the company's site near Hartford, Connecticut. Includes a history of the founding of the company in 1816 and its existence until the middle of the 1820s. Illustrations of a few surviving pieces and documentation of the factory's technological equipment.

986 _____. "The Mt. Washington Glass Company and Its English Relationships in the Late Nineteenth Century." GLASS CLUB BULLETIN 77 (March 1966): 3-7, 10-12.

Illustrations of influences between the American and British work.

987 _____. "Serendipity and an Amelung Tumbler." CONNECTICUT HISTORICAL SOCIETY BULLETIN 29 (April 1964): 33-41.

The discovery of a bona fide work of the New Bremen Glass Factory of Amelung. Explains the rarity of authentic, dateable pieces.

988 Winter, Henry. THE DYNASTY OF LOUIS COMFORT TIFFANY. Boston: Privately printed, 1971. 280 p. Illus.

A personal, eclectic view of Tiffany and his production, which attempts to deal with analysis, a catalog, an appreciation, and documentation. Somewhat garbled but worth browsing through for enlightening tidbits. Poor to very good illustrations.

989 Wittman, Otto. DOMINICK LABINO: A DECADE OF GLASS CRAFTSMANSHIP, 1964-1974. Toledo: Toledo Museum of Art, 1974. Unpaged. Illus.

An exhibition catalog which documents and illustrates the work of one of the principal figures in the growth of glassmaking in America since 1963. Individual works and the changes in form are discussed.

990 Wray, T. Donham. "The Stained Glass of Frank Lloyd Wright, and

His Theory of Ornament." GLASS 6, no. 2 (October 1978): 8-23.

Quotes Wright on his glass and ornamental work and analyzes the stained glass in terms of the artist's definitions. Traces the evolution of his work.

Chapter 10

AMERICAN METALWORK

More Americans used pewter than silver objects through the colonial period and well into the nineteenth century, but relatively little pewter or information about the alloy metal survives. This is due to its twin features of reusability and lesser comparative cost. Pewter was also made with expensive molds, thus insuring less change in style. Gold was only available to the wealthiest, and was never a very popular ingredient in functional objects. Silver remains the most written about and best documented among the metals, as is attested to by the proportion of writings on the various metals.

GENERAL HISTORIES OF AMERICAN GOLD AND SILVER

991 Bohan, Peter [J.]; Ebendorf, Bob; and Raleigh, Henry P. PRECIOUS METALS: THE AMERICAN TRADITION IN GOLD AND SILVER. Coral Gables, Fla.: Lowe Art Museum, 1976. 79 p. Illus. Bibliog., pp. 74-77.

> The catalog of an exhibition of work from the colonial period to the present. Brief biographies, essays on contemporary historical material, and clear illustrations, supplemented by a categorized bibliography. One of the few works to carry both gold and silver up to the present.

992 Cornelius, Charles O. "Early American Jewelry." METROPOLITAN MUSEUM OF ART BULLETIN 21 (April 1926): 99-101.

> Plates illustrating several high-quality early pieces.

993 Kovel, Ralph M., and Kovel, Terry H. A DICTIONARY OF AMERICAN SILVER, PEWTER, AND SILVER PLATE. New York: Crown Publishers, 1961. 352 p. Bibliog., pp. 345-47.

> An exhaustive dictionary of known silversmiths and pewterers in this country since colonial times. A basic source. Smiths' marks and initials used as marking devices are provided through line drawings.

994 Luck, Robert, and Smith, Paul. FORMS IN METAL: 275 YEARS OF
METALSMITHING IN AMERICA. New York: Finch College Museum
of Art, Museum of Contemporary Crafts. 36 p. 70 illus. Bibliog.

The catalog of a joint exhibition of some 275 objects, presented chronologically. Major divisions are 1700 to 1940 and
1940 to 1975. Discussion of function of objects in American
society and stylistic influences from abroad. Both everyday
ware and one-of-a-kind precious objects are illustrated, cataloged, and described.

995 Phillips, John M. "Gold and Silver in the Prentis Collection." NEW
YORK HISTORICAL SOCIETY QUARTERLY 35, no. 2 (1951): 165–69.

Various American pieces in this important collection with illustrations.

996 Thorn, C. Jordan. THE HANDBOOK OF AMERICAN SILVER AND
PEWTER MARKS. New York: Tudor, 1950. xii, 289 p. 310 illus.

Lists about 3,500 marks, all produced in the text, with information about dates and locations of the smiths they document,
and a brief technical history of metal smithing. A handy one-
volume reference tool.

AMERICAN GOLD

997 Bober, Harry. THE GOLDSMITH: AN EXHIBITION OF WORK BY
CONTEMPORARY ARTISTS-CRAFTSMEN OF NORTH AMERICAN.
Washington, D.C.: National Collection of Fine Arts, Smithsonian In-
stitution, 1974. 50 p. 39 illus.

The catalog of an exhibition of 164 pieces produced for a
national competition. The essay traces the history of the ancient craft to present. Catalog entries include information on
the mixed media of materials used by contemporary craftsmen.
Clear illustration.

998 Bohan, Peter J. AMERICAN GOLD. 1700–1860. New Haven: Yale
University Art Gallery, 1963. 52 p. Illus. Bibliog., p. 51–52.

This monograph is based on a loan exhibition at Yale University in 1963. Documents how gold work, often in tandem
with silver, was used for both secular and religious presentation pieces, and provides biographical information on major
practitioners.

999 Hipkiss, Edwin J. "Some Early American Objects of Gold." BULLE-
TIN OF THE MUSEUM OF FINE ARTS, BOSTON 44 (October 1946):
63–66.

This brief article discusses and illustrates a snuff box by Jacob Hurd and a couple of freedom boxes, presented to honor prominent men.

GENERAL AND PERIOD SURVEYS OF AMERICAN SILVER

1000 Andrus, Vincent D. EARLY AMERICAN SILVER, A PICTURE BOOK. New York: Metropolitan Museum of Art, 1955. 32 p. Illus.

One of a series of introductions to the various American crafts. Some information on periods and styles.

1001 "Articles on Silver in 'Antiques.'" ANTIQUES 51 (January 1947): 61-62, 64, 66.

A list of dozens of articles from 1922 to 1947, with many on American silversmiths and their work.

1002 Avery, Clara L. AMERICAN SILVER OF THE XVII AND XVIII CENTURIES: A STUDY BASED ON THE CLEARWATER COLLECTION. New York: Metropolitan Museum of Art, 1920. clix, 216 p. Illus. Bibliog., pp. clv-clix.

A survey of colonial and early federal period silver based on the over 500 pieces in the Clearwater Collection. Short chapters on individual forms combine historical and stylistic information and precede the chronological catalog of the collection. Descriptions, measurements, exhibition records, and illustrations. Still a basic tool.

1003 _____. "Colonial Silver in the Collection of the New York Historical Society." NEW YORK HISTORICAL SOCIETY QUARTERLY BULLETIN 4 (April 1921): 3-12.

Illustrates some of the major examples and lists and describes others in this very important collection.

1004 _____. EARLY AMERICAN SILVER. New York: Century Co., 1930. Reprint. New York: Russell and Russell, 1968. xliv, 378 p. 63 illus. Bibliog., pp. 361-64.

A standard well-illustrated and carefully documented study of the stylistic development and history of types in the colonial and early national periods of our history.

1005 Belden, Bauman L. UNITED STATES WAR MEDALS. New York: American Numismatic Society, 1916. 71 p. 10 illus.

More the product of the manufacturer than the craftsman, this work provides an authoritative chronology and catalog of the medals to date of publication.

1006 Bigelow, Francis H. HISTORIC SILVER OF THE COLONIES AND ITS
MAKERS. New York: Macmillan, 1917. Reprint. New York: Tudor
Publishing Co., 1948. xxiv, 476 p. Illus.

Concentrates on the work of the better-known smiths and those
who signed or marked their work. The illustrated objects have
historical as well as aesthetic value.

1007 Brooklyn Museum. CONTEMPORARY INDUSTRIAL AND HAND-
WROUGHT SILVER. Brooklyn: Brooklyn Institute, 1937. Unpaged.
Illus.

The catalog of an exhibition of primarily twentieth-century
silver pieces. Includes some fine earlier and some non-American examples of the presentation tradition. Includes jewelry
and domestic silverware. Description of manufacturing and
hand shaping techniques in the introductory essay.

1008 Buck, John H. OLD PLATE, ITS MAKERS AND MARKS. New York:
Gorham Manufacturing Co., 1903. 268 p. 82 illus.

A very old but still useful study. Chapters which trace the
silver field up through early American, discussion of forgery,
and "transformations," and a lengthy section on documented
ecclesiastical plates by colony. Various useful indexes relating to European and, primarily, American marks and types.

1009 Buffalo Historical Society. DRINKING VESSELS FROM THE COLLEC-
TION OF THE DARLING FOUNDATION. Buffalo, N.Y.: 1960.
11 p. Plates.

All cups, tankards, and other items, that were made by New
York silversmiths. Adequate illustrations.

1010 Buhler, Kathryn C. AMERICAN SILVER. American Arts Library Series.
Cleveland: World Publishing Co., 1950. 64 p. Illus. Bibliog.,
p. 64.

A brief introduction to American silver by a noted authority.
The series is devoted to introducing various decorative art
forms to the general public.

1011 _____. AMERICAN SILVER, 1655-1825, IN THE MUSEUM OF FINE
ARTS, BOSTON. 2 vols. Greenwich, Conn.: New York Graphic
Society, 1972. xx, 740 p. 650 illus. Bibliog., pp. xv-xx.

A well-documented study and survey of the fine collection in
the museum. Information on each piece, its type, maker,
and provenance is provided. Good illustrations.

1012 _____. COLONIAL SILVERSMITHS, MASTERS AND APPRENTICES. Boston: Museum of Fine Arts, 1956. 98 p. Illus.

Traces the development of the silversmith's art, through the works of both the masters and their followers, with attention to both the famous and the little known. The detailed catalog illustrates the variations in craftsmanship and style.

1013 _____. MASSACHUSETTS SILVER IN THE FRANK L. AND LOUISE C. HARRINGTON COLLECTION. Worcester, Mass.: Barre, 1965. 121 p. Illus.

Full biographical material, excellent histories and descriptions of individual pieces, background and provenance, and high-quality illustrations make this catalog an important reference for seeing and placing some of the finer examples of the silversmith's art. An excellent survey of the range and scope of colonial through federal period works in Massachusetts.

1014 _____. MOUNT VERNON SILVER. Mt. Vernon, Va.: Mount Vernon Ladies Association, 1957. 75 p. 37 illus.

Based on research into Washington's books and invoices, this volume lists the works and names of the smiths, both American and British, patronized by the first president. As the author discusses all the silver forms and general questions of style, this work is a useful introduction to the whole field of American silver.

1015 Buhler, Kathryn C., and Hood, Graham. AMERICAN SILVER IN THE YALE UNIVERSITY ART GALLERY. 2 vols. New Haven: Yale University Press, 1970. Vol. 1: xviii, 344 p. Illus. Bibliog., pp. xv-xvi. Vol. 2: xii, 300 p. Illus.

Each craftsman represented has his works consecutively listed. The catalog entries are fully documented, including the provenance for each object.

1016 Comstock, Helen. "The John Marshall Phillips Collection of Silver." CONNOISSEUR YEAR BOOK (London), 1957, pp. 28-33.

Discusses the Marshall Collection at the Yale University Art Gallery. Descriptions, dating, and analysis of styles and quality.

1017 Crosby, Sylvester S. THE EARLY COINS OF AMERICA; AND THE LAWS GOVERNING THEIR ISSUE. Boston: Privately printed, 1875. Reprint. Ann Arbor, Mich.: Token and Medal Society, 1965. 378 p. Illus.

Many useful illustrations and information about various colonial coins, medals, and tokens. The role of the silversmith in producing objects to external specifications is discussed.

1018 Currier, Ernest M. MARKS OF EARLY AMERICAN SILVERSMITHS. Portland, Maine: Southworth-Athoensen Press, 1938. Reprint. Harrison, N.Y.: R.A. Green, 1970. 179 p. Illus. Bibliog., pp. 172-76.

Includes notes on silver; discusses and illustrates spoon types. The various smiths' marks are documented and illustrated, and a list of New York City silversmiths of the early nineteenth century is provided.

1019 Delieb, Eric. INVESTING IN SILVER. New York: C.N. Potter, 1967. 152 p. Illus. Bibliog., p. 152.

A book for beginning collectors. Many examples, but not all, are of American pieces.

1020 Elwell, Newton W. COLONIAL SILVERWARE OF THE 17TH AND 18TH CENTURIES. Boston: G.H. Polley and Co., 1899. 2 p. 40 plates.

Beautiful large folio plates of candlelabras, communion service, tea sets, and other items.

1021 English Speaking Union. AMERICAN SILVER AND ART TREASURES. London: 1960. 88 p. 31 plates.

An essay on American silver, followed by a catalog arranged by geographical area, a biographical index of smiths, and a well-illustrated set of plates. Interesting as a perspective of of English taste in American work.

1022 Ensko, Stephen G.C. AMERICAN SILVERSMITHS AND THEIR MARKS. New York: Robert Ensko, 1948. 285 p. 193 illus. Bibliog., pp. 28-85.

Brief biographies of silversmiths, good photographs of their best work, and a complete listing of works from 1650 to 1850.

1023 Fales, Martha G. AMERICAN SILVER IN THE HENRY FRANCIS DU PONT WINTERTHUR MUSEUM. Winterthur, Del.: Winterthur Museum, 1958. 171 illus.

The work of eight-six individual silversmiths, primarily from New England, is examined and illustrated. Each of the approximately sixty forms is documented, and detailed provenance is given. Excellent-quality photographs and clear, readable introduction.

1024 _____. EARLY AMERICAN SILVER. Rev. and enl. ed. New York: E.P. Dutton, 1973. 336 p. Illus. Bibliog., pp. 298-313.

Revised and enlarged edition of the 1970 EARLY AMERICAN SILVER FOR THE CAUTIOUS COLLECTOR (see below). Fales's strength is in the discussion of stylistic differences between American pieces and their prototypes.

1025 _____. EARLY AMERICAN SILVER FOR THE CAUTIOUS COLLECTOR. New York: Funk and Wagnalls, 1970. x, 329 p. 226 illus. Bibliog., pp. 303-13.

Written for the collector rather than the scholar, this volume provides sections on stylistic development, both in general and for the specific forms. Discusses regional variations and design sources, and concentrates on connoisseurship features.

1026 Freeman, Graydon L. (Larry). VICTORIAN SILVER; PLATED AND STERLING; HOLLOW AND FLATWARE. Watkins Glen, N.Y.: Century House, 1967. 400 p. Illus. Bibliog.

Covers the entire range of silver production in the United States from 1830 to 1930. One thousand patterns are illustrated in encyclopedic format.

1027 Freeman, Graydon L. (Larry), and Beaumont, Jane. EARLY AMERICAN PLATED SILVER. Rev. ed. Watkins Glen, New York: Century House, 1973. 160 p. Illus.

Written for the collector. The author discusses types, firms that made plated silver, scarcity, and value.

1028 French, Hollis. A SILVER COLLECTORS GLOSSARY AND A LIST OF EARLY AMERICAN SILVERSMITHS AND THEIR MARKS. New York: Walpole Society, 1917. Reprint. New York: Da Capo, 1967. ix, 164 p.

A basic dictionary of the smiths, facsimilies of the marks, and line drawings. Useful information on types of objects, their decoration, and major styles are all covered in the glossary.

1029 Graham, James. EARLY AMERICAN SILVER MARKS. New York: Privately printed, 1936. 81 p. Illus.

A small but accurate dictionary of marks, centered on the eighteenth and the early part of the nineteenth century. The author, a dealer, had limited interest but specific concentration on the period.

1030 Green, Robert A. MARKS OF AMERICAN SILVERSMITHS. Harrison,

N.Y.: Privately printed, 1977. x, 245 p. 300 illus. Some 4,000 drawings. Bibliog., pp. 165–180.

An ambitious undertaking which provides individual chapters on trademarks, updates the standard works by Ensko (see 1022) and Currier (see 1018), contains an index of initialed marks including those of jewelers, watchmakers, and vendors. Introductory material on collecting silver and determining value. The bibliography is annotated.

1031 Hammerslough, Philip H. AMERICAN SILVER COLLECTED BY PHILIP H. HAMMERSLOUGH. 3 vols. (2 supplements). Hartford, Conn.: Privately printed, 1958, 1960, 1965. Unpaged. Illus.

The piece-by-piece catalog of one of the major collections of American silver is compiled by the collector. Excellent descriptions, references, and photographs. One of the great surveys of the work of the silversmith in America.

1032 Hammerslough, Philip H., and Feigenbaum, Rita F. AMERICAN SILVER COLLECTED BY PHILIP H. HAMMERSLOUGH. Hartford, Conn.: Privately printed, 1973. vi, 142 p. Illus.

Detailed catalog of the silver not included in the first three volumes of the Hammerslough collection (see no. 1031). Very high-quality illustrations, and valuable references and comparisons to other known pieces.

1033 Henry Francis du Pont Winterthur Museum. SPANISH, FRENCH, AND ENGLISH TRADITIONS IN THE COLONIAL SILVER OF NORTH AMERICA. Winterthur, Del.: 1968. 109 p. Illus.

A series of papers on the various influences on what is now primarily the area of the United States. Of particular importance are the papers dealing with American church silver.

1034 Hepburn, John M., and Bloomer, Jerry M. MEDALLIC ART OF THE UNITED STATES, 1800–1972. Shreveport, La.: R.W. Norton Art Gallery, 1972. 40 p. 105 illus. Bibliog.

Covers both coins and commemorative medals during the period. A background history traces medals from ancient Greece to the present. Discusses technical processes and illustrates a wide variety of examples.

1035 Hipkiss, Edwin J. THE PHILLIP LEFFINGWELL SPALDING COLLECTION OF EARLY AMERICAN SILVER. Cambridge: Harvard University Press, 1943. 84 p. Illus. Bibliog., pp. 81–84.

The catalog of one of the primary public collections of American silver; one of the best cataloged. Extensive description, documentation, biographical information of known smiths, and references.

1036 Holland, Margaret. SILVER: AN ILLUSTRATED GUIDE TO AMERICAN AND BRITISH SILVER. London: Octopus, 1973. 144 p. Illus.

A well-done general guide to both American and British work of the eighteenth and part of the nineteenth centuries. A chapter on collecting includes illustrations of museum-quality pieces. Entries are arranged by types of objects. Includes a selective guide to marks.

1037 Holloway, H. Maxson. "American Presentation Silver." NEW YORK HISTORICAL SOCIETY QUARTERLY 30 (October 1946): 215-33. Illus.

A broad view, written for the general audience, that illustrates the scope and range of objects and sets which were made both for institutions and in honor of individuals.

1038 Hood, Graham. AMERICAN SILVER: A HISTORY OF STYLE, 1650-1900. New York: Frederick A. Praeger, 1971. 256 p. 286 illus. Bibliog., pp. 247-50.

The introduction discusses the origins and practice of the craft, problems of dating, and manufacturing techniques. The history of style in American silver is traced from the seventeenth-century cups and beakers through the varied products of the end of the nineteenth century. Stylistic considerations and changes include discussion of political, social, and economic factors.

1039 Hornung, Clarence P., ed. A SOURCE BOOK OF ANTIQUES AND JEWELRY DESIGNS, CONTAINING OVER 3800 ENGRAVINGS OF VICTORIAN AMERICANA, INCLUDING JEWELRY, SILVERWARE, CLOCKS, CUTLERY, GLASSWARE, MUSICAL INSTRUMENTS, ETC. New York: G. Braziller, 1968. x, 244 p. Illus.

Essentially a useful picture book, containing designs for silverware, art, metal jewelry, and all sorts of related and unrelated ephemera.

1040 Jones, Edward A. THE OLD SILVER OF AMERICAN CHURCHES. Letchworth, Engl.: Arden Press, 1913. lxxxvii, 566 p. Over 1,000 illus.

Although extremely old, there is little out-of-date in this valuable and magnificently illustrated, oversized volume. Colonial churches are each carefully examined for silver pieces, works are attributed or their documentation is provided, and both description and history of piece and owner are provided.

Available in many good libraries and a must for the study of
ecclesiastic silver.

1041 Kauffman, Henry J. THE COLONIAL SILVERSMITH: HIS TECH-
NIQUES AND HIS PRODUCTS. Camden, N.J.: Thomas Nelson and
Sons, 1969. 176 p. Illus. Bibliog., p. 173.

Chapters on the metal and its general usage, on the process
of the workshop, and on the various products made by the
silversmith of the colonial period.

1042 Kernan, John D. "The Dating of Early American Silver." ART QUAR-
TERLY 25 (Spring 1962): 54-66.

Questions of style related to influences from abroad. Shapes
and regional variations are useful in the process.

1043 Klapthor, Margaret B. "Presentation Pieces in the Museum of History
and Technology." CONTRIBUTORS FROM THE MUSEUM OF HISTORY
AND TECHNOLOGY: PAPERS 47 (1965): 83-107. Illus.

Primarily illustrations of the collection of presentation pieces
eventually donated to or collected by the Smithsonian. More
concerned with the history of the pieces than the aesthetics
or technology.

1044 Langdon, John E. AMERICAN SILVERSMITHS IN BRITISH NORTH
AMERICA, 1776-1800. Toronto: Stinehour Press, 1970. 82 p. Illus.

The silversmiths were so well established in major American
cities that this useful study traces their influence into Canada.

1045 Los Angeles County Museum. EARLY SILVER IN CALIFORNIA COL-
LECTIONS. Los Angeles: 1962. 35 p. Illus.

The catalog of a loan exhibition of both early American and
some old English silver in major California collections. Covers
the whole country with natural weight toward the areas of
greatest manufacture.

1046 McClinton, Katharine [M.]. COLLECTING AMERICAN 19TH CENTURY
SILVER. New York: Charles Scribner's Sons, 1968. viii, 280 p.
Illus. Bibliog., pp. 274-76.

Of greatest use to the collector and connoisseur, this volume
is divided into chapters on the chronological periods and major creations within those periods, and a series of chapters on
special collectables, presentation pieces, swords, church silver and Masonic jewels. Helps any reader become familiar
with basic styles and designs.

1047 Metropolitan Museum of Art. EARLY AMERICAN SILVER, A PICTURE BOOK. New York: 1945. 30 p. Plates.

One of a series of general introductory picture books to promote public understanding of art.

1048 Montgomery, Charles F., and Maxwell, Catherine H. EARLY AMERICAN SILVER: COLLECTORS, COLLECTIONS, EXHIBITIONS, WRITINGS. Portland, Maine: Anthoensen Press, 1969. 60 p. Bibliog., pp. 51-60.

A scholarly oriented reference tool. It discusses the state of research, the important scholars involved, and lists major exhibitions, and those responsible for the catalogs.

1049 Norman-Wilcox, Gregor. "American Silver at the Los Angeles County Museum (the Marble Collection)." CONNOISSEUR YEAR BOOK (London), 1956, pp. 62-70.

A major collection of American silver, representing both high-style and modified pieces from throughout the country. Emphasis on eighteenth-century work.

1050 Peterson, Harold L. AMERICAN SILVER MOUNTED SWORDS, 1700-1815. Washington, D.C.: Corcoran Gallery of Art, 1955. 58 p. Illus.

This is the catalog of an exhibition of the swords used by the uniformed forces of the United States through the War of 1812. It actually serves as a supplement to Peterson's THE AMERICAN SWORD (see below).

1051 _____. THE AMERICAN SWORD, 1775-1945. Rev. ed. Philadelphia: Ray Riling Arms Books Co., 1965. xvi, 286 p. Illus.

A massive survey of swords, both useful and ceremonial work from the birth of the nation through the Second World War. Clear illustrations and useful, though often anecdotal, historical information.

1052 Phillips, John M. AMERICAN SILVER. New York: Chanticleer Press, 1949. 128 p. 32 illus. Bibliog., pp. 127-28.

A scholarly study that traces the history of style and deals with regional differences. Careful documentation of original points and careful selection of illustrations.

1053 _____. EARLY AMERICAN SILVER SELECTED FROM THE MARBLE BRADY GARVAN COLLECTION. Edited and notes by Meyric Rogers. New Haven: Yale University Art Gallery, 1960. Unpaged. 27 plates.

Published after the death of Phillips, Rogers edits some of the massive amount of research on the earlier collection previously undertaken by Phillips.

1054 Prime, Mrs. Alfred C. THREE CENTURIES OF HISTORIC SILVER. Philadelphia: Pennsylvania Society of Colonial Dames of America, 1938. 191 p. 141 illus.

Excluding a small selection of foreign pieces, this small volume is a biographical dictionary and exhibition catalog which concentrates on the production of Philadelphia silver makers of the prerevolutionary era. A useful tool for finding early known examples before they all settled into the museums.

1055 Rainwater, Dorothy T. AMERICAN SILVER MANUFACTURERS. Hanover, Pa.: Everybody's Press, 1960. xi, 223 p. Illus. with drawings. Bibliog., pp. 215-223.

An extensively researched guide to manufacturers, their marks, symbols, locations, and active dates. Arranged in alphabetical order by last name and contains a detailed glossary of general and specific terms relating to both objects and styles.

1056 _____, ed. STERLING SILVER HOLLOWARE. Princeton, N.J.: Pyne Press, 1973. 17 p., plus 140 plates. Bibliog., p. 16.

The brief text provides a neglected historical introduction to the field of holloware, outlines the stylistic relation to solidware, and discusses the use of the catalog. The rest of the value is reproductions of the catalogs of such major firms as S. Kirk, Gorham Manufacturing Company, and Unger Bros. A valuable guide to the taste of the times.

1057 Rainwater, Dorothy T., and Felger, Donna H. AMERICAN SPOONS: SOUVENIR AND HISTORICAL. Camden, N.J.: Thomas Nelson and Sons; Hanover, Pa.: Everybody's Press, 1968. 416 p. Illus. Bibliog., pp. 412-13.

A complete collector's guide to the variety of commemorative, subject, and souvenir spoons produced and patented in this country. Arranged according to subject or occasion and provides information on manufacture, designer, patent number and date. One entire section provides facsimiles of advertisements and original illustrations. A biographical list concentrates on designers.

1058 Rainwater, Dorothy T., and Rainwater, H. Ivan. AMERICAN SILVERPLATE. Nashville: Thomas Nelson and Sons, 1968. 480 p. Illus. Bibliog., pp. 461-65.

Provides the historical background of silverplate, discusses the development of electroplating and the methods of manufacturing. The various objects created from this material are discussed and illustrated, and a final chapter is devoted to care and restoration.

1059 Reed, Helen S. "Church Silver: A Colonial Tradition." ARTS IN VIRGINIA 10, no. 1 (1970): 2-9. Plates.

Discusses the tradition of presenting silver to a church as part of an ongoing tradition, with particular attention to examples and local implications for Virginia institutions.

1060 Schwartz, Marvin D. COLLECTORS GUIDE TO ANTIQUE AMERICAN SILVER. New York: Doubleday, 1975. xvii, 174 p. Illus. Bibliog., p. 169.

A popular and well-written survey of colonial and nineteenth-century silver in all forms. General information on style, regional variations, and quality.

1061 Semon, Kurt M., ed. A TREASURY OF OLD SILVER. New York: R.M. McBride, 1947. 112 p. Illus.

The articles in this volume cover a variety of silver-related questions, and are taken from the periodical THE AMERICAN COLLECTOR.

1062 Storer, Malcolm. "Pine Tree Shillings and Other Colonial Money." OLD TIME NEW ENGLAND 20, no. 2 (October 1929): Unpaged.

Useful for information on Hull and the role of coinage in the development of the work and status of the silversmith in colonial America.

1063 Stow, Millicent. AMERICAN SILVER. New York: Barrow and Co., 1950. 170 p. 81 illus.

A chatty pocket handbook that divides the history of American silver into three periods and presents chapters on marks and makers, museums to visit, and terms to know. Written for the beginning collector; it contains a lot of useful connoisseurship hints.

1064 Stutzenberger, Albert. AMERICAN HISTORICAL SPOONS: THE AMERICAN STORY IN SPOONS. Rutland, Vt.: Charles E. Tuttle, 1971. xviii, 535 p. Illus. Bibliog., pp. 512-30.

The first edition of this book was THE AMERICAN STORY IN SPOONS in 1953. Short to lengthy biographies and histories behind the events or about the individuals who were the subjects

of the spoon succeeds an introduction to the spoon and explains its popularity as the form for souvenir use. More important for subject than for discussion of style or period.

1065 Tiffany and Company. A COLLECTION OF EARLY AMERICAN SIL-
VER. New York: 1920. Unpaged.

A tiny catalog of seventy-five pieces of colonial and nineteenth-century silver in the company's collections. Lists silversmith, dates, object, dimensions, weight, description,
marks, and provenance. An important collection for comparative purposes and standards of quality.

1066 Turner, Noel D. AMERICAN FLATWARE, 1837-1910. South Brunswick, N.J.: A.S. Barnes, 1972. 473 p. Illus. Bibliog., pp. 413-
22.

A broad general history of manufactured work that provides a
surprisingly large amount of information on some of the larger
firms. Although the bibliography is not well organized, the
index of manufacturers, marks, and trade names is a more valuable tool for the collector, researcher, and general reader.

1067 ·Vermeule, Cornelius C. NUMISMATIC ART IN AMERICA: AESTHET-
ICS OF THE UNITED STATES COINAGE. Cambridge: Belknap Press
of Harvard University Press, 1971. xix, 266 p. Illus. Bibliog., pp.
229-31.

A serious discussion of the role of the craftsman as well as the
designer. The early coins are explained in terms of the role
of the silversmith as craftsman and worker. Goes beyond the
limitations of aesthetic questions.

1068 Wenham, Edward. THE PRACTICAL BOOK OF SILVER. Philadelphia:
J.B. Lippincott Co., 1949. 275 p. 45 plates. 197 fig. Bibliog.,
pp. 215-67.

Traces forms and styles back to Old World sources, dividing
the book into many small chapters. Mixed quality and with
some errors, but the sections on colonial saltcellars and on
forks are still worth reading.

GEOGRAPHICAL STUDIES OF AMERICAN SILVER

1069 Andrews, Ruth. THE METAL OF THE STATE. New York: Museum of
American Folk Art, 1973. 24 p. 13 illus.

Over 200 metal objects made in New York from the colonial
period through the Depression. Both handmade and manufactured

objects, traditional decorative art objects and others, are discussed and illustrated. Technical information on using copper, iron, lead, pewter, silver, and other metals.

1070 Avery, Clara L. EARLY NEW YORK SILVER. New York: Metropolitan Museum of Art, 1932. ix, 20 p. 104 illus.

An early but important exhibition catalog, documenting and illustrating work of forty silversmiths working in New York before the Revolution. Clear, useful illustrations, a list of smiths and their marks, and a brief essay on the silver market in colonial New York.

1971 Beckman, Elizabeth D. CINCINNATI SILVERSMITHS, JEWELERS, WATCH AND CLOCKMAKERS. Cincinnati: B.B. and Co., 1975. xvi, 168 p. Illus. Bibliog., pp. 156-60.

The bulk of this volume is an alphabetical listing and biographical treatment of all known craftsmen in the field. Includes dates, advertisements, marks, and photographs of actual pieces. An addendum lists smiths and watchmakers only listed in one of the directories. Lack of references in the body of text or footnotes provides frustration for researchers.

1072 Bohan, Peter J., and Hammerslough, Philip. EARLY CONNECTICUT SILVER, 1700-1840. Middleton, Conn.: Wesleyan University Press, 1970. xi, 288 p. 184 illus. Bibliog., pp. 279-83.

Contains a history of the silversmith, a chapter on technique, biographies of the smiths, a detailed catalog, and an index of marks. The illustrated catalog is especially useful in developing an idea as to the particular forms.

1073 Boylan, Leona D. SPANISH COLONIAL SILVER. Santa Fe: Museum of New Mexico Press, 1974. vii, 202 p. 97 illus. Bibliog., pp. 159-62.

General historical background of the geographical region, documentary evidence of silver plate during the colonial era, and descriptions of specific pieces of silver plate. A section on domestic silver and on accessories makes comparisons and analyzes reasons for attribution to the area. High-quality illustrations, facsimiles of marks, and catalogs of major collections.

1074 Bridwell, M.M. "Kentucky Silversmiths." FILSON CLUB HISTORY QUARTERLY (Louisville, Ky.) 16, no. 2 (April 1942): 111-26.

Primarily a listing of the smiths who worked in Louisville at any point in their career. Based on primary archival research, it lays the ground for serious study of an ignored area of southern silver.

1075 Brix, Maurice. LIST OF PHILADELPHIA SILVERSMITHS AND ALIEN
ARTIFICERS, 1682-1850. Philadelphia: Privately printed, 1920. vii,
125 p.

> An early but still useful and authoritative guide to who was
> working in the Philadelphia area through the early nineteenth
> century. Based on extensive primary research.

1076 Buck, John H. THE EARLY CHURCH PLATE OF SALEM. Salem,
Mass.: Essex Institute, 1907. 18 p. Illus.

> This pamphlet has been reprinted from the Essex Institute's his-
> torical papers. Documents the pieces presented to the reli-
> gious institutions of the area, and ties in the historical occa-
> sions for such donations.

1077 Burton, E. Milby. SOUTH CAROLINA SILVERSMITHS, 1690-1860.
Charleston, S.C.: Charleston Museum, 1942. xvii, 311 p. Illus.
Bibliog., pp. 291-302.

> A biographical dictionary of craftsmen working in metal in the
> state, arranged by geographic area. Included is a lengthy ta-
> ble of the initials stamped on the metal by the smith, and a
> detailed bibliography of primary and secondary sources.

1078 Carlisle, Lilian B. VERMONT CLOCK AND WATCHMAKERS, SILVER-
SMITHS, AND JEWELERS, 1778-1878. Burlington, Vt.: Stinehour
Press, 1970. xi, 313 p. Illus.

> A directory of approximately 1,000 craftsmen working with the
> precious metals between the years 1778 and 1878. Dates,
> names, locations, biographical material, and specific refer-
> ences to primary sources such as newspaper advertisements and
> account books. Illustrations of objects and marks, and facsim-
> iles of advertisements.

1079 Casey, Dorothy N. "Rhode Island Silversmiths." RHODE ISLAND
HISTORICAL SOCIETY COLLECTIONS 33 (July 1940): 1-64. Illus.

> A surprisingly thorough searching out of Rhode Island's smiths,
> documentations of their activity, and illustrations of their
> work. Comparisons of style to the mainstream Boston tradition.

1080 Corcoran Gallery of Art. A CENTURY OF ALEXANDRIA, DISTRICT
OF COLUMBIA AND GEORGETOWN SILVER, 1750-1850. Washington,
D.C.: 1966. 28 p. Illus.

> The catalog of a loan exhibition organized by the Corcoran
> and including work known or assumed to have been produced
> in the District of Columbia area in the one hundred years
> covered by the exhibition. Several otherwise unknown crafts-
> men were highlighted in this showing.

1081 Crosby, Everett U. BOOKS AND BASKETS, SIGNS AND SILVER OF OLD TIME NANTUCKET. Nantucket, Mass.: Inquirer and Mirror Press, 1940. 72 p. Illus.

Includes basket makers and street signs, but is primarily useful as a history of Nantucket silversmithing. Somewhat chatty, but carefully researched from primary sources.

1082 Currier, Ernest M. EARLY AMERICAN SILVERSMITHS, THE NEWBURY SPOON MAKERS. New York: Currier and Roby, 1930. 15 p. Illus.

The pamphlet is devoted exclusively to this one enterprise.

1083 Curtis, George M. EARLY SILVER OF CONNECTICUT AND ITS MAKERS. Meriden, Conn.: International Silver Co., 1913. 115 p. 33 plates.

A chatty but useful history of the role of the silversmith as banker, creator of currency, artisan, and merchant. The second half is a biographical dictionary that concentrates on basic data about each craftsman's life and dates of practice. Plates present provenance and measurements. Little or no stylistic analysis.

1084 Cutten, George B. SILVERSMITHS OF GEORGIA, TOGETHER WITH WATCHMAKERS AND JEWELERS, 1733-1850. Savannah, Ga.: Pigeonhole Press, 1958. 154 p. Illus.

Covers the entire range of documented and attributable work in Georgia, illustrations of individual works, biographical material, and marks of smiths.

1085 _____. THE SILVERSMITHS OF NORTH CAROLINA. Rev. ed. by Mary R. Peacock. Raleigh, N.C.: State Department of Archives and History, 1973. 93 p. 28 illus.

A brief introduction to the story of silversmithing in the state followed by biographical entries on almost 200 eighteenth- and early nineteenth-century smiths. Illustrations of both their work and available marks.

1086 _____. THE SILVERSMITHS OF VIRGINIA. Richmond, Va.: Dietz Press, 1952. xxiv, 259 p. Illus.

A brief history of silver and silversmithing in Virginia is followed by a biographical survey by city of the known figures working at the craft. Illustrations of the available surviving works are provided and show the high quality of native work. Present-day West Virginia is also included in this organization.

1087 _____. "Ten Silversmith Families of New York State." NEW YORK
HISTORY 27 (January 1946): 88–95; (April 1946): 224–230.

A small and highly specialized pamphlet that is completely
devoted to sorting out the various hands involved when silver
was attributed to or even signed by different craftsmen with
the same names. The families under discussion are Adriance,
Burr, DeRiemer, Fellows, Langworthy, Morgan, Munger, Stan-
ton, Stiles, and Stores.

1088 Cutten, George B., and Cutten, Minnie W. SILVERSMITHS OF UTI-
CA. Hamilton, N.Y.: Privately printed, 1936. 67 p. Illus. and
facsimiles.

A small but useful biographical dictionary of the smiths in the
Utica area from 1799 to about 1860. Information about the
illustrations of marks, references to advertisements, and many
indications about backgrounds and training are provided.

1089 Cutten, George B., and VerNooy, Amy P. THE SILVERSMITHS OF
POUGHKEEPSIE, N.Y. Poughkeepsie, N.Y.: Privately printed, 1945.
23 p. Illus.

A biographical treatment of the little-known silver workers
and a brief analysis of the development of style away from
the major silver centers.

1090 Darling, Sharon S. CHICAGO METALSMITHS. Chicago: Chicago
Historical Society, 1977. xvi, 141 p. 155 illus. Bibliog., pp. 137–
39.

An exhibition catalog and history of Chicago metal smithing
(mostly silver) from 1804 to 1970, with emphasis on the era
of the arts and crafts movement and on modern craftsmen. A
detailed catalog of the illustrated pieces and specific documentation about each important shop and its workers. The
only work to bring the long history of Chicago silver to our
attention.

1091 Darling Foundation. NEW YORK STATE SILVERSMITHS. Eggertsville,
N.Y.: 1965. 228 p. Illus. Bibliog., pp. 197–200.

A very complete, alphabetized list of all known silversmiths
who worked in the state from the earliest years through the
nineteenth century. Photographs of over 400 of the marks,
active dates, and locations.

1092 Dauterman, Carl C. CHECKLIST OF AMERICAN SILVERSMITHS WORK,
1650–1850, IN MUSEUMS IN THE NEW YORK METROPOLITAN AREA.
New York: Metropolitan Museum of Art, 1968. Unpaged. Bibliog.

Arranged alphabetically by craftsmen, and includes place of
operation, dates, and list of all known work in area collections. Helpful to the person who wishes to find a specific
type by a particular silversmith.

1093 de Matteo, William. THE SILVERSMITH IN EIGHTEENTH CENTURY
WILLIAMSBURG; AN ACCOUNT OF HIS LIFE AND TIMES, AND HIS
CRAFT. Williamsburg, Va.: Colonial Williamsburg, 1956. 36 p. Plates.

Describes the life, role, and status of the silversmith in colonial America in general and in Williamsburg in particular.
Meant for a general reader and aimed at placing the craftsman in his proper historical context.

1094 Fales, Martha G. JOSEPH RICHARDSON AND FAMILY: PHILADEL-
PHIA SILVERSMITHS. Middletown, Conn.: Wesleyan University Press,
1974. xviii, 340 p. 182 illus. Bibliog., pp. 312-20.

Traces the family from Francis Richardson (1681-1729) through
Nathaniel Richardson (1754-1827) and assesses their work and
influence with greatest attention to Joseph, Sr. Includes various appendixes: a commonplace book, letter book, and information on scales and weights of Joseph, Sr., plus a shop
inventory of Joseph and Nathaniel.

1095 Farham, Katherine G., and Elfird, Callis H. "Georgia Collects American Silver 1780-1870." HIGH MUSEUM ANTIQUES SHOW CATA-
LOGUE, pp. 57-88. Atlanta: High Museum, 1970.

Silver from all over the colonies and from the early federal
years, not just southern silver. Owned by both private collectors and institutions, showing that taste is more national
than regional.

1096 Flynt, Henry N., and Fales, Martha G. THE HERITAGE FOUNDA-
TION COLLECTION OF SILVER. Old Deerfield, Mass.: Heritage
Foundation, 1968. xiv, 391 p. 118 illus., hundreds of drawings.
Bibliog., pp. 367-82.

Individual brief essays on six New England states, each by a
noted authority, set the background for dozens of individual
works which together present the history of early New England
silver. Finally, a careful biographical dictionary provides
basic and specialized information, and illustrates the silversmiths' individual marks. Exhaustive bibliography.

1097 Fredyma, James P. A DIRECTORY OF MAINE SILVERSMITHS AND
WATCH AND CLOCK MAKERS. Hanover, N.H.: Privately printed,
1972. v, 26 p. Bibliog., pp. 24-26.

Each of the volumes in this small series is a simple but inclusive directory. Each lists names, location, active dates,
and bibliographic references. A good starting place for the
individual with nothing more than a name and probable state
of origin.

1098 Fredyma, John J. A DIRECTORY OF CONNECTICUT SILVERSMITHS
AND WATCH AND CLOCK MAKERS. Hanover, N.H.: Privately
printed, 1973. iv, 60 p. Bibliog., pp. 59-60.

For main entry, see no. 1097.

1099 Fredyma, Paul J., and Fredyma, Marie-Louise. A DICTIONARY OF
MASSACHUSETTS SILVERSMITHS AND THEIR MARKS. Hanover, N.H.:
Privately printed, 1972. iv, 27 p. Bibliog., pp. 25-27.

For main entry, see no. 1097.

1100 _____. A DICTIONARY OF RHODE ISLAND SILVERSMITHS AND
THEIR MARKS. Hanover, N.H.: Privately printed, 1972. v, 21 p.
Bibliog., pp. 20-21.

For main entry, see no. 1097.

1101 _____. A DIRECTORY OF BOSTON SILVERSMITHS AND WATCH
AND CLOCK MAKERS. Hanover, N.H.: Privately printed, 1975.
iv, 46 p. Bibliog., pp. 43-46.

For main entry, see no. 1097.

1102 _____. A DIRECTORY OF NEW HAMPSHIRE SILVERSMITHS AND
THEIR MARKS. Hanover, N.H.: Privately printed, 1971. v, 17 p.
Bibliog., pp. 15-17.

For main entry see, no. 1097.

1103 _____. A DIRECTORY OF VERMONT SILVERSMITHS AND WATCH
AND CLOCK MAKERS. Hanover, N.H.: Privately printed, 1974.
iv, 58 p. Bibliog., pp. 51-58.

For main entry, see no. 1097.

1104 Gerstell, Vivian S. SILVERSMITHS OF LANCASTER, PENNSYLVANIA,
1730-1850. Lancaster, Pa.: Lancaster County Historical Society,
1972. ix, 145 p. Illus. Bibliog., pp. 143-45.

A brief introduction to the historical development of the area
precedes a detailed catalog of individual smiths and their
work. Extensive documentary footnotes on each craftsman,
illustrations of representative work, and discussion of marks.
Based on primary source investigation.

1105 Gibb, George S. THE WHITESMITHS OF TAUNTON, A HISTORY OF REED AND BARTON. Cambridge: Harvard University Press, 1946. xxiii, 419 p. Illus.

> A volume in both business and decorative arts history. The progress of individuals and the firm over a hundred-year period is based on much of the firm's primary data. The relationship of manufactured products to handmade goods is explored, and questions of taste are raised.

1106 Gillingham, Harrold E. COUNTERFEITING IN COLONIAL PENNSYLVANIA. New York: American Numismatic Society, 1939. 52 p. Illus.

> The subject is a fascinating one, and the potential for its practice was great in an era when coinage depended more on content than it does today. Facsimiles of several spurious coins of the colonial era.

1107 _____. INDIAN ORNAMENTS MADE BY PHILADELPHIA SILVERSMITHS. New York: Museum of the American Indian. Heye Foundation, 1936. 26 p. Illus.

> This pamphlet deals with the traditional American craftsmen who, in the Philadelphia area at least, created a second set of wares for the Indian market.

1108 Goldsborough, Jennifer F. EIGHTEENTH AND NINETEENTH CENTURY MARYLAND SILVER IN THE COLLECTION OF THE BALTIMORE MUSEUM OF ART. Baltimore: Baltimore Museum of Art, 1975. ix, 204 p. Illus. Bibliog., pp. 201-4.

> A major exhibition catalog illustrating, describing, and documenting 207 pieces. References, provenance, descriptions, and illustrations of marks of craftsmen both illustrated and not, are in the catalog. Biographical information and a detailed bibliography.

1109 _____. AN EXHIBITION OF NEW LONDON SILVER, 1700-1835. New London, Conn.: Lyman Allyn Museum, 1969. 72 p. Illus. Bibliog., p. 40.

> A very brief introduction to the history of New London silver, followed by a catalog arranged by a known silversmith. References are to catalog entries, only some of which are illustrated, and provides information on marks, dimensions, owners, and brief descriptions. Very useable illustrations.

1110 Gourley, Hugh J. THE NEW ENGLAND SILVERSMITH: AN EXHIBITION OF NEW ENGLAND SILVER FROM THE MID-SEVENTEENTH

CENTURY TO THE PRESENT. Providence: Rhode Island School of Design, 1965. Unpaged. 84 illus.

The catalog of an important exhibition of a cross section of silver work from the colonial period to the present. Each of the 327 catalog entries is described with physical detail.

1111 Halsey, R.T. Haines. CATALOGUE OF AN EXHIBITION OF SILVER USED IN NEW YORK, NEW JERSEY AND THE SOUTH. New York: Metropolitan Museum of Art, 1911. 75 p. 36 plates.

One of the earliest of the major exhibitions of silver in the twentieth century. The author comments particularly on New York silversmiths, and the plates are of excellent quality.

1112 Harrington, Jessie. SILVERSMITHS OF DELAWARE: 1700-1950. Wilmington, Del.: National Society of Colonial Dames of America, 1939. x, 132 p. Illus. Bibliog., pp. 131-32.

Essentially devoted to the donated church plate in Delaware, with some material on the history of the craft in that state. Large clear plates for study of forms and decoration. Based on primary documentary sources.

1113 Hiatt, Noble U., and Hiatt, Lucy F. THE SILVERSMITHS OF KENTUCKY. Louisville, Ky.: Standard Printing Co., 1954. xxi, 135 p. Illus. Bibliog., pp. 119-26.

An annotated checklist of approximately 250 silversmiths recorded or known to have been working in Kentucky from 1785 to 1850. Includes a chart of their marks and discussion of some thirty unidentified craftsmen.

1114 Hill, Harry U. MARYLAND'S COLONIAL CHARM PORTRAYED IN SILVER. Baltimore: Waverly Press, 1938. xvii, 200 p. 38 illus. Bibliog.

Descriptions of the silver presentation service given by the citizens of Maryland to the cruiser MARYLAND and later moved to the battleship of the same name. Good background on colonial silversmiths and identifications of the various scenes on the silver pieces themselves.

1115 Hindes, Ruthanna. "Delaware Silversmiths 1700-1850." DELAWARE HISTORY 12, no. 4 (October 1967): 277-321. 54 illus.

A substantial and well-illustrated article which identifies many of the craftsmen who worked in the state for their entire career or for a short time. More historical than stylistic information; useful biographical data.

1116 Jayne, Horace F., and Woodhouse, S.W., Jr. "Early Philadelphia Silversmiths." ART IN AMERICA 9 (1959): 248-59. Illus.

A survey of the prominent craftsmen, particularly of French Huguenot descent, who developed Philadelphia as a major center of silver making at the end of the colonial era.

1117 Kernan, John D. AN EXHIBITION OF EARLY SILVER BY NEW HA-VEN SILVERSMITHS. New Haven, Conn.: New Haven Colony Historical Society, 1967. 103 p. Illus. Bibliog., p. 62.

Treats all silversmiths known to have spent any time working in New Haven from the beginning of the eighteenth through the first third of the nineteenth century. Each object is meticulously documented and described, inscriptions and marks are recorded, and such biographical information as available is noted.

1118 KIRK SILVER IN U.S. MUSEUMS. Baltimore: Samuel Kirk and Son, 1967. 22 p. Illus.

Published by the Baltimore firm of Samuel Kirk and Son, to document and commemorate the history of the firm and the place of its silver in American history.

1119 Knittle, Rhea M. EARLY OHIO SILVERSMITHS AND PEWTERERS 1787-1847. Cleveland: Calvert-Hatch Co., 1943. 63 p. Illus. Bibliog., p. 63.

Unusually valuable in that it starts with the Ohio Indians before treating colonial and early nineteenth-century silver forms in the area. Covers the major geographical divisions in a historical manner and provides checklists of silver and pewter makers. Based on primary source investigation of newspapers, account books, and others.

1120 May, Earl C. A CENTURY OF SILVER: CONNECTICUT YANKEES AND A NOBLE METAL. New York: Robert M. McBride, 1947. 388 p. 40 illus.

A history of the old silver manufacturers in Connecticut, their growth with the Rogers Brothers, and their electroplating contribution to the creation of the International Silver Company. Much of the early part of the book is concerned with early nineteenth-century silver.

1121 Meeks, E.V. MASTERPIECES OF NEW ENGLAND SILVER. Cambridge: Harvard University Press, for the Gallery of Fine Arts, Yale University, 1939. 97 p. 15 plates.

A survey of New England work from 1650 to 1800, based on

666
6666

American Metalwork

the Gorham Collection, but also pulling together many fine examples from other sources. Meticulous descriptions, documentation, and some editorial commentary.

1122 Miller, V. Isabelle. NEW YORK SILVERSMITHS OF THE SEVENTEENTH CENTURY. New York: Museum of the City of New York, 1962. Unpaged. 20 illus.

An exhibition catalog presenting the work of both established figures and more elusive early craftsmen of the area. Descriptions, measurements, inscriptions, and illustrations. A most basic survey.

1123 _____. SILVER BY NEW YORK MAKERS: LATE SEVENTEENTH CENTURY TO 1900. New York: Museum of the City of New York, 1937. xvi, 71 p. Illus.

A catalog of 383 items by New York craftsmen, listed alphabetically. Each work is described, markings are indicated, and weight is given. The illustrations cover a wide variety of objects, and the original owners, when known, are listed.

1124 Miller, William D. THE SILVERSMITHS OF LITTLE REST. Kingston, R.I.: D.B. Updike, 1928. xii, 50 p. Illus.

Discusses, documents, and illustrates the work of Samuel Casey, John Waite, Joseph Perkins, and other Kingston area colonial and early nineteenth-century smiths.

1125 Museum of Fine Arts, Houston. SOUTHERN SILVER: AN EXHIBITION OF SILVER MADE IN THE SOUTH PRIOR TO 1860. Houston, Tex.: 1968. Unpaged. Illus.

The work of important silversmiths of the South is presented with a descriptive entry on each piece. The introduction describes the general distribution and types of silver from the South and correctly points to the need for a great deal of research in the field.

1126 New Haven Colony Historical Society. AN EXHIBITION OF EARLY SILVER BY NEW HAVEN SILVERSMITHS. New Haven, Conn.: 1967. 99 p. Illus. Bibliog., p. 62.

A good catalog on a special area, arranged alphabetically by craftsmen. Brief biographical information, descriptions, and measurements of individual works, and a brief note on flatware from the New Haven area.

1127 Newman, Eric P. COINAGE FOR COLONIAL VIRGINIA. New York: American Numismatic Society, 1956. 57 p. Illus.

One of a series of monographs of the society, this volume
narrowly focuses on the relationship of the silversmith, both
in and out of Virginia, in producing standardized coins for
the colony.

1128 Noe, Sydney P. THE NEW ENGLAND AND WILLOW TREE COIN-
AGES OF MASSACHUSETTS. New York: American Numismatic Society, 1943. 55 p. 16 illus.

The early silversmith was usually as much involved in producing coins as he was in producing silver for domestic use. A
careful examination of some of the major early attempts at
developing a standardized coinage.

1129 Peale Museum. THE WARNER FAMILY, SILVERSMITHS TO BALTI-
MORE. Baltimore: 1971. 17 p. Plates.

A brief but important catalog which defines and analyzes the
work of a long-ignored family firm of craftsmen. Illustrates
their place in the larger Baltimore tradition.

1130 Philadelphia Museum of Art. PHILADELPHIA SILVER, 1682-1800.
Philadelphia: 1956. 32 p. Plates.

The catalog of an important exhibition of Philadelphia's silver,
with careful descriptions, discussion of external influences,
and good illustrations.

1131 Pleasants, J. Hall. MARYLAND SILVERSMITHS, 1715-1830. Baltimore: Lord Baltimore Press, 1930. Reprint. Harrison, N.Y.: Robert
A. Green, 1972. xiv, 320 p. 67 illus.

Discusses the individual smiths and their work, and illustrates
not only the fine examples of silver, but also the marks. A
design book.

1132 Porcher, Jennie R., and Rutledge, Aaron. THE SILVER OF ST.
PHILIP'S CHURCH, CHARLESTOWN, 1670-1970. Charleston, S.C.:
St. Philip's Church, 1970. 27 p. Illus.

A carefully documented examination of the presentation silver
in the collection of this old established Charleston institution.
Based on careful documentation, the work provides useful historical material on the role of silver in this major southern
city.

1133 Reed, Helen S. CHURCH SILVER OF COLONIAL VIRGINIA. Richmond: Virginia Museum of Fine Arts, 1970. 112 p. 79 illus.

Seventeenth- and eighteenth-century ecclesiastical silver, with

a map showing locations and attention to the role of Royal
gifts. Carefully presented history of religious developments
in Virginia and fully descriptive catalog entries.

1134 Rhode Island School of Design. THE NEW ENGLAND SILVERSMITH.
Providence: 1965. 40 p. Plates.

The catalog of an important loan exhibition of silver made in
New England between ca. 1650 and the middle of the twenti-
eth century. All works were loaned from prominent New
England collections. Useful source for tracing provenance.

1135 Rice, Norman S. ALBANY SILVER, 1652-1825. Albany, N.Y.:
Albany Institute of History of Art, 1964. 81 p. 156 illus. Bibliog.,
pp. 78-81.

This study of the production of one city is arranged by individual smiths. Illustrations, provenance, various data about
each piece, and historical material in the introduction.
Strong bibliography and solid biographical data.

1136 Roach, Ruth H. ST. LOUIS SILVERSMITHS. St. Louis, Mo.: Eden,
1967. 107 p. Illus.

Discusses the major developments of silver in the area, stylistic variations, and identifiable craftsmen. Some discussion of
Indian silver products as well.

1137 Rumford, Beatrix T. SAMUEL KIRK AND SON: AMERICAN SILVER
CRAFTSMEN SINCE 1815. Chicago: Chicago Historical Society,
1968. 31 p. Illus.

The catalog of a traveling exhibition which described, discussed, and documented the work of this long-time Baltimore
firm of silversmiths.

1138 Smith, Sidney A. MOBILE SILVERSMITHS AND JEWELERS, 1820-1867.
Mobile, Ala.: Historic Preservation Society, 1970. 12 p. Illus.

A brief survey of all the known Mobile smiths of the era,
based on local primary research and illustrated with examples,
for the most part, still in the area.

1139 Warren, David B. SOUTHERN SILVER, AN EXHIBITION OF SILVER
MADE IN THE SOUTH PRIOR TO 1860. Houston, Tex.: Museum of
Fine Arts, 1968. 92 p. Illus.

The catalog of the only major exhibition devoted exclusively
to the silver of the South from the years prior to 1860. Un-
even distribution of work, but good-quality text and illustrations. Descriptions of objects, discussion of marks and provenance, and basic data on the silversmith.

1140 Williams, Carl M. SILVERSMITHS OF NEW JERSEY, 1700-1825. Philadelphia: George S. MacManus Co., 1949. xii, 164 p. 46 illus. Bibliog., pp. 153-57.

A geographical division of the locations where smiths were active in the period under discussion. Lengthy biographical entries on the individual craftsmen and illustrations of their work.

INDIAN SILVER

1141 Adair, John. THE NAVAJO AND PUEBLO SILVERSMITHS. Norman: University of Oklahoma Press, 1944. xvii, 220 p. Illus. Bibliog., pp. 213-16.

The basic scholarly monograph on the development, tools, techniques, and creations of the Southwest Indian silversmiths. Discusses questions of the traditional tribal artist and the commercial world and majority culture. Much of the material is based on thorough, basic anthropological research.

1142 Beauchamp, William M. METALLIC ORNAMENTS OF THE NEW YORK INDIANS. Albany: University of the State of New York, 1903. 120 p. 37 illus.

A very old but still useful study of the jewelry and functional items made by nineteenth-century American Indians in the New York area. Primarily derived from archeological-anthropological research, but also of use to the art historian and collector.

1143 Bedinger, Marjery. INDIAN SILVER: NAVAJO AND PUEBLO JEWELERS. Albuquerque: University of New Mexico Press, 1973. xiv, 264 p. 100 illus (8 in color). Bibliog., pp. 243-55.

Includes information on a wide variety of objects ornamented by the silversmith, including ceremonial objects.

1144 _____. NAVAJO INDIAN SILVERWORK. Denver: J. Van Marle, 1936. 43 p. Illus. Bibliog., pp. 42-43.

Traces the development of the Navajo silver craft, discusses tools and types of articles by type, and has a few illustrations. Includes information on the Navajo forge and bellows, and the addition of stone settings.

1145 Belden, Bauman L. INDIAN PEACE MEDALS ISSUED IN THE UNITED STATES, 1789-1889. New York: American Numismatic Society, 1927. Reprint. New Milford, Conn.: N. Flayderman and Co., 1966. 46 p. Illus.

An exotic area of collecting historical research is documented
in this volume. More important as historical documentation
than as discussion of style (as the form remains static). Belden
does provide an exhaustive and reliable documentation of suc-
cessive commemorative issues.

1146 Colton, Mary R. "Hopi Silversmithing--Its Background and Future."
PLATEAU 12 (1939): 1-7.

Discusses the comparatively new Hopi craft, its adaptation to
both home and market needs, and the effect of working for
the marketplace.

1147 Harrington, M.R. "Iroquois Silverwork." AMERICAN MUSEUM OF
NATURAL HISTORY, ANTHROPOLOGICAL PAPERS 1, no. 6 (September 1908): 351-69. Plates.

An important pioneering study of the creation and use of the
work of this Indian tribe. Illustrates both objects and tools
and discusses the work from an anthropological rather than
artistic point of view.

1148 Hodge, Frederick W. "How Old is Southwestern Indian Silverwork?"
EL PALACIO 25 (October 1928): 224-32.

Grapples with the question of the start of the craft in the
area. Explores relations with majority culture and raises additional questions. A seminal article.

1149 Kirk, Ruth F. "Southwestern Indian Jewelry." EL PALACIO 52
(February 1945): 21-32; (March 1945): 41-50.

Discusses an important recent Indian art form and traces its
tribal use to that of a commercial staple. Mentions the use
of stones and variety objects within the various tribal groups.

1150 Mera, Harry P. "Indian Silverwork of the Southwest." LABORATORY
OF ANTHROPOLOGY. BULLETIN 17-19 (1944). Unpaged. Illus.

A three-part series on field and stamped bridles, band bracelets, and embossed band bracelets. Well-illustrated and carefully described. Brief studies of the various techniques used
by the area tribes.

1151 Tanner, Clara L. "Contemporary Southwest Indian Silver." KIVA.
Arizona State Museum 25, no. 1 (1960): 1-22.

Illustrates and discusses the work of various tribal craftsmen,
their use of the material, and the originality of their approaches, all tied to local traditions.

1152 Van Horn, Elizabeth H. IROQUOIS SILVER BROOCHES IN THE
ROCHESTER MUSEUM. Rochester, N.Y.: Rochester Museum of Arts
and Sciences, 1971. 70 p. Illus.

A catalog of the museum's holdings of the New York State
Indian's silver work in this form. Known as "as-ne-as-ga"--
an important item in their economy.

1153 Woodward, Arthur. A BRIEF HISTORY OF NAVAJO SILVERSMITHING.
Rev. ed. Flagstaff, Ariz.: Northland Press, 1971. xii, 103 p.
Illus. Bibliog., pp. 91-100.

A good basic yet scholarly survey of the work, tools, and
methods of the Navajo craftsman. The placement of the silver work within the broader Indian view of the arts is ana-
lyzed and the relationship of the creations to majority culture
is examined.

1154 Wright, Margaret N. HOPI SILVER: THE HISTORY AND HALLMARKS
OF HOPI SILVERSMITHING. Flagstaff, Ariz.: Northland Press, 1972.
xiv, 104 p. 37 illus. Bibliog., pp. 99-100.

Discusses the brief (since 1900) history of Hopi silver jewelry
work and the place of the craft in the life of the tribe and
provides biographical information about individual craftsmen.
Explains techniques, and most important, contains a full
checklist of craftsmen's hallmarks and a helpful glossary.

AMERICAN PEWTER

1155 Albany Institute of History and Art. ALBANY PEWTER AND ITS
MAKERS. Albany, N.Y.: 1942. 8 p. Plates.

The catalog of the 1942 exhibition of locally made pewter
includes that made by both long-time Albany residents and
others who might have had a brief sojourn in the city. An
early attempt to sort out a lot of forgotten material.

1156 Brandt, Frederick R. AMERICAN PEWTER. Richmond: Virginia Museum, 1976. 84 p. Illus. Bibliog., p. 83.

This catalog of an important and comprehensive exhibition includes an introduction to American pewter, a glossary of relevant terms, and 230 catalog entries of unusual items.

1157 Cocks, Dorothy. THE PEWTER COLLECTION OF THE NEW CANAAN
HISTORICAL SOCIETY. New Canaan, Conn.: New Canaan Historical
Society, 1967. 24 p. Illus.

The catalog of a small but choice collection of American

pewter; New England pieces almost to the exclusion of other geographical places, but not just a local focus.

1158 Colonial Williamsburg. PEWTER IN COLONIAL WILLIAMSBURG AND VIRGINIA. Williamsburg, Va.: 1935. 23 p. Illus.

This pamphlet is primarily concerned with references to the use of pewter in the Old South, particularly Virginia, during the colonial period, and makes reference to contemporary sources.

1159 Currier Gallery of Art. PEWTER IN AMERICA, 1650-1900. Manchester, N.H.: 1968. 73 p. Illus.

The catalog of an exhibition based on the holdings of the Currier Gallery but also supplemented by loans. Covers the entire range of American pewter, but very heavily weighted toward New England.

1160 Ebert, Katherine. COLLECTING AMERICAN PEWTER. New York: Charles Scribner's Sons, 1973. 163 p. 159 illus. Bibliog.

Well-written survey of pewter from the colonial period through 1860, the heyday of American pewter manufacture. Biographical information on pewters, with a checklist, based on documentary sources. Includes illustrations of both pewter objects and marks.

1161 Fairbanks, Jonathan. AMERICAN PEWTER IN THE MUSEUM OF FINE ARTS, BOSTON. Boston: Museum of Fine Arts, 1974. 140 p. 323 illus. Bibliog.

The catalog of over 400 pieces of American pewter in the museum collection, from the mid-eighteenth century through the third quarter of the nineteenth century. Illustrations include pewterers' marks. Text includes a brief history of pewter, changes in technology, and its place in the social order.

1162 Giffen, Jane C., and Taggart, Ida F. PEWTER IN THE COLLECTIONS OF THE NEW HAMPSHIRE HISTORICAL SOCIETY. Concord: New Hampshire Historical Society, 1968. 18 p. Illus.

A catalog based on the first full exhibition of the pewter holdings of the museum. Some pieces are illustrated; basic information on all others.

1163 Graham, John M. AMERICAN PEWTER. Brooklyn: Brooklyn Museum, Brooklyn Institute of Arts and Sciences, 1949. 36 p. Illus.

The catalog of a loan exhibition which surveyed pewter developments and evolution, with an emphasis on New England ware.

1164 Hirsch, Richard, ed. EARLY AMERICAN PEWTER. JOHN J. EVANS, JR., COLLECTION. Allentown, Pa.: Allentown Art Museum, 1966. 13 p. Illus.

> The catalog of 149 pewter art-related items from one of the first private collections in the country. Arranged by alphabetical lists of pewterers with heaviest representation devoted to the art of Philadelphia and its environs. Good illustrations.

1165 Hood, Graham. AMERICAN PEWTER: GARVAN AND OTHER COLLECTIONS AT YALE. New Haven: Yale University Press, 1965. 59 p. Illus.

> A catalog and description of the pewter holdings in one of the major American collections.

1166 Jacobs, Carl. GUIDE TO AMERICAN PEWTER. New York: McBride, 1957. 216 p. 57 illus.

> Primarily an alphabetically arranged guidebook to availability and price of the works of individual pewterers. Although the prices are obviously out-of-date, the descriptions of work, examples of marks, and dates still serve as useful tools for the collector.

1167 Jacobs, Celia. POCKET BOOK OF AMERICAN PEWTER: THE MAKERS AND THE MARKS. Southwick, Mass.: Privately printed, 1960. 85 p. Illus.

> A pocket dictionary, alphabetically arranged with illustrations of the most widely available and documented marks of pewterers.

1168 Kauffman, Henry J. THE AMERICAN PEWTERER, HIS TECHNIQUES AND HIS PRODUCTS. Camden, N.J.: T. Nelson, 1970. 158 p. Illus. Bibliog., p. 155.

> As with other volumes by the same author, there is great attention paid to the tools and methods of production. The use of pewter as a substitute for silver is discussed, and presentation of the slow evolution of forms and scarcity of remaining early pieces is provided.

1169 Kerfoot, J.B. AMERICAN PEWTER. New York: Bonanza Books, 1924. xxiii, 236 p. 500 illus.

> An account of every known American pewterer with dates, type of work, marks, and scarcity factors. Very old but useful source for research on pewter.

1170 Laughlin, Ledlie I. PEWTER IN AMERICA: ITS MAKERS AND THEIR MARKS. New ed. 2 vols. Barre, Mass.: Barre Publishers, 1969. Vol. 1: xix, 242 p. Illus. Bibliog., pp. 163-92. Vol. 2: xiv, 276 p. Illus.

A major study of the work in a once major craft form. As well as historical documentation, a checklist of American makers of pewter and an inventory of pewter shops are provided. The bibliography is both extensive and exhaustive.

1171 Marvin, Pearson. AMERICAN PEWTER (c. 1730- c. 1870) IN THE COLLECTION OF DR. AND MRS. MELVYN D. WOLF. Flint, Mich.: Flint Institute of Arts, 1973. 41 p. 48 illus.

A brief introductory history of pewter in America, from Jamestown through the mid-nineteenth century, precedes a catalog of over 200 pieces of East Coast pewter. Brief catalog entries, including descriptive data and good illustrations. Significant craftsmen include Bassett, Boardman, Will, and Young.

1172 Montgomery, Charles F. A HISTORY OF AMERICAN PEWTER. Rev. ed. New York: E.P. Dutton, 1978. 307 p. Illus. Bibliog., pp. 301-12.

An excellent and concise survey and history of the use of this material in America. Chapters on pewter in everyday life, the craft of the pewterer, and connoisseurship are followed by sections on the varieties of objects made from pewter. Well illustrated.

1173 Myers, Louis G. SOME NOTES ON AMERICAN PEWTERERS. New York: Country Life Press, 1926. xiii, 96 p. Illus.

Based on the author's own collection of pewter, it supplements the Kerfoot volume by noting some pewterers that escaped the earlier author's attention. Slightly updates work on touchmarks and provides clear illustrations of both objects and the marks. Very old but still useful; unfortunately, no references.

1174 New Haven Colony Historical Society. AN EXHIBITION OF CONNECTICUT PEWTER. New Haven: 1969. 72 p. Illus.

Chronological treatment of pewterers active in the area now called Connecticut.

1175 Osborne, Arthur D. A FEW FACTS RELATING TO THE ORIGIN AND HISTORY OF JOHN DOLBEARE OF BOSTON. New Haven: Privately printed, 1893. 32 p. Illus.

A history of an important early Boston pewterer. Excellent plates.

1176 Rogers, Malcolm A., Jr. AMERICAN PEWTERERS AND THEIR MARKS.
2d ed. Southampton, N.Y.: Cracker Barrel Press, 1968. 22 p.
Illus.

A handbook of pewterers and their marks.

THE NONPRECIOUS METALS IN AMERICA

1177 Cardinale, Robert. COPPER, BRASS, BRONZE EXHIBITION. Tuscon:
University of Arizona Press, 1977. 64 p. 48 illus.

The catalog of an exhibition of 236 works by contemporary
metal smiths in the three metals and alloys: copper, brass,
and bronze. Both functional and sculptural forms are included
and discussed with forty-eight illustrated. Descriptions, measurements, materials.

1178 Coffin, Margaret. THE HISTORY AND FOLKLORE OF AMERICAN
COUNTRY TINWARE, 1700-1900. Camden, N.J.: T. Nelson, 1968.
226 p. Illus. Bibliog., pp. 212-15.

A popular survey of tinware and the smiths who made it. Information on identification and care for the collector.

1179 Deas, Alston. THE EARLY IRON WORK OF CHARLESTON. Columbia, S.C.: Bostick and Thornley, 1941. 111 p. Illus. Bibliog.,
p. 111.

Discusses the architectural and decorative ornament in the
Charleston area. Illustrations are of architectural details and
the various usages of metal in gratings, window coverings,
sconces, and general ornament. A much-ignored area.

1180 DeVoe, Shirley S. THE TINSMITHS OF CONNECTICUT. Middletown,
Conn.: Published for the Connecticut Historical Society by Wesleyan
University Press, 1968. xxiv, 200 p. Illus. Bibliog., pp. 195-200.

Explores the work of a craftsman type whose products have all
but disappeared. With none of the intrinsic value of the precious metals, there was no heirloom or financial value to
keeping tin products. Based on primary archival sources and
illustrated with objects in both public and private hands.

1181 Gunnion, Vernon S., and Hopf, Caroll J. THE BLACKSMITH: ARTI-
SAN WITHIN THE EARLY COMMUNITY. Harrisburg: Pennsylvania
Historical and Museum Commission, 1972. 64 p. Illus. Bibliog.,
p. 12.

The catalog of an exhibition of late colonial and nineteenth-
century ironwork. Illustrates and describes the variety of

utilitarian objects created by the metal smith and traces their
evolution and tradition.

1182 Hummel, Charles F. WITH HAMMER IN HAND: THE DOMINY
CRAFTSMEN OF EAST HAMPTON, NEW YORK. Charlottesville:
Published for Henry Francis du Pont Winterthur Museum by University
Press of Virginia, 1968. xiv, 424 p. Illus. Bibliog., pp. 407-14.

Traces and discusses the Dominy family involvement in all aspects of metalcraft, general metalwork, and clock and watch
making. A good basic source for understanding; illustrations
of relevant tools.

1183 Kauffman, Henry J. AMERICAN COPPER AND BRASS. Camden,
N.J.: Thomas Nelson and Sons, 1968. 288 p. Illus. Bibliog.,
pp. 282-83.

Two main sections, one on the products of the coppersmith
and one on the products of the Brass Founder. Lists of craftsmen are included with locations and active dates.

1184 _____. EARLY AMERICAN COPPER, TIN, AND BRASS. New York:
McBride, 1950. 112 p. 90 illus.

Checklist of over 400 smiths follows discussion of these metals
in our history. Includes information about forms of manufacture and the development of certain functional objects.

1185 _____. EARLY AMERICAN IRONWARE, CAST AND WROUGHT.
Rutland, Vt.: Charles E. Tuttle Co., 1966. 166 p. 210 illus.

Discusses the types of ironwork produced on the forge, through
the blast furnace, and by the nailer, wheelwright, and tin-
smith, to name a few. Illustrations of tools, objects, and
advertisements and period prints. Brief mention of known
craftsmen makes this popular volume the standard in the field.

1186 Lindsay, J. Seymour. IRON AND BRASS IMPLEMENTS OF THE ENG-
LISH AND AMERICAN HOUSE. Rev. ed. Bass River, Mass.: Carl
Jacobs, 1964. 88 p. Illus.

Fireplace tools, kitchen implements, and other forms created
by the metalsmith and in common use in both England and the
United States. Adds to the small amount of literature on this
taken-for-granted subject.

1187 Longenecker, Elmer Z. THE EARLY BLACKSMITHS OF LANCASTER
COUNTY. Lancaster, Pa.: Community Historians, 1974. 44 p.

Blacksmithing among the various settlers in the area, illustrations, and descriptions of the creations of practical artisans.

1188 Scott, Mary W. "Cast-Iron Ornament in Richmond." ARTS IN VIR-
GINIA 2 (Winter 1962): 20–29. Illus.

> Cast-iron work tends to be anonymous, but is still a living
> record of the metal smith's art. This article traces develop-
> ments during the heyday of metal ornamentation.

1189 Sonn, Albert H. EARLY AMERICAN WROUGHT IRON. 3 vols. New
York: Charles Scribner's Sons, 1928. Vol. 1: xvi, 262 p. Vol. 2:
vi, 204 p. Vol. 3: vii, 263 p. 320 illus.

> Iron was used for all sorts of practical implements and for or-
> nament and decoration as well. This serves as an encyclo-
> pedia of the uses for wrought iron. Well illustrated, with
> examples from all regions.

1190 Southern Illinois University at Carbondale. IRON, SOLID WROUGHT/
USA. Carbondale: University Museum and Art Galleries, 1976.
72 p. 74 illus.

> The theme of this exhibition was "The Blacksmith as Artist and
> Craftsman in the United States, 1776–1976." Some 117 his-
> torical items and seventy pieces by contemporary craftsmen
> point out both the continuity and the change in craft creations
> by metal smiths. Some background on the European smith and
> his decline at the time of the Industrial Revolution.

1191 Wallace, Philip B. COLONIAL IRONWORK IN OLD PHILADELPHIA:
THE CRAFTSMANSHIP OF THE EARLY DAYS OF THE REPUBLIC. New
York: Architectural Book Publishing Co., 1930. 3 p. 147 plates.

> Measured drawings, an introduction to the use of ironwork for
> architectural decoration and ornament by Fiske Kimball, and
> 147 plates illustrating its use.

INDIVIDUAL CRAFTSMEN IN METALS

Most of the information about individual metal smiths is to be found in general, period, or regional surveys.

1192 Buhler, Kathryn C. "The Ledgers of Paul Revere." BULLETIN OF
THE MUSEUM OF FINE ARTS 34, no. 201. (1936): 38–45.

> Records of the famous metal smith and patriot indicate the
> range of his activities. Useful primary material.

1193 _____ . PAUL REVERE: GOLDSMITH, 1735–1818. Boston: Museum
of Fine Arts, 1956. 44 p. Illus.

Discusses the man, his general involvement in American life, and his work as a smith. Documents particular Revere works.

1194 Clarke, Hermann F. JOHN CONEY, SILVERSMITH. Boston and New York: Houghton Mifflin Co., 1932. xv, 92 p. 31 illus.

A biography and discussion of the work of the important American-born colonial silversmith. Meticulously researched and documented, it remains the standard work in spite of new additions to his oeuvre and more recent analysis of his place in the period. High-quality plates and full description of each work illustrated.

1195 _____. JOHN HULL, A BUILDER OF THE BAY COLONY. Portland, Maine: Southworth-Anthoensen Press, 1940. xiv, 221 p. 15 plates. Bibliog., pp. 195-99.

The standard monograph on this important colonial smith. Carefully researched and clearly documented biography, background of his times, and a wealth of information about coinage and the profession. A list of documented works and illustrations of marks, but weak on qualitative analysis.

1196 Clarke, Hermann F., and Foote, Henry W. JEREMIAH DUMMER: COLONIAL CRAFTSMAN AND MERCHANT. Boston: Houghton Mifflin Co., 1935. Reprint. New York: Da Capo Press, 1970. xix, 205 p. 23 plates.

The life and work of this silversmith is presented as completely as possible. Contains the hypothesis that Dummer may have painted portraits as well.

1197 Davis, Myra T. SKETCHES IN IRON: SAMUEL YELLIN, AMERICAN MASTER OF WROUGHT IRON, 1885-1940. Washington, D.C.: George Washington University, 1971. 20 p. Illus. Bibliog., pp. 18-19.

The catalog of an exhibition of one of the few well-documented early twentieth-century craftsmen to work with wrought iron. Illustrates the range and diversity of his production.

1198 de Jonge, Eric. "Johann Christoph Heyne: Pewterer, Minister, Teacher." WINTERTHUR PORTFOLIO 4 (1968): 168-84.

A Moravian pewterer's career traced from Europe to his death in Lancaster, and a study of his known work. Presents a tentative typology and illustrates over twenty pieces of his art.

1199 Forbes, Esther. PAUL REVERE AND THE WORLD HE LIVED IN. New York: Literary Classics, 1942. xiii, 510 p. Illus. Bibliog., pp. 491-96.

An anecdotal yet well-written historical biography of the metal smith and patriot, with emphasis on the politics rather than art. Based on serious research, but lack of specific documentation makes it frustrating to consult.

1200 French, Hollis. JACOB HURD AND HIS SONS NATHANIEL AND BENJAMIN, SILVERSMITHS 1702-1781. Cambridge: Riverside Press, 1939. Reprint. New York: Da Capo Press, 1972. 154 p. 27 illus.

Presents biographical information and a discussion of the type and quality of the Hurd silver work and its place in America's craftsmanship.

1201 Gillingham, Harrold E. "Ceaser Ghiselin: Philadelphia's First Gold and Silversmith 1693-1733." PENNSYLVANIA MAGAZINE OF HISTORY AND BIOGRAPHY 57 (July 1933): 244-59.

An early article which explores the life and work of a previously underrated figure in the development of metal smithing in America. Points out the importance of Huguenot craftsmen in establishing the craft in Philadelphia.

1202 _____. "Indian Trade Ornaments Made by Joseph Richardson, Jr." PENNSYLVANIA MAGAZINE OF HISTORY AND BIOGRAPHY 67 (January 1943): 83-91.

Richardson was one of a large family of Philadelphia silversmiths, and just one of those involved in this aspect of the Indian trade.

1203 Hamilton, Suzanne. "The Pewter of William Will: A Checklist." WINTERTHUR PORTFOLIO 7 (1972): 129-60.

A careful and detailed checklist of 197 pieces identified as the work of Will, 128 being marked. Each work is described, measured, and dated, and names of owners and bibliography are provided. Includes a brief summary of one of the great eighteenth-century pewterers.

1204 Hoopes, Penrose K. SHOP RECORDS OF DANIEL BURNAP, CLOCKMAKER. Hartford: Connecticut Historical Society, 1958. 188 p. Illus.

Brings the activity of the metal smith and clockmaker alive for both the collector and the general enthusiast of American culture. Documentation of prices, activity, and demand.

1205 Nichols, Arthur H. "Bells of Paul and Joseph Revere." ESSEX INSTITUTE, HISTORICAL COLLECTIONS 47 (1911): 293-316; 48 (1912): 1-16.

The Reveres were famous for cast work as well as for the better-known gold of Joseph and the silver of Paul. Description
and discussion of the bells designed by the two metal smiths.

1206 Rosenbaum, Jeanette W. MYER MYERS: GOLDSMITH, 1723-1795.
Philadelphia: Jewish Publication Society of America, 1954. 141 p.
30 illus. Bibliog., pp. 139-41.

A biographical study of the smith and patriot. Illustrations
of his work, identification of his marks, and a technical discussion of his various works are provided.

1207 Schwartz, Marvin D. ELIAS PELLETREAU, LONG ISLAND SILVER-
SMITH AND HIS SOURCES OF DESIGN. Brooklyn: Brooklyn Institute
of Arts and Sciences, Brooklyn Museum, 1959. Unpaged. Illus.

A small catalog of a heretofore little-known and almost documented silversmith. Discusses broader cultural influences and
defines the limits of the craftsman.

1208 Scott, Kenneth. "Daniel Greenough, Colonial Silversmith of Ports-
mouth." HISTORICAL NEW HAMPSHIRE 17 (November 1960): 26-31.

The reconstruction of the identity and work of an elusive historical figure who produced significant conventional work before the Revolution. The only real source of information on
Greenough.

1209 Singleton, Esther. "The Halsey Collection of Paul Revere Silver."
ANTIQUARIAN 3 (November 1924): 10-14. Illus.

An illustrated article that introduces us to one of the five
groupings of authentic Revere pieces. Corrections to the article are found in volume 3, January 1925, p. 29.

1210 Smith, Helen B. "Nicholas Roosevelt--Goldsmith (1715-1769)." NEW
YORK HISTORICAL SOCIETY QUARTERLY 34 (October 1950): 301-
14. Illus.

A documentation of the known bibliographical material and
examination of the work of an eighteenth-century New York
craftsman. Discussion of his place in the Dutch-American
stream and illustrations of attributable work.

1211 Tapley, Harriet S. "The Ledger of Edward Lang, Silversmith of Salem."
ESSEX INSTITUTE HISTORICAL COLLECTIONS 66 (1930): 325-29.

Presentation and analysis of this interesting and useful historic
document. Illustrates the diverse roles and activities of the
silversmith not only in Salem, but throughout the colonial and
early federal periods.

1212 Warren, David B. "Bancroft Woodcock: Silversmith, Friend and Land-
holder." DELAWARE ANTIQUES SHOW CATALOGUE, 1967, pp. 89-
97. Illus.

The life and work of an important local craftsman and several
examples of his work. Discusses external influences on his
style.

1213 Weaks, Mabel C. CAPTAIN ELIAS PELLETREAU, LONG ISLAND
SILVERSMITH. Southampton, N.Y.: Yankee Peddler Book Co., 1966.
10 p. Plates.

More a biography and a history of the times than a scholarly
analysis of the work of the craftsman. The illustrations include things not found in the work by Marvin D. Schwartz.

1214 Wood, Elizabeth. "Thomas Fletcher, A Philadelphia Entrepeneur of
Presentation Silver." WINTERTHUR PORTFOLIO 3 (1967): 136-71.
Illus.

Fletcher, of Fletcher and Lardner, and the other large presentation pieces made after his move from Boston to Philadelphia.
Traces the concept of commemorative pieces since antiquity
and points out the European influences on Fletcher's work.

1215 Worcester Art Museum. PAUL REVERE, 1735-1818. Worcester, Mass.:
1965. 86 p. Plates.

The catalog of an exhibition of both his silver and prints,
along with paintings by A. Ripley that document key events
in the life of the craftsman-patriot. Of both artistic and historical interest to the general public.

1216 Wroth, Lawrence C. ABEL BUELL OF CONNECTICUT, SILVERSMITH,
TYPE FOUNDER AND ENGRAVER. Rev. ed. Middletown, Conn.:
Wesleyan University Press, 1958. xiv, 102 p. Illus.

The life of this controversial figure. Involved in questionable
business practices and changes of career, he was an important
silversmith nonetheless. Based on documentary research and
utilizes extracts from local records. An interesting case study.

Chapter 11
AMERICAN TEXTILES

Americans have made textiles since the earliest colonial days, but printed fabrics were imported in the nineteenth century. Home weaving gave way to the work of professionals and fabric making became increasingly an industrial operation. Quilting and embroidery never went out of style and have been treated continuously, while all forms of textile work have been part of the rebirth of interest in handcrafts in the middle of the twentieth century. Many of the sources deal with both the technical and the visual aspects of creating textiles.

GENERAL STUDIES AND SURVEYS OF AMERICAN TEXTILES

1217 Bendure, Zelma, and Pfeiffer, Gladys. AMERICA'S FABRICS: ORIGIN AND HISTORY, MANUFACTURE, CHARACTERISTICS AND USES. New York: Macmillan Co., 1946. xv, 688 p. Illus. Bibliog., pp. xi-xii.

> Primarily concerned with manufactured rather than cottage-industry textiles, with a concentrated examination of developments in New England. Useful background information for the study of the effect of industrialization on design.

1218 Bowles, Ella. HOMESPUN HANDICRAFTS. Philadelphia: J.B. Lippincott Co., 1931. 251 p. 60 illus.

> Includes information about a variety of textile crafts, both that of the occasional producer and that of the cottage-industry variety. Some background history with attention to fabrics, patterns, and colors. Chatty but perceptive comments.

1219 Cummings, Abbott L., ed. BED HANGINGS, 1650-1850. Boston: Society for the Preservation of New England Antiquities, 1961. ix, 60 p. Illus.

> The collected papers presented at a conference on the subject of bed hangings. Includes sections on "Fabric and Documentary Sources" and "Pictorial Sources." Good illustrations

and valuable technical information about materials and their decoration.

1220 Frankl, Paul T. AMERICAN TEXTILES. Leigh-on-Sea, Engl.: Lewis, 1954. 20 p. Illus.

This brief survey is one of a British series on world textiles. Adequate coverage and good illustrations.

1221 Gordon, Beverly. DOMESTIC AMERICAN TEXTILES, A BIBLIOGRAPHIC SOURCEBOOK. Pittsburgh, Pa.: Center for the History of American Needlework, 1978. 217 p. Bibliog.

A basic though flawed bibliography which is devoted to textiles and needlework produced or used in this country. Primarily an annotated bibliography arranged by the author.

1222 Harbeson, Georgiana B. AMERICAN NEEDLEWORK. New York: Coward-McCann, 1938. Reprint. New York: Bonanza Books, 1972. xxxviii, 232 p. Illus. Bibliog., pp. 225-26.

Chapters on the various forms of embroidery and religious and secular samplers, of both native Americans and European settlers and their descendants. Explains how work was used and methods of creation.

1222a Heisey, John W.; Andrews, Gail C.; and Walters, Donald R. A CHECKLIST OF AMERICAN COVERLET WEAVERS. Williamburg, Va.: Colonial Williamsburg Foundation, 1978. x, 149 p. Illus. (some in color), Bibliog., pp. 139-42.

An illustrated alphabetical checklist of over 900 weavers. An introduction presents background on the weavers and the technical developments which affected them, especially the invention of the Jacquard mechanism.

1223 Little, Frances. EARLY AMERICAN TEXTILES. New York: Century Co., 1931. xvi, 267 p. 62 illus. Bibliog., pp. 249-53.

Discusses the early colonial history of hand and wheel work, the development of an industry, and the types of materials produced. Other chapters cover the rise of the Machine Age, American silk manufacture, and a discussion of early cotton printing. An old, but still useful source.

1224 Swan, Susan B. PLAIN AND FANCY: AMERICAN WOMEN AND THEIR NEEDLEWORK, 1700-1850. New York: Rutledge Books, Holt, Rinehart, and Winston, 1977. 240 p. 123 illus. Bibliog., pp. 235-37.

Explores the role of needlework and textile craft in the life of the American woman until 1850. Careful explanation of

the methods of stitchery, a survey of the types of objects
made, and an examination of the woman's place in the home.
Particular attention is paid to the sampler and crewelwork.

1225 _____ . A WINTERTHUR GUIDE TO AMERICAN NEEDLEWORK. New
York: Crown Publishers, 1976. 144 p. 100 illus. Bibliog., pp.
142-44.

A concise pocket-sized guide to the various needlework forms:
samplers, canvas work, crewel, silk work, quilts, tambour,
knitting, and white work. Brief introductory essays, with
many detailed descriptions accompanying the illustrations.

1226 Woodward, Paul J. CATALOGUE OF EARLY AMERICAN HANDI-
CRAFT. Brooklyn: Brooklyn Museum Press, 1924. 76 p. 16 illus.

The catalog of an exhibition which included coverlets, embroidery, lace, quilts, and samplers. Old but still useful
survey of the broad range of textile arts in the United States.

GEOGRAPHICAL STUDIES OF TEXTILES

1227 Browne, George W. THE AMOSKEAG MANUFACTURING CO. OF
MANCHESTER, NEW HAMPSHIRE. Manchester, N.H.: Privately
printed, 1915. 288 p. Illus.

A history of one of the early and important textile firms op-
erating in New England. Describes the development, growth,
and decline of the firm seen as a New Hampshire social institution. Some discussion of the variety of products.

1228 Fennelly, Catherine. TEXTILES IN NEW ENGLAND, 1790-1840.
Old Sturbridge Village booklet series, no. 13. Sturbridge, Mass.:
Old Sturbridge Village, 1961. 40 p. Illus.

Provides historical background on the creation of material in
the early federal period in New England and a catalog of
works in the Old Sturbridge Village Collection. A good introduction for the novice.

1229 Giffen, Jane C. "The 1967 Summer Exhibition, Household Textiles."
HISTORICAL NEW HAMPSHIRE 22, no. 4 (Winter 1967): 19-33.

An illustrated review of the exhibition.

1230 Griffin, Richard U. "An Origin of the Industrial Revolution in Maryland: The Textile Industry, 1789-1826." MARYLAND HISTORICAL
MAGAZINE 61, no. 1 (March 1966): 24-36.

Describes the growth and development of the industry, relating technological advances to social questions. The range

and diversity of manufactured goods, in comparison with home
industry, is also presented.

1231 Hemphill, Herbert W., Jr., and Weissman, Julia. THE FABRIC OF
THE STATE. New York: Museum of American Folk Art, 1972. 28 p.
12 illus.

The hand weaving and needlework of New York State's craftsmen from the late colonial period to the present. Both domestic and factory textile production is examined and techniques are described. Needlepoint and quilting are discussed
as ongoing home crafts. Catalog entries with good illustrations.

1232 Jardine, Josephine. "Moravian and Other Work." NEEDLE ARTS 1,
no. 9 (Fall 1971): 8-13.

Illustrates and discusses the specialized iconography and style
of the Moravian women in the American settlements.

1233 Montgomery, Florence. "Fortunes to be Acquired." RHODE ISLAND
HISTORY 31, nos. 2, 3 (May, August 1972): 53-64.

A brief history of the development of the textile industry in
eighteenth-century Rhode Island. Illustrative of the types of
cloth made in the mills; discusses ties to European traditions.

1233a Museum of International Folk Art. SPANISH TEXTILE TRADITION OF
NEW MEXICO AND COLORADO. Santa Fe, N.Mex.: 1979. xii,
264 p. Illus. Bibliog., pp. 252-59.

A major survey of the weaving arts of a large part of the
American Southwest. Essays by specialists on both the history
and style of the works, as well as on particular media such
as embroidery and handspun cotton. A series of special appendixes covers the technical areas quite well.

1234 Schiffer, Margaret B. HISTORICAL NEEDLEWORK OF PENNSYLVA-
NIA. New York: Charles Scribner's Sons, 1968. 160 p. Illus.
(some in color). Bibliog.

Examines the various kinds of needle craft produced in Pennsylvania in the colonial era and, more completely, during the
nineteenth century. Particularly interested in the homemade
work done in the eastern part of the state.

1235 Sinclair, J. Bruce. "The Merrimack Valley Textile Museum." CO-
LONIAL SOCIETY OF MASSACHUSETTS PUBLICATIONS 43 (n.d.):
406-16.

Discusses the holdings in the collection.

1236 Weiss, Harry B., and Ziegler, Grace M. THE EARLY FULLING MILLS OF NEW JERSEY. Trenton: New Jersey Agricultural Society, 1957. 79 p. Illus.

> Describes the historical background of New Jersey's early growth, the rise of the textile industry, and its place in the society. More concerned with technological developments and processes than questions of style, but design is not excluded.

EMBROIDERY

1237 Baker, Muriel L. A HANDBOOK OF AMERICAN CREWEL EMBROI-DERY. Rutland, Vt.: Charles E. Tuttle Co., 1966. 67 p. Illus. Bibliog., p. 67.

> A brief survey of the history of crewel embroidery and its place in the home crafts of our society. Illustrations of popular patterns and stitches.

1238 Bowen, Richard L. "The Scott Family Needlework." RHODE ISLAND HISTORY 2, no. 1 (1942): 11-21; no. 2 (1942): 49-57.

> Discusses the work of several generations of the women of a Rhode Island family. Traces images, lettering styles, and technique.

1239 Cavallo, Adolph S. "New England Crewel Embroideries." CON-NECTICUT HISTORICAL SOCIETY BULLETIN 24 (April 1959): 33-43.

> A general survey of the style and imagery in New England, in the colonial and early federal periods.

1240 Davis, Mildred J. EARLY AMERICAN EMBROIDERY DESIGNS. New York: Crown Publishers, 1969. 159 p. Over 300 illus. (56 in color). Bibliog., pp. 154-56.

> Primarily concerned with illustrating the range and variety of the actual designs, rather than analyzing sources or technology. A sampling of both geometric and subject-oriented designs found throughout the colonies and country.

1241 _____. EMBROIDERY DESIGNS 1780 THROUGH 1820. New York: Crown Publishers, 1971. xiii, 94 p. Illus.

> The trade edition of the catalog of an exhibition held at the Valentine Museum in Richmond, Virginia. A scholarly examination of the designs, where they came from, and how they were used in American textile creation.

1242 Hanley, Hope. NEEDLEPOINT IN AMERICA. New York: Charles

Scribner's Sons, 1969. 160 p. Illus. (9 in color). Bibliog., pp. 153–57.

A short chapter on European origins of needlepoint is followed by a thorough discussion of the colonial period and the heyday of the "Berlin pattern." The revival of the craft and ways of doing popular stitches is useful for understanding the appearance of needlework designs. The illustrations are quite good.

1243 Hedlund, Catherine A. A PRIMER OF NEW ENGLAND CREWEL EMBROIDERY. 3d ed. Old Sturbridge Village booklet series, no. 17. Sturbridge, Mass.: Sturbridge Village, 1971. 72 p. Illus.

One of a series of general works published by an important decorative arts museum, based primarily on their holdings. Traces the origin and development of interest in this textile art, illustrates a variety of patterns and designs, and provides some technical material on the way it is done.

1244 Howe, Margery B. EARLY AMERICAN EMBROIDERIES IN DEERFIELD. Deerfield, Mass.: Heritage Foundation, 1963. 40 p. Illus.

A catalog which provides information on designs and materials, and some historical background.

1245 Kassell, Hilda. STITCHES IN TIME: THE ART AND HISTORY OF EMBROIDERY. New York: Duell, Sloan, and Pearce, 1967. 108 p. Illus. Bibliog., pp. 107–8.

Traces the technical evolution and stylistic changes from the colonial period to the middle of the twentieth century. Information for the practitioner on how to use the various stitches.

1246 Katzenberg, Dena S. THE GREAT COVER-UP: COUNTERPANES OF THE EIGHTEENTH AND NINETEENTH CENTURIES. Baltimore: Baltimore Museum of Art, 1971. 48 p. Illus.

Introductory essay covers the variety of techniques and designs used by the craftsmen. Special attention is paid to "white work," the difficult stuffed and stitched work done throughout the nineteenth century. Eighty-four cataloged items; dimensions, dating, probable location of origin, and description.

1247 Landon, Mary T., and Swan, Susan B. AMERICAN CREWEL WORK. New York: Macmillan, 1970. 192 p. Illus. (some in color).

Describes the history of this home craft, illustrates and discusses some of the more popular designs and stitches through the years, and makes it practical for the contemporary worker.

1248 Rowe, Ann P. "Crewel Embroidered Bed Hangings in Old and New England." BOSTON MUSEUM BULLETIN 71, no. 365 (1973): 101–66.

Discusses the rise of the form in England and shows its evolution during colonial days in New England. Careful comparison of imagery and technique.

1249 Schiffer, Margaret B. "Early Embroidery in Pennsylvania's Chester County." NEEDLE ARTS 2, no. 4 (Fall 1977): 4-16.

Specific analysis and discussion of the stitches, color, and imagery of the area. Some pieces included are not found in the author's general survey.

1250 Stearns, Martha G. HOMESPUN AND BLUE: A STUDY OF AMERICAN CREWEL EMBROIDERY. New York: Charles Scribner's Sons, 1940.

Discusses crewelwork as an American form, concentrating on providing many specific examples of the art and on the technical aspects as well. Would be of interest to both the collector and the practitioner.

1251 Townsend, Gertrude. "An Introduction to the Study of Eighteenth Century New England Embroidery." BOSTON MUSEUM OF FINE ARTS BULLETIN 39 (April 1941): 19-25.

An illustrated article that emphasizes connoisseurship. How to recognize eighteenth-century work by designs, material, and colors. Points out origins and foreign influences.

1252 Vanderpoel, Emily N. AMERICAN LACE AND LACEMAKERS. New Haven: Yale University Press, 1924. xx, 14 p. Illus.

Still probably the standard account of this genre in America. Extremely well illustrated and enables the reader to examine and trace forms through two centuries. Traces the ups and downs of interest in lace making at various times in our history.

1253 Wheeler, Candace. THE DEVELOPMENT OF EMBROIDERY IN AMERICA. New York: Harper and Bros., 1921. x, 152 p. Illus.

An old and chatty survey which begins with a view of the needle in history before dividing into chapters on the various crafts: crewelwork, samplers, quilts, embroidery, and tapestry.

1254 Wilson, Erica. CREWEL EMBROIDERY. New York: Charles Scribner's Sons, 1962. 153 p. Illus.

A survey of the long-popular needlework form. Both technical and aesthetic issues are discussed.

PRINTED FABRICS

1255 New York Historical Society. AMERICAN SCENES AND EVENTS ON
      TEXTILES. New York, 1941. 33 p. Illus.

> The catalog of an exhibition of a variety of textiles, cotton,
> linen, and silk, on which American historical events and spe-
> cific scenery are illustrated. Covers the colonial-printed cot-
> tons through later manufactured wares.

1256 Penn, Theodore Z. "The Introduction of Calico Cylinder Printing in
      America: A Case Study in the Transmission of Technology." In TECH-
      NICAL INNOVATION AND THE DECORATIVE ARTS, edited by Ian
      M.B. Quimby and Polly Anne Earl, pp. 235–55. Charlottesville:
      University of Virginia Press, 1974.

> How British skills and equipment were brought to America and
> adapted for use in the developing American textile industry.

1257 Pettit, Florence. AMERICA'S INDIGO BLUES. New York: Hastings
      House, 1974. 256 p. 150 illus. (8 in color).

> A successful attempt at deciding whether or not resist-dyed
> fabrics were produced in America in the eighteenth century.
> She decides that they were, documents the designs in about
> twenty museums, and presents a broad picture of the use of
> indigo and other dyes across the world. Includes a survey of
> fabric printing from the seventeenth to the nineteenth century.

1258 _____ . AMERICA'S PRINTED AND PAINTED FABRICS, 1600–1900.
      New York: Hastings House, 1970. 256 p. 175 illus. (6 in color).
      Bibliog., pp. 245–47.

> The first section discusses and illustrates the different methods
> of hand and machine printing, another is concerned with tech-
> nical and stylistic developments in the colonial period, and
> the last traces developments to 1900.

1259 Preston, Paula S. PRINTED COTTONS AT OLD STURBRIDGE VIL-
      LAGE. Sturbridge, Mass.: Sturbridge Village, 1969. 36 p. Illus.

> Background information on the history of printed materials
> abroad and the development of the industry in late colonial
> America. Illustrated entries of particular printed fabrics,
> their designs and colors, and works at this museum of folk
> arts.

1260 Sloat, Caroline. "The Dover Manufacturing Company and the Integra-
      tion of English and American Calico Printing Techniques, 1825–29."
      WINTERTHUR PORTFOLIO 10 (1975): 51–68.

> A study of the Dover Manufacturing Company and its difficult

attempt to develop suitable techniques for printing on cotton
textiles. Based on three surviving company letter books, and
serves as a case study of industrial development.

QUILTS

1261 Bacon, Lenice I. AMERICAN PATCHWORK QUILTS. New York:
Wm. Morrow and Co., 1973. 190 illus. (32 in color). Bibliog.

A history of the creation of patchwork quilts in this century
throughout the country, including Hawaii. Discusses the hu-
man element in the creation of each work discussed.

1262 Bishop, Robert C. NEW DISCOVERIES IN AMERICAN QUILTS. New
York: E.P. Dutton and Co., 1975. 127 p. 240 illus. Bibliog.

A survey of American quilt-making technique and imagery.
Illustrations of popular images which reappear throughout
American quilt-making history.

1263 Bordes, Marilynn J. TWELVE GREAT QUILTS FROM THE AMERICAN
WING. New York: Metropolitan Museum of Art, 1974. 36 p. 17
illus. (10 in color).

The text accompanies the exhibition of a wide variety of
American quilts, dating from 1800 to 1920. Descriptive entries on such types as federal, crazy, mosaic, and log cabin,
include technical background and excellent illustrations.

1264 Carlisle, Lilian B. PIECED WORK AND APPLIQUE QUILTS AT SHEL-
BURNE MUSEUM. Shelburne, Vt.: Shelburne Museum, 1957. 95 p.
Illus.

A handbook and guide to the collection of this genre of work
in a major museum of Americana. Some background and historical information.

1265 Colby, Averil. PATCHWORK. New York: B.J. Batsford, 1958.
201 p. Illus.

A study of patchwork as applied to quilting, an essentially
American form. Illustrates the different patterns and approaches
of the mid to late nineteenth century, the heyday of the craft.

1266 _____. PATCHWORK QUILTS. New York: Charles Scribner's Sons,
1965. 94 p. Illus. (some in color).

A survey of this popular nineteenth-century American form.
Information about the range of taste in patchwork and many
illustrations of popular varieties.

1267 DeGraw, Imelda. QUILTS AND COVERLETS. Denver: Denver Art
Museum, 1974. 160 p. 144 illus. (7 in color). Bibliog.

Updates a 1963 publication of the Denver Museum's impressive
holdings of American quilts and coverlets. The two forms are
discussed individually, each with historical notes. Brief essay
on dating, designs, and techniques, and descriptions of illustrated works. Clear illustrations and general background bibliography.

1268 Dow, George F. "The Patchwork Quilt and Some Other Quilts."
OLD-TIME NEW ENGLAND 17, no. 4 (April 1927): 156-73.

Discusses the arrival of quilting from English and European
sources and points out the uses of quilts in early America.
Speaks to both utilitarian and aesthetic issues and to the importance of this as a form of disciplined needlework for young
women.

1269 Dunton, William K. OLD QUILTS. Catonsville, Ind.: Privately
published, 1947. 276 p. 125 illus. Bibliog., pp. 5-16.

Chapters on a variety of practical and decorative quilted objects, with major emphasis on detailed description and with
narrative about each individual work. Quotes many primary
and newspaper sources for information about the designer or
owner of each piece. Some attributions as to date based on
author's own connoisseurship.

1270 Fayerweather, Eleanor, and Rockefeller, Sharon P. MOUNTAIN AR-
TISANS APPALACHIA: AN EXHIBITION OF PATCHWORK AND
QUILTING. Providence: Museum of Art, Rhode Island School of
Design, 1970. 52 p. 27 illus. Bibliog.

One essay presents the development and background of quilting in America from the earliest known work through the nineteenth century while the other concentrates on the rural sur-
vival of the craft. The catalog entries describe the various
patterns and colors used by the contemporary hand workers and
relates their production to their isolated rural society.

1271 Finley, Ruth E. OLD PATCHWORK QUILTS AND THE WOMEN WHO
MADE THEM. Philadelphia: J.B. Lippincott, 1929. 202 p. 96 illus.

Provides a brief history of quilt making and describes processes.
Included is a checklist of types of quilts by name.

1272 Haders, Phyllis. SUNSHINE AND SHADOW: THE AMISH AND THEIR
QUILTS. New York: Universe, 1976. 72 p. 48 illus. (12 in color).

A rich variety of the quilts used by this isolated sect. Drawn
from widely scattered Amish communities and emphasizing the
richness of the stitching tradition.

1273 Hall, Carrie A., and Kretsinger, Rose. THE ROMANCE OF THE
PATCHWORK QUILT IN AMERICA. Coldwell, Idaho: Coxton Printers,
1935. Reprint. New York: Bonanza Books, 1972. 299 p. Illus.
Bibliog., p. 202.

> The history of the development of the genre and the techniques
> and personal tricks used in the making thereof. Examples from
> all over the country, and some accounts of the personal rea-
> sons many were created.

1274 Holstein, Jonathan. ABSTRACT DESIGNS IN AMERICAN QUILTS.
New York: Whitney Museum of American Art, 1971. 16 p. 6 plates.

> An exhibition catalog which concentrates on visual and aes-
> thetic rather than technical considerations. Color, pattern,
> and line in sixty nineteenth-century American quilts. Brief
> bibliography and information on all exhibited works.

1275 _____. AMERICAN PIECED QUILTS. Washington, D.C.: Smithsonian Institution, 1972. 94 p. 84 illus. (15 in color).

> The catalog of an exhibition of this important form of Ameri-
> can decorative arts. Although occasionally made by the spe-
> cialist, it is a genre that was widely developed with interest-
> ing regional variations.

1276 _____. THE PIECED QUILT: AN AMERICAN DESIGN TRADITION.
Greenwich, Conn.: New York Graphic Society, 1973. 192 p. 155
illus. (some in color). Bibliog., pp. 188-89.

> The pieced quilt is presented as one of the great folk art
> forms of American art. The types of patterns and decoration
> are amply illustrated.

1277 Ickis, Marguerite. THE STANDARD BOOK OF QUILT MAKING AND
COLLECTING. New York: Dover Publications, 1959. xi, 270 p.
Illus.

> Although primarily a "how-to-do-it" book, there is some ma-
> terial of broader interest: chapters on collecting quilts, a
> brief history of the craft, and historical information on the
> variety of techniques, plus many good illustrations.

1278 Lithgow, Marilyn. QUILTMAKING AND QUILTMAKERS. New York:
Funk and Wagnells, 1974. 100 p. 59 illus. (18 in color).

> A well-written concise history of American quilt making, including
> a brief chapter on how to actually do quilting. For the beginner.

1279 Orlofsky, Patsy, and Orlofsky, Myron. QUILTS IN AMERICA. New
York: McGraw-Hill, 1974. xiv, 368 p. 310 illus. (105 in color).
Bibliog., pp. 351-57.

A general survey of quilt making in America, followed by
specific chapters on techniques, tools and equipment, types
of quilts, and a discussion of patterns and pattern names.
Information on the care of quilts and information on dating.

1280 Peto, Florence. AMERICAN QUILTS AND COVERLETS. New York:
Chanticleer Press, 1949. 63 p. Illus. (some in color). Bibliog.

A history of this form of American craft endeavor and a section for the layman on how quilts and coverlets can be made
today.

1281 _____. HISTORIC QUILTS. New York: American Historical Co.,
1939. xix, 210 p. Illus.

A general discussion of quilts in America, their background
and sources, regional variations and characteristics, and description of the designs. Old but still useful survey.

1282 _____. "New York Quilts." NEW YORK HISTORY 30, no. 3
(July 1949): 328-39.

Provides some brief background on quilt making in America in
general and then comments on some particular examples of
known and attributed works of New York quilt makers. Indicates the prevalence of certain motifs and colors.

1283 Robacker, Earl F. "Piece-Patch Artistry." PENNSYLVANIA FOLKLIFE
15 (July 1963): 2-10.

A modest exploration of the role of patchwork quilts in Pennsylvania. Discusses and illustrates several examples of the
local tradition and mentions the broader spectrum of the quilt
in America.

1284 Robertson, Elizabeth W. AMERICAN QUILTS. New York: Studio
Publications, 1948. 152 p. Illus. Bibliog., pp. 151-52.

The first chapter provides a general background statement
about early American quilts while the second presents the history of manufactured textiles used in quilts and comments on
various aspects of the craft as relates to the Industrial Revolution. Other chapters are concerned with techniques of decoration, sources of design and nomenclature, and information
about quality itself. Many good black and white illustrations.

1285 Safford, Carleton L., and Bishop, Robert. AMERICA'S QUILTS AND
COVERLETS. New York: Weathervane Books, 1974. 313 p. 462
illus. (some in color). Bibliog., p. 310.

Provides a history of both the technical changes and varieties

of the genre and discusses the changes in taste. Various types
are documented and illustrated, including the crazy quilt,
candlewick spread, and the applique quilt.

1286 White, Margaret E. QUILTS AND COUNTERPANES IN THE NEWARK
MUSEUM. Newark, N.J.: Newark Museum, 1948. 90 p. Illus.
Bibliog., pp. 89-90.

A discussion of quilting as a popular form of textile creation
in the United States and some historical background. Catalog
entries are primarily concerned with designs, images, and the
variety of approaches to quilting. Adequate illustrations.

RUGS AND TAPESTRIES

1287 Bowles, Ella S. HANDMADE RUGS. Garden City, N.Y.: Garden
City Publishing Co., 1937. xv, 205 p. Illus. (some in color).
Bibliog., pp. 204-5.

A very chatty and anecdotal survey of the hooked, braided,
crocheted, and woven rug in America, with chapters on making the rugs and how to dye the fibers. A wide variety of
illustrations and some useful technical information.

1288 Bunker, Cameron F., et al. SYLVIA HEYDEN RECENT TAPESTRIES.
Durham, N.C.: Duke University Museum of Art, 1972. 65 p. 12
illus. Bibliog.

The catalog of a retrospective exhibition of the weavings of
an artist concerned with classical and biblical myths. Contains a biography, essays on her work and imagery, and clear
illustrations.

1289 Burroughs, Bryson. MEMORIAL EXHIBITION OF THE WORK OF
ARTHUR B. DAVIES. New York: Metropolitan Museum of Art, 1930.
xviii, 36 p. Plates.

The catalog of an exhibition of Davies's work presented soon
after his death. Includes a list, measurements, and illustrations of the tapestries and rugs made to the artist's designs.

1290 Kent, William W. THE HOOKED RUG. New York: Tudor, 1937.
xiii, 210 p. 175 illus.

The hooked rug was a very common type of homecraft, and
this volume provides historical background as to its use, describes materials of creation, and provides information about
design sources.

1291 Kopp, Joel, and Kopp, Kate. AMERICAN HOOKED AND SEWN
RUGS: FOLK ART UNDERFOOT. New York: E.P. Dutton, 1975.

128 p. 213 illus. (100 in color). Bibliog., p. 128.

A history and development of the hooked rug, including discussion of how this imagery often is related to that used in other folk art forms. Individual chapters on bed, yarn-sewn, and embroidered and braided rugs. Detailed attention to hooked rugs and a special section on the care of these rugs.

1292 _____. HOOKED RUGS IN THE FOLK ART TRADITION. New York: Museum of American Folk Art, 1974. 40 p. 70 illus.

A catalog of one of the only exhibitions devoted exclusively to the hooked rug, with sixty-five examples from the nineteenth century to the present. Background material on materials and techniques, a historical view of function, and an examination of images and color combinations used by the folk artist.

1293 Roth, Rodris. FLOOR COVERINGS IN 18TH CENTURY AMERICA. Washington, D.C.: Smithsonian Press, 1967. 63 p. Illus.

As the colonial period drew to a close, bare or painted floors were replaced by a variety of coverings. Discusses both the how and why of floor coverings.

SAMPLERS

1294 Bolton, Ethel S., and Coe, Eva J. AMERICAN SAMPLERS. Boston: Massachusetts Society of the Colonial Dames of America, 1921. Reprint. New York: Dover, 1973. xii, 416 p. 126 illus. (some in color).

An old but extremely thorough discussion of this textile form. Major value is its register of known eighteenth-century samplers. Well-spaced illustrations help document the earliest use of particular, favorite designs. A basic reference tool for purposes of identification.

1295 Harris, W.L. "Samplers and American History." ANTIQUARIAN 4, no. 3 (April 1925): 13-17.

Historical scenes as a source of inspiration for the sampler makers.

1296 Mercer, Mrs. William R. "Bucks County Samplers." BUCKS COUNTY HISTORICAL SOCIETY 5 (1926): 347-56.

An illustrated article which gathers together and documents the local works in this craft. Some discussion of popular images and colors.

1297 Miner, George L. "Rhode Island Samplers." RHODE ISLAND HISTOR-
ICAL SOCIETY COLLECTIONS 13, no. 2 (April 1920): 1-56.

> An illustrated major article on the sampler as developed in
> Rhode Island. Comparisons with the general sampler tech-
> niques and motifs, and particular attention to documentable
> and attributable local works.

1298 Townsend, Gertrude. "Judith Paul's Sampler." RHODE ISLAND HIS-
TORICAL COLLECTIONS 34, no. 3 (July 1941): 79-90.

> A detailed analysis of a sampler of 1791. Discussion of sam-
> pler technique and the variety of stitches, colors, and imagery
> in this early work.

WEAVING

1299 Atwater, Mary M. THE SHUTTLE-CRAFT BOOK OF HAND-WEAVING.
Rev. ed. New York: Macmillan Publishing Co., 1959. xv, 341 p.
Illus.

> Oriented toward both the collector and the weaving buff, this
> traces the history of weaving in brief, with emphasis on the
> colonial and early federal success of weaving. Discusses the
> resurrection of interest in hand weaving and is illustrated with
> patterns taken from early American designs.

1300 Ayres, James E. "American Coverlets." TEXTILE HISTORY 1, no. 1
(1971): 92-102.

> A survey article concerning coverlets, the way they were
> made, materials used, and their decoration.

1301 Constantine, Mildred, and Jaffe, Irma B. AMERICAN TAPESTRIES.
New York: Charles E. Slatkin Galleries, 1968. 52 p. 35 illus.
(27 in color).

> The tapestries described and illustrated in this catalog were
> all designed by contemporary American artists. Discussion of
> the relationship of texture and relief to the artists.

1302 Knodel, Gerhardt G. FABRICATIONS. Bloomfield Hills, Mich.:
Cranbrook Academy of Art, 1972. 45 p. 35 illus.

> The catalog of an invitational exhibition of thirty-five con-
> temporary American weavers. Artists' commentary on their
> work, catalog entries, exhibition record for each, and photo-
> graphs of the craftsmen.

1303 Montgomery, P.W. INDIANA COVERLET WEAVERS AND THEIR COV-
ERLETS. Indianapolis: Hoosier Heritage Press, 1974. x, 138 p. 124 illus.

Discusses the multitude of weaving-related activities of the
early settlers and notes how they produced dyed, homespun,
and overshot coverlets. Also documents how professional
weavers took over and created the jacquard weave coverlets
after 1820. Patterns and colors are classified, and a biographical dictionary is part of the work.

1304 Parslow, Virginia D. "Early American Fabrics and Colors." NEW
YORK HISTORY 29, no. 2 (April 1948): 203-13.

Although concentrating on the New York scene, there is good
general background information about both technical and stylistic developments in the creation of woven textiles in the
heyday of weaving activity early in the nineteenth century.

1305 _____. WEAVING AND DYEING PROCESSES IN EARLY NEW
YORK, WITH A DESCRIPTION OF SPINNING FIBERS. Cooperstown,
N.Y.: Farmer's Museum, 1949. 20 p. Illus.

This booklet is oriented to the understanding of the technical
processes involved in home weaving. The role of fabric production in the home is dealt with in a historical framework,
with modest attention to the designs and aesthetics.

1306 Rabb, Kate. INDIANA COVERLETS AND COVERLET WEAVERS. Indianapolis: Indiana Historical Society, 1928. 39 p. Illus.

A study of the regional work from the earliest days of settlement. Specific information on those specialists in the coverlet, and careful documentation.

1307 Reinert, Guy F. COVERLETS OF THE PENNSYLVANIA GERMANS.
Allentown: Pennsylvania German Folklore Society, 1949. iv, 264 p.
Illus.

A history of coverlet making in America is background for the
essay on the specific work of the Pennsylvania Germans. Influences from the Old World are discussed and particular attention is paid to choices of motifs, colors, and regional technical solutions. Catalog entries on illustrated works.

1308 Rossbach, Ed, and Salmon, Larry. JACK LENOR LARSEN RETROSPEC-
TIVE. Boston: Museum of Fine Arts, 1971. 30 p. 16 illus. (4 in
color).

The retrospective of the work created between 1956 and 1976
by a famous contemporary designer. Emphasis on Larsen's quality and experiments with both technique and materials. Catalog entries with good illustrations.

1309 Swygert, Mrs. Luther. HEIRLOOMS FROM OLD LOOMS. Chicago: Colonial Coverlet Guild of America, 1955. viii, 406 p. Illus.

A catalog of the important collection owned by the Colonial Coverlet Guild of America. This volume illustrates hundreds of different patterns, names and attempts to date them, and includes an alphabetical list of main weavers. A fine reference for those wishing to identify a particular pattern or its dating.

1310 Teleki, Gloria R. THE BASKETS OF RURAL AMERICA. New York: E.P. Dutton and Co., 1975. xx, 202 p. 74 illus. Bibliog., pp. 193-95.

Divided into three main sections: technical, commercial, and regional varieties described and information on various aspects of collecting. Collectors are directed to sources; and methods of identification, condition of the baskets, their care and display are also covered. A good sampling of traditional baskets.

1311 Thieme, Charles, and Marguess, Joyce. AMERICAN COVERLETS OF THE NINETEENTH CENTURY FROM THE HELEN LOUISE ALLEN TEXTILE COLLECTION. Madison, Wis.: Elvehjem Art Center, 1974. 108 p. 41 illus. Bibliog.

Discusses the place of the handwoven coverlet in America during the nineteenth century, with reference to materials, techniques, and patterns. Illustrated with works from an important collection and provides technical information about the individual woven patterns.

1312 Warren, William L., ed. BED RUGS: 1722-1833. Hartford, Conn.: Wadsworth Atheneum, 1972. 80 p. Illus.

The catalog of an exhibition of a now very rare textile form, the colonial and early nineteenth-century "bed rug." Traces the history of this form from its European antecedents, discusses its maturation as a form here, and illustrates how various natural dyes and colors were used in developing the designs.

1313 White, Margaret E. HANDWOVEN COVERLETS IN THE NEWARK MUSEUM. Newark, N.J.: Newark Museum, 1947. 83 p. 32 illus. Bibliog., p. 83.

A brief introduction on loom houses informs us as to the places early weaving was done. The catalog itself is divided into classifications of weaves: overshot, doubleweave, and jacquard. Identifies weavers, patrons, style, and design. Good black-and-white illustrations.

INDIAN TEXTILES

1314 Brody, Jerry J. BETWEEN TRADITIONS: NAVAJO WEAVING TO-
WARD THE END OF THE NINETEENTH CENTURY. Indianapolis: Indianapolis Museum of Art, 1976. 64 p. 40 illus. (5 in color).

Concentrates on the transitional "Eye-Dazzler" work of 1880-
1910 and places it between the traditional classic work and
the revival work of the twentieth century. Development,
techniques, and the society of the women artists are all discussed, with each work illustrated.

1315 Cerny, Charlene. NAVAJO PICTORIAL WEAVING. Santa Fe, N.
Mex.: Museum of International Folk Art, 1975. 32 p. 24 illus. (4
in color). Bibliog.

A brief but solid history of the comparatively unknown pictorial weavings which Navajo women created in the 1880s and
1890s. Animal and plant motifs and landscapes are discussed
and illustrated, and their creation in relationship to white influence is explored.

1316 Fallon, Carol. THE ART OF THE INDIAN BASKET IN NORTH AMER-
ICA. Lawrence: University of Kansas Museum, 1975. 56 p. 69
illus. Bibliog.

One of the few studies which concentrates on the work as art
objects rather than from the ethnographic vantage point. Variety of form, weave, and usage are explored, and historical
information on the various tribes is presented. Construction
and decorative techniques.

1317 Houlihan, Patrick T. INDIAN BASKET DESIGN OF THE GREATER
SOUTHWEST. Salt Lake City: Museum of Fine Arts, University of
Utah, 1976. 48 p. 30 illus.

This exhibition catalog emphasizes the design styles of the
baskets. The three great processes--coiling, plaiting, and
twining--are explained and their history developed. The catalog is divided by tribe, and illustrations of the design specialties of each are provided.

1318 James, George W. INDIAN BLANKETS AND THEIR MAKERS. Chicago: A.C. McClurg and Co., 1914. xvi, 213 p. Illus.

An old but careful study of the blanket weaving of the American Indians with particular reference to and concentration on
the work of the Navajo. Much of the pioneering documentation is still valid, and this remains the only source for several
of the illustrations of works whose locations are now unknown.

1319 Kahlenberg, Mary Hunt, and Berlant, Anthony. THE NAVAJO BLAN-
KET. Catalog of an Exhibition first held at Los Angeles County Museum
of Art, June 27-August 27, 1927. New York: Frederick A. Praeger,
1972. 112 p. 97 illus. (16 in color). Bibliog., p. 111.

A history of the techniques and style of the blanket and its
place in the life of the Navajo is followed by a discussion
of more recent changes and the impact of cultural change.
The catalog of the exhibition has well-documented entries.

1320 Katzenberg, Dena S. "And Eagles Sweep Across the Sky." INDIAN
TEXTILES OF THE NORTH AMERICAN WEST-NAVAJO BLANKETS AND
RUGS, BASKETS OF THE WEST. Baltimore: Baltimore Museum of
Art, 1977. 166 p. 131 illus. (7 in color). Bibliog.

The catalog of an impressive museum collection of American
Indian textiles. Blankets, rugs, and baskets are illustrated
and described, and historical material is provided, particularly
on the production of the Southwest tribes. Good illustrations,
maps, and catalog of the individual objects. Relationships
between history and techniques.

1321 Mason, Otis T. "Aboriginal American Basketry: Studies on a Textile
Art Without Machinery." ANNUAL REPORT OF THE SMITHSONIAN
INSTITUTION, 1902, pp. 171-548. Plates 1-248.

A very old but highly detailed, scholarly, and well-illustrated
survey of American Indian basket work done before the later
developments of tourist-oriented work produced a confusion of
dates. A historical and anthropological view rather than an
aesthetic view, but very valuable for understanding techniques
and tribal variations.

1322 Mera, Harry P. PUEBLO INDIAN EMBROIDERY. Memoirs of the
Laboratory of Anthropology, vol. 4. Santa Fe: University of New
Mexico Press, 1943. 73 p. 21 plates. Drawings by the author.

Discusses the techniques and tools of the Pueblo Indians and
the general characteristics of their work, and surveys the most
frequently used designs. Historical notes are provided with
adequate illustrations of their craft.

AUTHOR INDEX

In addition to authors, this index includes all editors, compilers, translators, and other contributors to works cited in the text. Numbers refer to entry numbers and alphabetization is letter by letter.

Author Index

Author Index

Author Index

Lanmon, Dwight P. 775, 952
Laughlin, Ledlie I. 1170
Lavine, Sigmund A. 92, 383
Lea, Zilla R. 704
Lechler, Doris 893
Lee, Ruth W. 776, 837-38, 865, 894, 953
Lee, Sherman E. 100
Leed, Gretel 415
LeFevre, Leon 129
Lehmann, Henri 163
Leeper, Jeannette 503
Lerch, Lila 416
Lessard, Michel 65
Lewis, Albert 954
Libbey Glass Co. 955
Lichten, Frances 52, 365
Lindsay, J. Seymour 1186
Lindsey, Bessie M. 777
Link, Eva M. 265
Lipkowitz, Freda 880
Lipman, Jean 366
Lippert, Catherine 813
Lister, Florence C. 554
Lister, Robert H. 554
Lithgow, Marilyn 1278
Little, Frances 1223
Little, Nina F. 346, 367
Littleton, Harvey 956
Liverani, Giovanni 164
Loar, Peggy 485
Lockschewitz, Gertrud 9
Lockwood, Luke V. 640, 679
Lockwood, Sarah M. 580
Lohmann, Watson M. 957
London, Mary T. 1247
Long, Deborah 417
Longenecker, Elmer Z. 1187
Lord, Priscilla S. 368
Lorrain, Dessamae 839
Los Angeles County Museum 1045
Low, J.C. 504
Low, John 504
Lucas, E. Louise 10
Luck, Robert 994
Luft, R.W.P. 219
Luddington, John 266
Luther, Clair F. 705
Lyman, Susan E. 814

Lynch, Ernest C. 641
Lyon, Irving W. 642

M

Maas, John 384
McCauley, Robert H. 165, 505
McClelland, Nancy 751
McClinton, Katharine M. 30, 53, 78, 184, 347, 385, 778, 1046
McClure, Abbott 337
MacDonald, William H. 706
Macdonald-Taylor, Margaret S. 31, 210
McEldowney, B.A. 8
McElroy, Cathryn J. 643
MacFarland, Anne S. 709
MacKay, James A. 54
McKean, Hugh F. 386
McKearin, George S. 779-80
McKearin, Helen 779-81, 895
Mackenna, Francis S. 166
McKinnell, James 463
McLaughlin, Warner 958
McMurray, Charles 896
McQuade, Arthur J. 782
McVean, Albert F. 526
Madigan, Mary J. 722
Madsen, Stephen T. 55
Makinson, Randell L. 752
Mankowitz, Wolf 167
Margon, Lester 581-82
Marguess, Joyce 1311
Mariacher, Giovanni 248
Marriott, Alice 555
Marsh, Tracy H. 783
Marvin, Pearson 1171
Mason, Otis T. 1321
Maurer, Evan M. 439
Maust, Don 784
Maxwell, Catherine H. 1048
Maxwell Museum of Anthropology 556
May, Earl C. 1120
Mayer, Christa M. 303
Meader, Robert F. 723
Meals, Moscile T. 606
Measell, Brenda 815
Measell, James 815, 959
Mebane, John 56
Meeks, E.V. 1121
Melvin, Jean S. 897

TITLE INDEX

This index includes the titles of all books cited in the text. In some cases titles have been shortened. Numbers refer to entry numbers and alphabetization is letter by letter.

C

Title Index

Title Index

Phillip Leffingwell Spalding Collection of Early American Silver, The 1035

Pictorial Encyclopedia of Antiques, The 23

Picture Book of Philadelphia Chippendale Furniture, 1750-1780, A 717

Picture History of Furniture 177

Pieced Quilt, The 1276

Pieced Work and Applique Quilts at Shelburne Museum 1264

Pine Furniture of Early New England, The 635

Pittsburgh Glass 1797-1891 808

Plain and Fancy 1224

Pocket Book of American Pewter 1167

Popular American Ruby-Stained Pattern Glass 849

Porcelain 123

Porcelain through the Ages 132

Portland Glass Company, The 976

Potters and Potteries of Bennington 490

Potters and Potteries of Chester County, Pennsylvania, The 482

Pottery 538

Pottery: A Utilitarian Folk Craft 470

Pottery and Ceramics 3

Pottery & Ceramics: From Common Brick to Fine China 130

Pottery and Porcelain 127

Pottery and Porcelain Collector's Handbook, The 449

Pottery and Porcelain in Colonial Williamsburg's Archaeological Collections 467

Pottery and Porcelain of New Jersey, The 478

Pottery and Porcelain of the United States, The 444

Pottery and Porcelain 1700-1914 151

Pottery in the United States 453

Pottery of Marguerite Wildenhain 541

Pottery of San Ildefonso Pueblo, The 543

Pottery of the American Indians 561

Pottery of the Santo Domingo Pueblo, The 544

Pottery of the Southwestern Indians 550

Pottery of the State, The 484

Pottery Sketchbook, A 517

Practical Book of American Antiques, The 337

Practical Book of American Furniture and Decoration, The 678

Practical Book of Chinaware, The 125

Practical Book of Italian, Spanish, and Portuguese Furniture, The 197

Practical Book of Silver, The 1068

Precious Metals 991

Pre-Columbian Ceramics 163

Prentis Collection of Colonial New England Furnishings, The 405

Pressed Glass Salt Dishes of the Lacy Period, 1825-1850 898

Price Guide to English 18th Century Drinking Glasses, The 255

Primer of American Antiques, The 335

Primer of New England Crewel Embroidery, A 1243

Printed Cottons at Old Sturbridge Village 1259

Printed Textiles 319

Pueblo Indian Embroidery 1322

Pueblo Indian Pottery 545

Pueblo Potter, The 542

Q

Quiltmaking and Quiltmakers 1278

Quilts, Counterpanes, and Related Fabrics 314

Quilts and Counterpanes in the Newark Museum 1286

Quilts and Coverlets 1267

Quilts in America 1279

R

Random House Collector's Encyclopedia, The 59

Random House Encyclopedia of Antiques, The 35

Random Notes on Colonial Furniture 672

264

SUBJECT INDEX

This index includes topics covered in the text. Underlined numbers refer to areas of emphasis of the topic. References are to entry numbers and alphabetization is letter by letter.

A

Abstract expressionism, in ceramics 458
Adam, Robert 208
Adriance family (silversmiths) 1087
Advertisements
    Civil War to World War I 379
    colonial newspaper 403
    by early chair-makers 695
    for ironware 1185
Aesthetics 42, 429
    of the Art Deco period 62
    in glass manufacture 227
    in Indian art 438
    of quilts 1274
    of pottery 538
    of pre-Columbian ceramics 163
    of samplers 315
    of 20th-century American ceramics 474
Africa
    decorative arts of 64
    influence on Afro-American art 432, 441
Afro-Americans. See Blacks
Albany, Ind., glass manufacture at 798
Albany, N.Y.
    pewter of 1155
    silver-work of 1135

Albany Glass Works 814
Albany Institute of History and Art, furniture collection of 651
Alexandria, Va., silver-work of 1080
Alfred University, ceramics program at 447
Allegany County, Md., glass manufacture in 796
Amana Church Society, furniture of 711
Amelung, John Frederick 924, 939, 948, 952, 987
American Indians
    ceramics of 542–63
    decorative arts of 431, 433–39
    glass trading beads of 800
    silver-work of 1119, 1136, 1141–54
    textile production by 1314–22
    See also Arikara Indians; Hopi Indians; Iroquois Indians; Navaho Indians; Pueblo Indians
Amish, quilts of 1272
Amoskeag Manufacturing Co. 1227
Andreson, Laura 525
Andrews (Faith and Edward Deming) Collection (Shaker items) 726

Subject Index

Annapolis, Md., cabinet-makers of
608
Appalachian region
decorative arts of 412
quilts of 1270
Applied arts
bibliography on 6
dictionaries and encyclopedias on
16, 34
as folk art 367
in 19th-century Detroit 426
Russian 109
Arab countries. See Near East
Architectural design 1179, 1191
Architecture
American 574
Pennsylvania 425
of the Art Deco period 44
French Louis XVI 75
relationship to furniture 588
use of pottery in 129
Arikara Indians, ceramics of 548
Art, survey of Chinese 73
Art Deco 44, 49, 53, 59
Art industries and trade. See
Applied arts
Art Institute of Chicago
exhibition catalog on Indian art
from 439
textile collection of 303
Artists
American 366
black 432
Essex County, Mass. 399
dictionaries on 16, 48
Art Nouveau 40, 43, 55-56, 61-62
American ceramics 447, 466, 515
glass 242
relationship of Gustav Stickley to
739
Arts and Crafts Exhibiting Society 320
Arts and crafts movement
American 375
ceramics 447
Chicago 1090
Detroit 426
European 389, 396
Ashbee, Charles R. 389
Asia, East, pottery and porcelain of
127, 169

Asia, quilts of 314. See also
China, People's Republic
of; Japan; Korea; Thailand
Austria, porcelain of 173

B

Bachman, Jacob 736
Bakewell Glass Co. 912
Baltimore
furniture and furniture-makers of
608, 618, 745
glass manufacture at 812, 964
silver-work of 1118, 1129
Baltimore Glass Works 964
Baltimore Museum of Art, silver
collection of 1108
Barbour, Frederick K. and Marga-
ret R. 638-39
Baroque period
decorative arts of 60
silk manufacture during 324
Baskets and basketry, American
1310
Indian 431, 1316-17, 1320-21
Shaker 430
Bassett family (pewterers) 1171
Bauhaus 82-84
Bedford Crown Glass Works 958
Beds, hangings and rugs for 1219,
1248, 1312. See also
Daybeds
Bell (pottery firm) 488
Bells 1205
Bennington, Vt., pottery and por-
celain of 475, 490,
509, 530
Bennington (Vt.) Museum, art glass
collection of 848
Bergstrom Art Center, paperweight
collection of 888
Biedermeier style 204
Biennial Crafts Exhibition, Eighth
(Sacramento), catalog
of 377
Blacks
art of 432, 441
as furniture-makers 754
Blacksmithing 1181
Lancaster County, Pa. 1187
See also Ironwork

270

Subject Index

Egerton, Matthew, Jr. 746
Egypt, furniture of 191
Elfe, Thomas 732
Elvehjem Art Center. Helen Louis
    Allen Textile Collection
    1311
Embroidery 300, 302, 323
    American 1237-54
        Chester County, Pa. 1249
        colonial period 1248, 1251
        designs 1240-41
        New England 1239, 1243,
            1251
        Pueblo Indian 1322
        Rhode Island 1238
        Southwest 1233a
    English 318
        Elizabethan period 310
        Victorian period 320
    See also Crewelwork, American;
        Lace and lacemakers;
        Needlepoint
Empire style 76, 202, 719, 729.
        See also Biedermeier style
Enameling, of glass 247, 902
Enamelware
    Battersea 91
    20th-century American 390
    See also Cloisonne
England. See Great Britain
Engraving and engravers
    colonial American 403
    Connecticut 1216
    glass 247
    New England 403
Esherick, Wharton 744
Essex County, Mass.
    artists and craftsmen of 399
    furniture of 621, 624
Etruscan civilization, furniture of
        212
Europe
    encyclopedia of the antiques of
        23
    glass of 229
    Japanese export porcelain made for
        158
    oriental rugs of 312
    painted furniture of 213
    paperweights of 221
    peasant art of 15

porcelain of 126-27, 141, 151
pottery of 126-27, 151
quilts of 314
samplers of 309, 315
silk manufacture in 324
silver-work of 264, 268, 286
Evans, David 698
Evans (John J., Jr.) Collection
        (pewter) 1164
Expressionism. See Abstract
        expressionism

F

Fabrics. See Textile and textile
        manufacture
Faience 146
Far East. See Asia, East
Fashion. See Costume and dress
Federal period
    furniture of 398, 678, 719
    goldsmiths of 1206
    silver-work of 398, 1002,
            1004, 1013, 1018,
            1095, 1124, 1211
    textiles of 1228
Fellows family (silversmiths) 1087
Fenton (pottery company) 490
Figurines, Indian clay 558
Findlay, Ohio, glass manufacture
        at 971
Fine arts
    American 331
        New Hampshire 420
    dictionaries and encyclopedias of
            12, 27, 38
    French Empire style 76
    Scottish 86
Firearms, Canadian 67
Fireplace accessories, American
        360, 1186
Fish, Frederick S. (Mrs.) 781
Flasks 895-96, 904-5
Flatware. See Tableware, American
Fletcher, Thomas 1214
Folk art
    American 354, 361-72
        Appalachian region 412
        pottery 455, 491, 498, 509
        Southern states 419

G

Subject Index

Germantown, Pa., furniture and
    furniture-makers of 740
Germany
  decorative arts of 82-84
  faience of 143
  furniture of 204
  porcelain of 143, 173
  Meissen 153
Ghiselin, Ceaser 1201
Gilding 247. See also Ormolu
Glass and glass manufacture
  American 331, 337, 374, 377
    forgeries of 775-76
    forms of 882-907
    general studies and surveys of
      766-93
    geographical studies of 794-
      828
      Albany, Ind. 798
      Boston 917, 972
      Bridgeport, Ohio 802
      California 799
      East Cambridge, Mass.
        944, 969-70, 978-79
      East Hartford, Conn. 972
      Greentown, Ind. 813, 815,
        937, 959
      Hartford, Conn. 985
      Jamestown, Va. 805
      Maryland 801
        Alleghany County 796
        Baltimore 812, 964
        New Bremen 924, 939,
          952, 962, 987
      New Bedford, Mass. 911,
        963, 986
      New England 827-28
      New Hampshire 420, 807,
        931, 951, 972
      New Jersey 817, 822,
        826, 965
        Glassboro 957
        Millville 810
      New York 415, 825, 932
        Albany 814
        Bedford 958
        Corning 918, 925, 933,
          938, 950, 967-68, 973-
          74
        Lancaster 803

        Lockport 803
        Saratoga Springs 811
      North Carolina 422
      Ohio 960
        Bridgeport 802
        Cambridge 913-14,
          983
        Findlay 971
        Fostoria 816
        Newark 881, 885, 921
        Toledo 929-30, 944,
          955
        Zanesville 821, 823
      Pacific Northwest 824
      Pennsylvania 795, 818,
        975
        Pittsburgh 806, 808,
        912, 922
        White Mills 935
      Sandwich, Mass. 917,
        919, 942-43, 953,
        961, 984
      Somerville, Mass. 966
      West Virginia 981
        Wheeling 809
    Indian beads 800
    individual makers and com-
      panies 766-67, 908-90
    period studies of 829-46
      colonial period 825, 902
      depression era 829, 831-
        32, 835-36, 842,
        844-45, 975
      Lacy period (1825-50) 875,
        898
      19th-century 394-95, 794
        798-99, 808, 834, 837,
        839, 863, 865, 929-
        32, 955, 960-61, 970
      20th-century 390, 392,
        833-34, 837, 840,
        843, 846, 925-26,
        933-34, 938, 941,
        957, 967
      Victorian period 838,
        1039
    prices of 836, 842, 844,
      852, 857, 861, 866,
      870-71, 938, 941,
      957

Subject Index

prices of 255
goldsmithing in 275, 287
pewter of 274, 276, 290
porcelain of 144, 147–48, 151,
154, 167, 170–71
for the American export market
492, 502, 505
Chelsea 166
Derby 138
Worcester 137
pottery of 147–48, 151, 154,
167, 171
for the American export market
161, 165, 512
Devon 512
Mason's 149
samplers of 315, 317
silver-work of 268, 272–73, 275,
278, 284, 287, 292,
294
Rococo period 281
textiles of 307, 319, 325
See also Ireland; Scotland
Greece
furniture of 191, 212
pottery of 145
silver-work of 293
Greene Brothers (furniture designers)
752
Greenfield Village, colonial furniture of 669
Greenough, Daniel 1208
Greentown, Ind., glass manufacture
at 813, 815, 937, 959
Greeting cards, American 379
Gregory, Mary 961
Grotell, Marja 522
Guimard, Hector 56

H

Hammerslough, Philip H. 1032
Harrington (Frank L. and Louise C.)
Collection (silver) 1013
Hartford, Conn.
cabinet-maker price list from
(1792) 636
furniture and furniture-makers of
652, 697, 709
glass manufacture at 985
See also East Hartford, Conn.

Heisey (A.H.) & Co. 881, 885,
921
Henchman, Daniel 699
Hepplewhite–Sheridan style 608
Hewes, Robert L. 972
Hewitt, John 748
Heyden, Sylvia 1288
Heyne, Johann Christoph 1198
Heywood–Wakefield Co. 694
Hispanic Society of America, silver
collection of 288
Hitchcock, L. 702
Holland. See Netherlands
Hooked rugs. See Carpets and rugs,
American
Hopi Indians, silver-work of 1146,
1154
Houghton, Arthur 934
Houghton, John 654
Hubbard, Elbert. See Roycrofters,
The
Hull, John 1062, 1195
Hungary, furniture of 192
Hunter, David 750
Hurd, Jacob 999, 1200

I

Icons, Russian 109
Illinois Glass Co. 941
Imagery
in quilt-making 1262
in rug-making 1291
in stained glass 954
in tapestries 1288
Implements, utensils, etc.,
American 381
glass 772
See also Kitchen-ware, American
India
decorative arts of 96
textiles of 305
Indiana
furniture and furniture-makers of
662
stoneware of 485
weaving in 1303, 1306
See also Albany, Ind.; Greentown, Ind.
Indiana Tumbler and Goblet Co.
813, 937, 959

280

Indians. See American Indians
Industrial design, German 84
Industrial Revolution
impact on Maine potters 477
textile manufacturing and 1230,
1284
Interior design and decoration 181,
190
American 333, 345, 349, 351,
355, 358-59
colonial period 387, 391
Victorian period 384
bibliography on 9
English 89, 199, 207
Georgian period 85
French 80
Italian 99
Mexican 104
Spanish 194
See also Furnishings
International Silver Co. 1120
Iowa City Flint Glass Manufacturing
Co. 819
Ireland
decorative arts of 94
glass of 239, 247
silver-work of 272
Ironstone china, Mason's 149
Ironwork 261
American 1185-86, 1189-90
Charleston, S.C. 1179
Philadelphia 1191
Richmond, Va. 1188
20th-century 1197
See also Blacksmithing; Castings,
iron
Iroquois Indians, silver-work of 1147
Islamic Empire, decorative arts of 97
Italy
decorative arts of 98-99
furniture of 180, 197
glass of 248
porcelain of 162
pottery of 164
textiles of 321
See also Roman Empire; Venice,
Italy
Ivory carving
African 64
Chinese 70, 74

J

Jade, Chinese 72-73
Jamestown, Va., glass manufacture
at 805
Japan
ceramics of 150, 152, 160
decorative arts of 100-103
export porcelain of 158
glass of 236
textiles of 313
Jarves, Deming 919, 943
Jefferson, Thomas 729
Jenkins (Henry W.) & Sons Co.
745
Jewelry and jewelers
American 992
Cincinnati 1071
Georgia 1084
Indian 431
Mobile, Ala. 1138
marks on 1030
19th-century 1138
silver 1007
Tiffany 386
Vermont 1078
Victorian period 1039
gold 267
See also Semiprecious stones
Joinery, in English furniture-
making 219

K

Kansas, University of. Museum,
samplers of 309
Keene and Stoddard (glass manu-
facturers) 951
Kemple Glass Works 908
Kentucky
furniture and furniture-makers of
648, 666
silver-work of 1113
See also Louisville, Ky.
Kimball, Abraham 734
Kimball, Fiske 1191
Kingston, R.I., silver-work of
1124
Kirk (Paul) & Son 1118
Kirk, S. 1056, 1137

Subject Index

pewter collection of 1162
New Haven, Conn.
China trade porcelain exported
through 168
furniture of colonial 634
silver-work of 1117, 1126
New Jersey
clockmakers of 746
decorative arts of 414, 427-28
furniture and furniture-makers of
664, 765
colonial period 631
19th-century 706
glass manufacture in 817, 822,
826, 965
pottery of 486, 494
silver-work of 1111, 1140
textile manufacture in 1236
New Jersey State Museum, porcelain
collection of 508
New London, Conn., silver-work of
1109
New Orleans, furniture of colonial
630
Newport, R.I., decorative arts of
401
New York
colonial glass manufacture in 825
colonial goldsmiths of 1210
decorative arts of 410, 415
furniture and furniture-makers of
615, 628, 644, 651,
748-49
metal-work of 1069
pottery of 446, 483-84
quilts of 1282
silver-work of 1009, 1018, 1087,
1091, 1111, 1123
colonial period 1070, 1122
Indian 1142
weaving in 1304-5
See also Albany, N.Y.; Buffalo,
N.Y.; East Hampton,
N.Y.; Lancaster, N.Y.;
Lockport, N.Y.; Long
Island; Orange County,
N.Y.; Poughkeepsie,
N.Y.; Rochester, N.Y.;
Saratoga Springs, N.Y.;
Utica, N.Y.

New York Historical Society
colonial New England furnishings
of 405
silver collection of 1003
New Zealand
decorative arts of 106
furniture of 211
Noguchi, Isamu 753
Norcross (Hiram) Collection
(bottles) 886
Norman, Edward 538
North America, pottery and porcelain 151. See also
Pre-Columbian art
North Carolina
decorative arts of 422
furniture and furniture-making
in 668
19th-century 754
Moravian pottery of 476
silver-work of 1085
Norton (pottery company) 490, 530
Norway, decorative arts of 107
Norwich, Conn., furniture and
furniture-makers of 609

O

Occupations, colonial American
403
Ohio
art pottery of 494
coverlets of 332
furniture of 606
glass manufacture in 960
silver-work of 1119
20th-century decorative arts of
429
See also Cincinnati; Findlay,
Ohio; Fostoria, Ohio;
Zanesville, Ohio
Old Deerfield, Mass., furniture of
622
Old Sturbridge Village, Mass.
glass collection of 827
textile collection of 1228
embroidery 1243
printed fabrics 1259
Ontario Glass Manufacturing Co.
932

Subject Index

English 147–48, 154, 165, 167, 171
  for the American export market 161, 165, 512
  Devon 512
  European 126
  Greek 145
  marks on 118, 121–22, 126, 128, 134, 167, 171, 443, 451–52, 459, 462, 477, 481, 483, 491, 502, 510
  pre-Columbian 140
  See also Faience; Majolica; Stoneware
Poughkeepsie, N.Y., silver-work of 1089
Prairie School of furniture design. See Furniture and furniture-making, American
Pre-Columbian art
  ceramics 163
  pottery 140, 448
  See also American Indians
Prentis Collection (furnishings) 405, 995
Price, Ken 458
Printing, cylinder 353
Providence, R.I., furniture and furniture-making in 645
Pueblo Indians
  embroidery of 1322
  pottery of 542–46, 549, 551–52, 555–57, 559–60, 563
  silver-work of 1141, 1143

Q

Queen Anne style 716
  chairs 692, 703
  in Maryland 718
Quilts and coverlets 314
  American 32, 1261–86, 1300, 1313
  Amish 1272
  Appalachian region 1270
  as folk art 362–63, 371, 1276
  Indian 1303, 1306
  New York 1282
  19th-century 1265–66, 1311
  Pennsylvania 1283, 1307
  20th-century 1261
  See also Blankets, Indian

R

Rammelsberg, Frederick (furniture-maker) 756
Reed and Barton (firm) 1105
Regency period, antiques of England from 93
Religious art
  gold 998
  needlework 1222
  silver 279, 1008, 1020, 1033, 1040, 1046, 1059, 1075, 1112, 1132-33
  See also Icons
Renaissance, decorative arts of 4
  Italian 98-99
Revere, Joseph 1205
Revere, Paul 336, 382, 1192–93, 1199, 1205, 1209, 1215
Rhode Island
  silver-work of 1019, 1100
  textile manufacture in 1233
    embroidery 1238
    samplers 1297
  See also Kingston, R.I.; Newport, R.I.
Richardson, H.H. 757
Richardson, Joseph, Jr. 1202
Richardson (Joseph) and family 1094
Richmond, Va., ironwork of 1188
Rippon, Ruth 536
Roberts, Aaron 609
Robineau, Adelaide Alsop 518
Rochester, N.Y.
  furniture and furniture-makers of 656
  pottery of 489
Rochester, (N.Y.) Museum of Arts and Sciences, Indian silver-work of 1152
Rococo period
  American furniture of 687
  decorative arts of 60
  silk manufacture during 324
  silver-work of 281
Rogers Bros. (silversmiths) 1120

Subject Index

Subject Index

Texas
  furniture and furnishings of 424, 659
  pottery of 521
Texas Christian University. Mills Collection 771
Textiles and textile manufacture
  American 319, 325, 337, 374, 377, 382
    bibliography on 1221
    colonial period 1233
    Federal period 1228, 1230
    as folk art 361
    general studies and surveys of 1217-36
    geographical studies of 1227-36
      Manchester, N.H. 1227
      Maryland 1230
      New England 1217, 1228
      New Jersey 1236
      North Carolina 422
      Rhode Island 1233
    Indian 431
    19th-century 394
    printed 1255-60
    20th-century 390
  of the Art Deco period 53
  catalog of indigo dyed 51
  Chinese 70, 74
  country and period studies (general) 305-25
  English 307, 319, 325
  French 77, 308, 325
  general works on 295-304
  Italian 321
  Japanese 313
  printing and dyeing of 299-300, 308, 319, 325
  terminology 295, 297, 300, 302
  See also Blankets, Indian; Carpets and rugs; Chintz, Indian (East); Costume and dress; Crewelwork, American; Lace and lacemakers; Needlepoint; Needlework; Quilts and coverlets; Samplers; Tapestry
Thailand, ceramics of 152
Thurston, John 654

Tiffany, Charles L. 393
Tiffany, Louis Comfort 56, 386, 923, 945-47, 988
Tiffany Glass Co. 841, 909, 915
  lamps of 899
Tiles and tilemaking 129
  American 444-45, 453, 504, 526, 531
Tinware and tinsmiths, American 1178, 1184-85
  Connecticut 1180
Tobey (furniture company) 764
Tokens, colonial silver 1017
Toledo, Ohio, glass manufacture at 929-30, 944, 955
Toys
  American 379
  bibliography on 7
  encyclopedia of 34
Trades. See Occupations, colonial American
Treenware. See Woodenware
Trotter, Daniel 741
Turnbridge wares 91
Type-founding 1216

U

Unger Bros. 1056
Union Glass Co. 966
Union of Soviet Socialist Republics. See Russia
United States, decorative arts of 326-441
  general studies and surveys 326-60
  geographical studies 397-429
  folk art 361-72
  period studies 373-96
  See also American Indians; Blacks; subheading "American" under classes of decorative arts (e.g., Silverwork, American)
United States Glass Co. 808
Upholstery 204
Utah, furniture and furniture-makers in 646
Utensils. See Implements, utensils, etc.

p